T0083530

Jan Sokol

Ethics, Life and Institutions
An Attempt
at Practical Philosophy

KAROLINUM PRESS
PRAGUE 2016

Originally published in Czech under the title
Etika, život, instituce: Pokus o praktickou filosofii
Prague: Vyšehrad 2014

KAROLINUM PRESS
Ovocný trh 5/560, 116 36 Prague 1
Czech Republic
Karolinum Press is a publishing department of Charles University
www.karolinum.cz

Layout by Jan Šerých
Typeset by DTP Karolinum Press
Printed in the Czech Republic by Karolinum Press
First English edition

The Cataloguing-in-Publication data is available from the National Library
of the Czech Republic

ISBN 978-80-246-3429-6
ISBN 978-80-246-3430-2 (pdf)

Contents

Introduction

In a usage that begins with Kant, 'practical' is the name given to that branch of philosophy which concerns itself with action, decision and judgment. It regards man first and foremost as a being which must act, and therefore judge. Against this stands theoretical philosophy, the investigation of existence and all that is. Theoretical philosophy is understood primarily as an instrument of understanding and so it asks what *is* and *is* not, while practical philosophy concerns itself with what is good and bad – what *should* and *should not* be. This fundamental distinction has been with us since ancient times. Socrates himself was primarily concerned with the question of how we ought to live; he repeatedly asks whether people err simply because they do not know any better. If right action were merely a question of correct knowledge, it would be possible to eliminate errors and learn how to live the good life. This question comes up repeatedly in many of Plato's dialogues. The answer is sometimes yes and sometimes no; or the question simply remains unanswered. Aristotle, on the other hand, sees two distinct areas of mental activity, governed by different principles. While only those things which do not change can become known, our actions could always have been different. In practical philosophy, or ethics, our task is not merely to learn and to know, but rather a more fundamental task – to act well (and better), gain skill and, in so doing, to *become good*. It is for this reason that ethics does not distinguish between truthful and untruthful, but rather between good and bad, better and worse. 'Since, then, the present inquiry does not aim at theoretical knowledge like the others (for we are inquiring not in order to know what virtue is but in order to become good, since otherwise our inquiry would have been of no use), we must examine the nature of actions, namely how we ought to do them.'[1]

---

1   Aristotle, *Nicomachean Ethics* (hereafter *NE*) 1103b26f. The writings of Plato and Aristotle are usually cited with a link to the page (sometimes even the paragraph and row) of the standard

By its very nature, therefore, practical philosophy is a rather delicate and precarious task. Unlike theoretical philosophy, which can aspire to a certain impartiality and neutrality, practical philosophy has to address those areas of life where people occupy some kind of standpoint toward the world and themselves, where decisions and value judgments are made. It seeks to investigate human freedom, a realm which we today consider almost intimate. What gives it the right to do this? Moreover, each new attempt in the centuries-long history of practical philosophy has of necessity something bold, immodest or disproportionate about it. And so the reader has every reason to be sceptical. 'Who does this author think he is – some kind of expert? What could he possibly know about it and how can there even be anything new to say about it? Am I a little child, to be told by somebody else how to live my life?' I cannot allay these doubts here; I can only appeal to the reader's patience in the hope that answers to them will be found in the book.[2] The aim of the book is indeed not a modest one, although it does not wish to moralise and does not claim any particular authority for itself.

In spite of all of these difficulties and doubts, practical philosophy currently enjoys considerable public interest, which, while perhaps unexpected, is probably not coincidental. The achievements of modern science, technology, economics and organisation have enormously broadened the scope of human possibilities; and millions of people around the world are dedicated to the continued expansion of these possibilities. However, there are also a growing number of people who are troubled by the use we make of these incredible possibilities. Among the first of these were the physicists who, after the explosion of the first atomic bomb, were genuinely horrified by the forces they had unleashed. And the expansion of such possibilities has only gathered pace since then, giving the ancient question – 'how ought we to live?' – a new meaning and a new urgency, as attested to by the rich literature, the plethora of ethical codices and commissions and even our everyday public debate.[3]

---

edition, which in modern translations is given in the margins. – The literature cited here is meant to serve as a prompt to independent study, not as an appeal to a higher authority or an alibi for the author. It should however help us keep in mind one of the theses of this book, namely that we rarely invent completely new ideas, but rather live from that which we have inherited.

2   Rousseau answers a similar question: 'I would not take it upon myself to try to teach people, if others did not keep on leading them astray.' Cited in Spaemann, *Basic Moral Concepts*.

3   The Illinois Institute of Technology database of ethical codes for various professions (http:// ethics.iit.edu.research/codes-ethics-collection) lists over 850 of them. While I certainly do not underestimate the practical importance of these professional 'ethics', they are beyond the scope of this book.

This book will certainly not be able to solve all the questions, doubts and disagreements that lie at the heart of these debates; it cannot relieve people of the need to make (or, for that matter, the pleasure and responsibility of making) their own moral evaluations and judgments; and it cannot deputise for them in these questions. We will not be dealing here with the specific problems of, say, medical ethics, or the moral demands on economics and politics as they are formulated by various social ethics. This is partly because I have no expertise in this area, but also to avoid weakening the philosophical, universal aim of the book: to point out what needs to be considered by everybody in his or her actions, and why. Any reader seeking more than this degree of clarification and orientation will most likely be disappointed. Wishing to remain philosophical, the book sets itself goals that are both more limited and more general – although it would also like to be worthy of the name 'practical' in the title.

It aims to pursue in particular the following goals:

- To contribute to a more lucid distinction between morally significant phenomena, in order that we may think and talk about them more precisely and meaningfully.
- To strengthen our awareness of the fact that morality is not merely a private quality of each individual, but rather that it plays out primarily in relationships between people.
- To remind us of the altered situation in which we, as acting people, find ourselves today: an interconnected, globalised world in which institutions and organisations play an ever more important role.
- To meet the urgent need for common starting points or fundamentals of a universal and *panhuman* morality, as called for by these profound transformations.[4]

To help us in this task, we will make use of two sources, which I consider complementary, neither of which our predecessors had at their disposal:

- An overview of thought-traditions and carefully examined historical experience, so that we do not lose sight of what has been achieved in the past, and;
- The findings of sciences, mainly biology and anthropology. It is for this reason that the concept and idea of *life* will play such a key role in this book.

---

4   Compare Ulrich Beck, *The Reinvention of Politics*; on the need to justify ethical judgment A. Honneth, *Pathologie des Sozialen*.

* * *

Man is clearly a social animal and cannot live in any other way than in some kind of group or community.[5] Even the task of biological reproduction cannot be achieved without one other person, and, in order to succeed in the world, we have to rely on an ever greater number of these others. Some two hundred years ago, even in Europe, every village was self-sufficient, with its own blacksmith, cobbler and carpenter, mayor, teacher and priest – and later even doctor. People would occasionally need to go to the city, to go to market, or on a faraway pilgrimage. But there the village's dependence on other people would end; everything else had to be provided for at home.

Today most of us live in cities surrounded by thousands of people all like each other, and in amorphous states, where there are millions of us. When in the mid-20th century the creators of 'real socialism'[6] attempted to create the self-sufficient state by limiting our dependence on the outside world as much as possible, it was already plain that this was impossible; the state had to import petrol or iron ore anyway. And since then our 'relationships' (or, more accurately, our dependence on the work of other people) have on the one hand become dramatically deeper while on the other spreading out across a 'global' network across the entire world. The fact that these relationships are entirely anonymous, mediated in large part by money, does not change this. When as children we would visit our grandmother we would admire a small hand-painted Italian pot – from so far away! Now if we wish to impress our guests we would do so with plums or radishes from our own garden. If you take a minute to look around you, at what you wearing today or at the objects on your table, you can draw your own conclusions. Whatever name may be written on these objects – Levi's, Adidas, or IBM – we can be fairly sure that they have come from China.

More and more, we are acquiring, not only things, but activities ('services') in exchange for money from entirely unknown people rather than performing these activities ourselves. Fewer and fewer people do their own sewing, knitting and cooking, or organise their own entertainment or holidays; more and more, we are entrusting the care of our children

---

5   'Who cannot live in a society, or is so self-sufficing that he has no need to do so, is no part of a state, but rather a beast or a god.' Aristotle, *Politics*, 1253a. So too are humans caught between the two fatal temptations of headless mass collectivity, and of the illusive absolute of our own ego.

6   Real Socialism has been the self-designation of the East European regimes before 1989.

to kindergartens. Only a truly exceptional individual could survive on a desert island; today's explorers and adventurers, travelling to the remotest corners of the earth, where cars and televisions are unknown, do not set out without their radio transmitters and satnavs. These devices (products of the work of thousands of unknown people) provide them with the all-important security of orientation and contact with 'civilisation' – that enormous human community which is, in reality, our home.

A fine home that is, you may object, where the majority of people speak languages we don't understand, where nobody is waiting to welcome us and where people are more interested in our money than our unique personalities – if they notice us at all. The sceptic Heidegger accurately observed that, while modern technology and society may have broken down distances, they cannot offer any closeness. That is definitely true, and yet millions of migrants the world over today and every day are proving that it is preferable to eke out a grim existence in vast slums, feeding off the waste of rich societies, than to starve to death in the supposed 'closeness' of their traditional rural homes.

This new situation of global possibilities and global dangers, which curious, conquest-minded Europeans have been building since the 15th century,[7] is not one that we are 'by nature' equipped for. The instinctive barriers between 'us' and 'them', just like our personal safe zones, are not compatible with life in big cities, and this leads to constant stress, which can only be weakened and suppressed through learning and experience.[8] The incomprehensible language and habits of foreigners outrage the settled natives, but are far worse for the unfortunate immigrant, who has no option but to live among 'foreigners'.

The attractive and yet oppressive openness of the modern rich world, often associated with the loss of closeness, homeland and firm ground beneath our feet, awakens an almost spontaneous dual response. As the world changes rapidly, it forces us to adapt and to make decisions for ourselves as the tried-and-trusted models are often lacking. Since the early modern era, the response of most Europeans to this growing dependence on millions of strangers, without whom we would not survive, to the feeling of being lost among enormous crowds and masses, has been a greater emphasis on his personal, individual autonomy. In opposition to the ever smaller degree of genuine self-sufficiency, we emphasise our

---

7   The Portuguese occupied Madeira in 1420 and the Azores in 1427; these were the first European colonies in the modern sense of the word.

8   According to ethologists, man, like other creatures, has his 'zone of distance', and if a stranger steps in, this can be perceived as an attack.

personal autonomy and individual freedom, which is no longer under threat from the state so much as from the reality of uniform consumption and mass culture, unwittingly cultivated by school and television. It is naturally harder to resist the pressure of the billions-strong global majority than in the times when society was formed of thousands of free members of elites, who everyone else imitated and obeyed without resistance. Those who wish to fight against this pressure at all costs may perhaps flirt with the idea of using explosives; but even that is unlikely to help them.

The second, more recent reaction to European globalism is less utopian than enlightened individualism, and perhaps more effective. It consists in seeking out and defending whatever remnants can be found of real or supposed 'closeness' – from folkloristic peculiarities to national or regional loyalty. The somewhat spoiled modern European starts to feel revulsion towards the globalised world, and has no wish to become a 'world citizen'. He instead holds onto his own homeland, language and culture and defends them from the onslaught of globalisation, which he perceives as a threat to his special status. Nazi ideology was able to latch onto the mass horror that Germans felt about military defeat and economic collapse, and it offered the people a tangible image of 'foreigners' as enemies. Communist ideology also had to underpin revolutionary fervour with the idea of a powerful internal and external enemy, in order to sustain the necessary social momentum. The concept of the enemy is an important one, and we shall return to it.

But justice requires us to provide a corrective to this overly dark picture of individualistic and collectivistic defence of European man against global reality. Enlightened and liberal individualism is not merely an instinctive reaction against a looming danger. It also signifies a fundamental breakthrough in human freedom – the ideal of freedom for each individual person. It is here that the concept of human rights and freedoms, the first attempt at a panhuman formulation of the foundations of the future global society, first arose. No matter how much we may criticise it, we cannot abandon it – not even in practical philosophy.

The Romantic stress on everything local, different and national has likewise been open to abuse, and yet it remains an important component of human life in society. Just as enlightened individualism is a constant antidote to tyranny and absolutism of all kinds, so Romantic particularism expresses an equally important resistance against the attempt to reduce human society to a set of identical, atomised and mutually indifferent individuals – and to treat it accordingly.

We can illustrate the factual significance of these two streams of thought with an example from political philosophy. One of the most significant intellectual feats of the early modern age is the idea of the social contract. Although we understand this as an attempt at a new way of thinking rather than an historical event, it provides us with a certain model of society, which establishes and runs itself without the need for any external authority. It follows from this that, while an organised society doubtless requires some kind of authority, it is able to secure this for itself and no government can claim to be the only possible one (and therefore irreplaceable).

All theories of the social contract, however, share the same weakness: the very term *contract* presupposes that people can trust each other and that they will keep their promises. Without this fundamental trust in the given word (which must operate without the support of government, power and law) the term 'contract' has no meaning.[9] And so the social contract can hypothetically create a state, but it must presuppose an organised society, whose members can rely on each other.

But we also now know that relations of such elementary mutual trust come into being in small, transparent societies, which tend to be 'closed' rather than 'open'. It is precisely in such places – where people have lived together for a long time and reached agreement on much more than merely enlightened postulates of equality and freedom of the individual – that firm relations of friendship and trust can emerge over time. It was in societies such as these, bound as they were by a common culture – usually language, religion, custom and habits, and perhaps also a common bond to a certain place or countryside – that there emerged the prerequisites for the foundation of the good society. And we can imagine the creation of some kind of 'social contract' (and a corresponding power or government which has no need to suppress freedom because freedom does not threaten it) as belonging among these prerequisites. It is societies such as these which have, throughout history, become models and crystallising cores for wider and more varied societies.

As Europeans, we are fortunate in that our ancestors (voluntarily or by necessity) set about this arduous task of finding a way of living, and even living freely, in the confusion of these large and varied societies – often at the cost of great societal conflict and human suffering. The method that they arrived at (the same method, incidentally, that the Roman Caesars adopted centuries before them) is based on three main principles:

9   See P. Barša, *Imanance a společenské pouto* (*Immanence and the social bond*), p. 13.

- The state must compensate for the loss of this cultural and intellectual 'glue' through strengthening its institutional rule – especially in administration and record-keeping, finance, policing and the military.[10]
- It must promote and support the new 'civic virtues', especially discipline and tolerance, and it must strictly enforce the observance of this reduced social order.[11]
- It must surrender those things which would be unacceptable to a large part of the society – for example, a state religion – and confine itself to a commonly agreed 'civic minimum'.[12]

This method has – despite all of the historical catastrophes – proved remarkably successful. It helped to radically reduce the proportion of violent death and to improve the conditions of life.[13] It has withstood the onslaught of totalitarian ideologies and it continues today in its task of reducing the compulsory minimum of civic accord even further. Of course the societies which have emerged in this way are very different from pre-modern societies. The main difference is that they are extremely large and complex, strongly individualised and usually rich. Life in such societies is organised through increasingly complex institutions, which understandably has a homogenising effect, with the result that people in such societies become more and more alike (or at least more interchangeable).

This similarity is mostly in the realm of 'external' things – speech, behaviour, clothing – whereas on the 'inside' people jealously guard their own identity and their deepest convictions, which they would rather keep secret. To this ever-advancing 'inner' individualisation, which began more than two thousand years ago with the 'discovery of the soul'[14]

---

10 That modern states have nonetheless been threatened by this 'emptying out' is demonstrated by the fate of the 'right of the subjected against the ruler'. While medieval political thought, starting with John of Salisbury (†1180) took this right as a given, it disappears from modern thought for a long time, in the light of the religious and civil wars of the 15th, 16th and 17th centuries. Jeremy Bentham was horrified by any idea of the 'right to rebel'.

11 Compulsory school attendance belongs in this category. See Gellner, *Nations and Nationalism*.

12 This is the political sense of Hobbes' and Spinoza's critiques of revealed religion. But in the case of Bodin, Locke and Spinoza there is also a connection with tolerance. The French *laïcité*, the effort to exclude elements of religion from public life, belongs in this context. See Kohen, *In Defence of Human Rights*. Against this, not only the theorists of the so-called Islamic State, but also Leo Strauss and others insist that politics must be founded upon an absolute religious background, even at the cost of dividing the world into friends and enemies (Carl Schmitt).

13 See S. Pinker, *The Better Angels of our Nature*. However surprising, the thesis of the book is well documented. On the other hand, its overall optimism might seem somewhat premature.

14 See B. Snell, *The Discovery of the Mind*. (In German: *Die Entdeckung des Geistes*) and Ch. 3.3. below.

and which continues unabated underneath the surface layers of mass uniformity and globalisation, we are indebted for many, many things; we will remind ourselves of this at a later point. At the same time, however, there has emerged (at least among more observant people, and among the young) a threefold unpleasant feeling, or perhaps rather three questions:

- The accumulated wealth of human possibilities and resources raises the urgent question: what are we to do with it all?
- Can we find it within ourselves, within the relaxed confines of free societies, to keep ourselves in check, or are our societies already headed for disaster?
- Do we have the creative power and imagination to give our lives some meaning in this spiritual void, or do we need to content ourselves with a comfortable existence, devoid of any prospects?[15]

This last question, in all its urgency, comprises the entire content of Nietzsche's work and nobody has put the question more poignantly. This book is for those who also feel the urgency of the question but who are not content with Nietzsche's precocious attempts at answering it – whether it be Superman, eternal return or immoralism. People who consider these questions to have been answered – either by tradition or through their own efforts – should probably not expect to find too much in this book; while those who do not even ask such questions would most likely regard the whole enterprise as ridiculous and a waste of time.

Practical philosophy came into being at a time when people realised that the traditional answers were insufficient and when they could no longer even rely on the automatic agreement of their fellow-citizens. If they did not want to accept the naive, and perhaps cynical, celebration of force, as embodied by Plato's Callicles,[16] they had no option but to set out on the problematic search for meaning – and moreover a meaning which all people could accept as their own. Having nothing but human reason (supposedly common to us all) to aid them, their labours must have resembled those of a man trying to lift himself up out of the swamp by pulling at his own hair. Even we today cannot avoid this comparison,

---

15 Nietzsche called this, contemptuously, 'little comfort' or also 'nihilism'.

16 'What do we do with the best and strongest among us? We capture them young, like lions, mould them and turn them into slaves by chanting spells and incantations over them which insist that they have to be equal to other and that equality is admirable and right. But I'm sure that if a man is born in whom nature is strong enough, he'll shake off all these limitations, shatter them to pieces and win his freedom ... and then natural right will blaze forth.' (Plato, *Gorgias*, 484a)

but if we can rid ourselves of a certain pedantry that even philosophy suffers from, we can also benefit from the findings of the empirical sciences, especially biology.[17]

These findings have played a significant part in the remarkable transformation of our picture of the world and our own position in it. The universe is in fact not eternal, rather it has a beginning (albeit one that is unknowable to us) and probably an end as well.[18] In contrast to the older ideas of diversity, as expressed by the Aristotelian families and species or the systematisation of Linnaeus, we now see the universe as a gigantic process of irreversible changes, within which this diversity has come into being. The individual categories of being are not to be found lying alongside each other in their insurmountable difference, but rather they signify certain stages of the process which binds them all together. The universe therefore presents itself to us as 'historical', and even man, in so many ways exceptional, nonetheless belongs to it; not only because he comes from it and lives in it, but also (and mainly) because he has the Earth more and more in his power. These are facts which practical philosophy cannot ignore today.

---

17 Attempts to establish human morality on the ordering of the Universe can be found in many cultures. (See Lovin – Reynolds, *Cosmogony and Ethical Order*) But whereas they sought there arguments for the immutability of the moral order, we shall be looking after scientific explanations of its developement.

18 The Big Bang theory, on which contemporary cosmology is based, speaks of a 'singularity' which evades direct observation.

1. Practical Philosophy

'For here the point is no less than how we ought to live.'
Plato, *Republic* 352d

Socrates' question forms the basis of practical philosophy and defines its terms and goals. But it raises a whole range of sceptical objections. What more is there to be said about it in the third millennium? It is clearly too brief and all of its five words – 'how ought we to live?' – raise further questions. What is 'to live'? Why 'ought' anyone do anything? And even if they 'ought' to do something, what exactly? And where to look for it? These questions are at the heart of this book and we will be returning to them throughout.

Each new attempt at practical philosophy must both remain philosophy and yet also validate itself through its results. In this context 'practical' means that it should be of some help to its readers or listeners in the difficult task that lies before them as people: namely, to lead their lives responsibly. That is, in such a way that they do not attempt to squirm out of the task and that they realise that it really does matter how they perform it. This can be expressed in the form of a metaphor, as if they would have to answer the question, why they did or did not do this or that.[19] That there is certain hopelessness to such a task is a point we need not labour; but I should perhaps explain why I wish to undertake it at all. There are two reasons: the first is that, over the last twenty years of living in a free society I have come to realise that if people stop talking about certain things, it is as if these things no longer exist. It is therefore essential to talk about them so that they are not forgotten about. There

---

19 This is what Sartre means by his famously paradoxical statement that man is 'condemned to freedom'. The question 'before whom' or 'to whom' man must answer is, at this stage, not yet asked. See below, Ch. 2.6.

is no shortage of critical observers of contemporary societies and their complaints often convey the impression that the general public has simply forgotten about moral questions. If a suspect politician can declare his case to be settled purely because he was not punished, it is as if there is no other aspect to be considered other than that of court procedure.[20] It is as if not being found guilty of a crime is in itself a qualification for public office.[21] This is surely not the case, because even in modern societies people somehow manage to live and to pursue goals; and, given that they have managed to do this without murdering each other, it is evident that their actions are being guided by something. Nonetheless in the public idea of society something substantial is definitely missing.

The second reason links directly to the first one. We do not speak about what it is that we are guided by in our actions, because we do not know how to. We do not have the words for it, or to put it more precisely, the words we do have are worn down through severe neglect. Whether we respond positively or negatively to Socrates' eternal questioning about whether the good life can be taught, one thing is clear – we must learn to speak about it. And so the first task of practical philosophy, in my opinion, must be an attempt to sharpen our linguistic tools, in order that we may distinguish better. I remember watching a televised debate on the topic of morality a couple of years ago. The panel was made up of distinguished, educated people. After a while, the entire debate became focused on whether we ought to give up our seats on the tram to older people. Now I am certainly not opposed to that, but it is surely a warning sign when a gathering of such distinguished people can confuse morality with politeness.

This fundamental task of distinguishing and sharpening words so that they may serve as terms is the subject of the second chapter of this book. The point is not to find out what the correct word for such and such a thing is, but rather to learn what we need to distinguish from what, so that our speech has some meaning. Of course, *distinguishing* is not the same as *separating*. Practical philosophy cannot be axiomatic, for the simple reason that it seeks to be practical. If it is to deal with how we lead our lives, it cannot sharply separate and sort its themes into discrete categories, as mathematics or bureaucracy do. Only in mathematics or in civil administration is it possible for us to define precisely delineated sets

---

20 It is surely unnecessary to add that the judicial system, according to the presumption of innocence, must regard these cases as closed.

21 I will just add as an aside here that many important politicians have spent periods in prison on their road to power: not only Hitler and Stalin, but also Nelson Mandela or Václav Havel.

with no overlap, such as *even numbers* or *people born in 1968*. Practical philosophy cannot aspire to the logically necessary judgments and proofs, which are the preserve of the axiomatic sciences and of administration.[22] But already in law, which must also strive for the same degree of precision, the sorting of human activity into legal categories is the hardest task of both prosecutor and judge – and those in the dock often have the impression that they have failed in it.

Moral theories, which will be the theme of chapter three, cannot therefore be understood as self-sufficient and mutually exclusive systems – even if Hobbes, Spinoza or Kant thought so. Bernard Williams ironically refers to this conception of moral theories as an 'aggressive weapon' against the 'prejudices' of others and compares defenders of this approach to superpowers who only feel secure when they are able to destroy their opponents.[23] But in this book, we shall conceive of the various moral theories as frequently complementary ways of looking at situations of action and judgment (which are of course rarely straightforward), which can clarify, or perhaps support, certain types of decision. My own contribution, which is the topic of chapter four, should also be read in this light.

In his *Nicomachean Ethics*, Aristotle introduces the important distinction between that which is relevant to practical ethics and that which is not.[24] In one regard in particular he restricts the realm of the morally significant quite narrowly; no citizen of Lacedaemon, in his view, contemplates how other communities should be run. So here 'contemplation' is restricted to the viewpoint of action, which seems to have been the case in the strictly segregated *poleis* of ancient Greece, whereas today we can no longer be so sure of this. After all, dictatorial and terrorist regimes are a menace not only to their own subjects. Aristotle correctly summarises that practical philosophy should concern 'that which is in our power and which we may carry out' – but 'our power' is substantially greater and further-reaching today than it was then.

A different, and altogether more radical, attempt at separating out that which does not concern moral thought was sketched out by David Hume: no 'ought' can follow on directly from an 'is', from a statement of

---

22 Aristotle states at the very beginning of the *Nicomachean Ethics* that 'it is the mark of an educated man to look for precision in each class of things just so far as the nature of the subject admits' (*NE*, 1094b). William Sweet also states that ethics cannot provide proof, but only suggestions of how to act. (*The Bases of Ethics*, p. 11)

23 Williams, *Ethics and the Limits of Philosophy*, p. 85 f.

24 *NE*, III.5, 1112a22–31; also *NE* 1139a.

facts.[25] This attractively simple idea is the subject of various polemics to this day, and from it Immanuel Kant constructed his concept of the 'two kingdoms': the 'kingdom of necessity', where the laws of nature hold sway, and the 'kingdom of ends' or freedom, in which we lead our lives through our own decisions. Descartes also arrived at a similar idea, but in his quest for precision the realm of what really matters shrunk almost to vanishing point; nothing that depends on others can, according to him, have any significance for one's own judgment.[26]

This general tendency to limit our responsibility to that which can undoubtedly and from without be 'ascribed' to us is, in my opinion, an expression of a certain conception of man which Nietzsche called 'otherworldly'; a person is put into the world and must somehow make the best he can of it, and is responsible only for those things that he himself has caused and what he could have prevented, whereas he can respond to the farther consequences of his action (or inaction) with a shrug of the shoulders: 'nothing to do with me'. While the law courts doubtless have to operate in this way, our understanding of our own responsibility needs to be much broader. For we know from bitter experience that consequences (whether we caused them or not) will fall upon us and our descendants. Moral thought cannot, therefore, proceed along the lines of the defendant seeking only to exculpate himself, but rather like the public prosecutor, actively seeking and facing up to potential threats.[27]

This 'exculpating' tendency we have just mentioned goes hand in hand with a narrower conception of free action, which culminated with Kant's conviction that only decisions and 'good will' have any moral significance. This stems from a strongly idealised conception of the acting person, who has through his decision created a kind of absolute beginning, brought about by nothing, leading on from nothing and connected to nothing. A free person, in this conception, may be strictly bound by his (highly abstract) 'categorical' responsibility but in reality does not suffer from hunger, is in no pain and in need of nothing and need not give too much consideration to anything. Here, however, I would like to conceive of action as something that is conditional on various things, limited in possibilities, very often brought about by external events, something more like an answer to a call, or a means towards some fur-

---

25 Hume, *Treatise*, III.I.I.

26 Descartes, *Passions of the Soul*, II, art. 146.

27 This corresponds to the contemporary concept of precautionary principle which would find no place in Kant's 'kingdom of ends'.

ther end.[28] Even moral theories can, for the most part, be understood as partial and historic attempts to respond to a challenge; Kant himself is a shining example of this.

Practical philosophy, if it wishes to be worthy of the name, must take notice of how people live their lives, make decisions and act – as is implied, albeit silently, by Socrates' question. It cannot simply limit itself to that area in which we voluntarily limit our behaviour, which can be expressed in rules and which I will call morality. It should instead take account of both the various conditionalities and social contexts, which I will call custom, and also goals and consequences, the positive motives to action. Indeed it is not always easy to distinguish between means and ends – and their interrelation plays an important role in moral evaluation.

As I have already mentioned, I shall use, more than is common, the findings of science, particularly of the life sciences. This may seem like a paradox; after all, we have already spoken of Hume's distinction between what is – the subject matter of science – and that which I should or should not do. This objection has been lent support by Max Weber's demand that science should avoid evaluations, which in turn has led to an even more radical claim, that of a supposed 'value-free' science. And because science today shapes our public discourse to such an extent, there has developed the slightly vague notion that reality itself is neutral as regards values and that a moral viewpoint is a kind of superstructure that has been grafted onto it. There are, I believe, several grave misunderstandings at work here.

First of all, it is clear that practical philosophy is about people, or – as Kant has it – about all rational and free beings. Bulls can no longer be put on trial for lacerating anyone, as was the case in the late Middle Ages.[29] So in that sense only man and his actions can be the focus of moral evaluation and judgment, primarily his own. But it does not by any means follow from this that we should regard everything else that surrounds us, and from which we live, as valueless or morally irrelevant.

Man is – like all other creatures – first and foremost living, and he relates everything to his own life. So he naturally judges the things around him as either beneficial or harmful – as good or bad, in a sense. This we obviously cannot change, but we should nonetheless judge in the light

---

28 We will return later to Heidegger's conception of human existence as 'thrown projection'.

29 Modern society deals with such animals in a different way and without anything as awkward as morality getting in the way. Of course the animal's owner or other 'responsible person' could still find himself in court.

of knowledge, and with the necessary distance. Having a snake in your sleeping bag is clearly a bad thing, and something has to be done about it. But it does not follow (as we should all know by now) that snakes as such are an evil which we need to exterminate. Funnily enough, we owe our knowledge of this to science, which, with all its detachment, managed to notice that even snakes can be good for something (provided they are not in your sleeping bag).

Scientists also relate their activities to their own lives, whether it be that they are slaking their thirst for knowledge, fulfilling their potential, seeking to excel in some way, or even simply earning a living. Only against the background of this natural evaluating stance, and of their attachment towards their own scientific work, does Weber's call for scientists to maintain the greatest possible distance towards their subject make sense, because only then can their results be universally valid and acceptable. That this is not a natural state is clear from the fact that Weber puts the point across to scientists in the form of a demand. No one needs to order them to eat or sleep. Objectivity as a relationship towards a thing is not some sort of 'zero state' of the thing itself but rather a strict cultural demand made of scientists – namely that they attempt, for a large part of their lives, to put aside their natural attitudes to the world and to approach their subjects as if they had no bearing on their lives, in order to benefit the rest of us. Plato spoke of the necessity to study things 'according to themselves' (*kata to auto*) and not in relation to our own needs and interests.

This example illustrates a certain division of the moral world, to which we will devote more attention later. I criticised Kant's division into two 'kingdoms' as it makes us look upon non-human reality as morally insignificant. Moral beings do not live in their exclusive kingdom of ends, limited only to moral beings. People on the other hand live only one life and their ends are mixed together with those of other people, and also infringe into the broader non-human reality. But because man alone is able to think, and to be responsible, he must take this responsibility upon himself even for those who do not speak. One of the important new moral demands of the present time states that man cannot separate himself from non-human reality, especially that of living things, as was propounded by early modern moral codes, but must rather draw the conclusions that follow from his belonging to the whole of nature. We will return repeatedly to this important question.

Classical moral theories presuppose that each person acts for himself and acts freely only towards that which belongs to him. This was always a considerable simplification, for actions as a rule influence the lives of others; in the context of modern societies it is more of a mistake than an oversimplification.[30] Today almost all of us spend part of our lives as free citizens, enjoying our privacy and our 'free time'. However we are only able to earn this life by spending the other half of our life going to work – by hiring ourselves out into the service of others, usually organisations. Even in this environment we remain to some extent ourselves, but nonetheless we act according to the commands of others and the authority and resources which we deploy do not belong to us. This fundamental difference between the free life of a private citizen and that of an employee who is only conditionally responsible for his actions, has led some social theorists to the hasty conclusion that there is no need for morals in large organisations. Sombre experience has taught us that we cannot agree with this; however it is the case that the moral problems of people in institutional roles are of a different character and must be measured according to different criteria. This is another theme that we will be returning to.

---

30 A good example here is that of a voter on election day, whose actions, albeit on a small scale, have an impact on everyone.

2. From Words to Terms

He learns well who distinguishes well
Bene docuit qui bene distinguit

Words are the only tools that philosophers have at their disposal, and we must therefore take good care of them, to ensure that they can function as terms – our only tools for the communication of thought, blunt tools though they often are.[31] They would perhaps be a good deal better if we treated them better, if we distinguished better between them rather than mixing them together. It really is not a matter of indifference what we call things, even if some people may think it is. Before we set out on the difficult path into the thicket of practical philosophy – 'where nothing indicates the presence of game'[32] – we should clarify as far as we can what our main terms are, what they mean and what they do not mean, how they differ from each other and why.

We have already said that distinguishing does not mean the same as dividing or separating. In the realm we are entering into, the meanings of terms cannot be strictly separated as in mathematics; they are not terms which arise out of definitions, but instead commonplace everyday words which people invented when they needed them. We have often treated these words shoddily, with the result that they have become confused and mixed up. This is less of a problem in common speech, which always takes place in some sort of context – the person receiving the communication can figure out what is being said or can ask. But, as Plato observed, as soon as something is written down, it stands alone by itself

---

31 'Those who wish to speak without terms may do so elsewhere but in philosophy they do not have that right.' Hegel, *Outlines of the Philosophy of Right*. Introduction.
32 Emmanuel Levinas, *Totality and Infinity*. Introduction.

and if we need clarification there is no one we can ask.[33] We therefore have no option but to attempt precision and accuracy, of course only to the extent that it is possible in the given subject area. We have already heard that 'we must not expect more precision than the subject-matter admits of'.[34] That the intricate sphere of human life and action does not permit of any great precision does not mean that we should give up on it.

2.1 Life

The world and life are one.[35]

When Immanuel Kant finally published his anthropology lectures in 1798, he was able to sum up the whole sphere of the physiological study of man (or 'what nature has made of man') in a few sentences, reaching the conclusion that 'all theorising about causes is nothing but a waste of time' and concentrating on purely 'pragmatic' observation.[36] This has radically changed over the last two hundred years; now we cannot avoid or ignore the findings of the natural sciences, not even in practical philosophy.[37] For example, as we will see, the life sciences have discovered and re-established the term 'human nature', with a meaning which extends far beyond the boundaries of the empirical sciences.[38]

Let us start with the term *life*, which has perhaps not received the attention it deserves from philosophers but will play a key role here. It is a very common word, one which we use daily, and so we perhaps overlook the fact that it has two very different – albeit related – meanings. It can mean both 'my life' and 'all life, life as such'. The first meaning can be interpreted as something internal and private, whereas the second pertains to everything that lives, and not only at the present moment,

---

33 Plato, *Phaedrus*, 275d.

34 Aristotle, *NE*, 1094b.

35 Wittgenstein, *Tractacus logico-philosophicus*, 5.621. On the 24th of June 1916, Wittgenstein wrote in his diary 'The world and life are one. Physiological life of course is not "life" and neither is psychological life. Life is the world.'

36 Kant, *Anthropologie in pragmatischer Hinsicht*. Preface. Akademische Ausgabe, (AA) VII, p. 119.

37 For more on the idea of life in the Western tradition, see Pichot, *Histoire de la notion de vie*.

38 Looking for a source of law, Cicero says: 'How much has been bestowed upon men by nature, and how great a capacity for the noblest enterprises is implanted in the mind of man, for the sake of cultivating and perfecting which we were born and sent to the world, and what beautiful association, what natural fellowship binds men together by reciprocal charities: and when we have explained these grand and universal principles of morals, then the true fountain of laws and rights can be discovered.'(Cicero, *De Legibus*, I.16.)

but also *diachronically*, stretching back into the past, from where all life originates, and into the future, which awaits it. The Spanish philosopher José Ortega y Gasset observed this duality and distinguished between *biographical* and *biological* life. We will start with the first of these.

Long ago, before there were banks, highwaymen would attack travellers in the forest with the cry 'Your money or your life!' The unfortunate victim of course knew that it was his own life that was being referred to, and it would never occur to him to start discussing biology with his tormentor. We use the word with this meaning in many other, more common situations too: 'bet your life!', 'I swear on my mother's life', but also 'lifelong' or 'life insurance'. Of course the life being referred to here is mine, yours, his, hers, theirs – an individual, unique life, from birth to death. Even the expression 'eternal life' is commonly understood to mean the continuation of this individual life. My life, or to put it more philosophically, *existence*, is the thing that children take joy in and which adults toil for. As great Romantic literature, from Goethe's *Werther* to Kafka's *Metamorphosis*, revealed the hidden recesses of our inner life, its expressive power bewitched philosophers – starting with Kierkegaard – to the extent that they were almost unable to see anything else. Even the sober Husserl was convinced that the self-exploration of the subject and his experiences was the key to everything else (to say nothing of those less sober thinkers, from Sartre and the existentialists to the postmodernists). Even Wittgenstein, in the quote above, understood 'the world' as 'his own world' – and life as his own life. But could that sentence not also mean something else?

Their enchantment with the depths of their inner lives was doubtless sincere, and is something we all went through in our youth. Those who have read Dostoyevsky or Proust will have learned to honour the abysses of passions, suffering and longing which accompany human lives. We will remain grateful to these great writers for their insight, and will not forget them, even if we perhaps also feel that this is not the whole story of life. However, the other, alternative picture of man, the direct counterpart to the melancholic enchantment with the tragic depths of one's own life, was too harsh and ugly for readers – or even philosophers – to stomach. Science had entered the scene, so drastically and scandalously, that there was nothing to do but ignore it – or, to use Freudian language, to *suppress* it.

The horror and revulsion aroused by Darwin's *Origin of Man* in 1871 were not of a metaphysical nature and could only secondarily be explained by religious feelings. Lamarck had written something very similar fifty years earlier and had met no such response.[39] Lamarck, however, was writing for scientists and dealt mainly with invertebrates; Darwin's message hit much deeper. It had such a severe impact on man's modern self-understanding that it even shook the objectivity of those scientists who could not reconcile themselves to it. If we had to give a name to the repulsion it aroused, we would have to call it *aesthetic*. In opposition to the Romantic image of suffering and longing man, Darwin had constructed as a paradigm that which was at the time regarded as the ugliest, nastiest thing possible: brutal apes, among whom only the strongest will survive. I do not suspect Darwin of having concocted this number on purpose, and not until Nietzsche did anyone savour it in full. But the bomb had nonetheless gone off and people were now divided into two camps: those who repudiated Darwin's apes with shock and horror, and those who took a certain malicious delight in them, the delight of *Schadenfreude*.

And yet Darwin had done nothing more than remind us all of the other, forgotten meaning of the word *life*. He also reminded us of our similarity to animals, something which must have been perfectly clear to our more distant ancestors. It was a matter of course to them that animals also have legs, heads and ears – even if they don't have mouths and lips. It was clear to them that animals also lived, slept, gave birth and died. And the similarity does not end there. Comenius, among others, emphasised that even acting people can learn from animals: 'the source of God's warning', his 'light' is, according to him, 'the example of other creatures, in whom we learn of how they maintain themselves in their being'.[40] Our ancestors also knew that, while each individual lives his own life, has his own experiences, his own character and his own name, nonetheless he is only here because his parents brought him into the world, and it is expected of him that he will treat his life not only as an end in itself. We cultivated, modern Europeans have somewhat forgotten this, as the idea has entered our heads that we are not only 'by ourselves' but also primarily 'for ourselves', as Hegel accurately observed.

---

39 Even Darwin's own *Origin of Species*, published in 1859, did not cause any comparable upset. It is however true that English society was better prepared for Darwin, at least since the time of David Hume.

40 Comenius (1592–1670) was the last bishop of the Czech Brethren church in exile and a pedagogical reformer. In his last work, on the improvement of human affairs (*De rerum humanarum emendatione*), he wrote: 'All which was created gives us, as a whole and individually, examples of reasonableness'. Cicero also starts his treatise on good action by showing what we have in common with animals; man differs from them, however, in his ability to remember and predict (*De officiis*, I.11).

We are now a century and a half removed from Darwin; the passions have cooled to some extent and the real horrors of the twentieth century have taught us to value ordinary life. The pathos of inner suffering and longing also seems to have lost its lustre to some extent. We all know that we are mortal, and we are more cautious when we speak of eternity. Resistance to the 'monkey theory' still rears its head every now and then, yet not to such an extent as to render discussion of it impossible. But for the present, let us leave the monkeys to themselves and return to the discussion of what the term *life* is meant to encompass. Because we are here pursuing philosophy and not science, we can allow ourselves some degree of simplification, and perhaps even say things that no conscientious scientist would allow himself to say, as he would immediately be confronted by some exception.

Life and living things can be roughly characterised by the following six important characteristics:[41]

1. Every organism builds up its own individual and internally unified whole, which *delimits itself* from its environment and the outside world – for example, by a cell wall, membrane or skin.

2. The organism cannot, however, separate itself entirely from its surroundings, as it *depends upon it* for its existence in many respects: it needs energy, water and various other materials, and also must excrete its waste products back into the environment.

3. The organism keeps itself alive by continuously *regulating* certain states and processes within its body.

4. Depending on their environment and having to select materials from it, living organisms have the ability to distinguish and to orient themselves; biologists refer to this as *irritability*.

5. Most living organisms have a pre-set, limited lifespan, and their own characteristic chronological form (*Zeitgestalt* in German): they are born, they grow, they age and they die.

6. This feature, although unexpected and almost suicidal as a strategy of being, is more than compensated for by the ability to *reproduce*: organisms can multiply.

Each of these characteristics is deserving of closer study. A living organism is primarily an *indivisible whole*, which cannot be taken apart and re-assembled like a machine. It is not only a mere object, but also a continuing process, which we cannot turn off and back on again like an en-

---

41 Much of this is from a standard Czech textbook on biology. S. Rozsypal, *Přehled biologie*, p. 163. It starts with the living cell, which would be Point 2 in this list.

gine. By delimiting itself from the world outside and constructing a clear boundary, it establishes a difference between the inside and the outside, between its own body and what surrounds it. Thanks to this division, the organism can maintain within itself conditions different to those that apply in the surrounding environment, from acidity levels to the concentration of various materials to a lower level of entropy. This characterises the organism's elemental 'being for itself'. Its own body enables it to govern itself according to its own needs and also limits the field of its self-concern which, in limitless space would disperse without any result.[42]

Early modern philosophy characterised substance as that which endures by itself and which needs nothing further for its own existence. We could imagine a granite boulder as representing the ideal of this kind of substance: hard, impervious and aloof. The superhero Iron Man is an expression of this naive ideal of man. With living organisms, the exact opposite is the case; living things live off of their environment, from the water, light and energy that they can draw from their surroundings. If they do not find them, they die. Life therefore means *dependence*. Organisms also choose what materials to accept and which to reject from their surroundings. Hans Jonas saw in this ability something resembling the roots of human freedom.[43]

Living organisms maintain themselves not only by growing and expanding but also by self-regulation or *self-limitation*. They do not spread out like a fire or an explosion, but rather contain themselves within certain dimensions and limits. Should this self-regulation fail, the organism will die, as is the case in malignant cancerous growths. So even in the simplest living organism the principle of limitation is encoded as a condition of its existence. No matter how much life may have seemed to Nietzsche as the 'will to power', a closer look demonstrates that life also contains the opposite of this within itself, as a kind of corrective. It is this that will be of most interest to us in what follows.

Because living things depend on their environment, they need to be acquainted with it, to be able to orient themselves, and move around if necessary. Plants turn towards the light, animals seek food and water while also trying to find a partner and avoiding danger. Unlike trees which have no option but to wait for rain and cannot escape forest fires, animals can run to sources of water and away from fire. So living things

---

42 On a different level, man achieves a structurally similar 'separation' from his environment by building houses with windows and doors. See Lévinas, *Totality and Infinity*, Ch. II. D. On the need for the cultural separation of groups, see Richerson – Boyd, *Not by Genes Alone*, Ch. 4.

43 Jonas, *Evolution and Freedom*.

need what biologists, with typical understatement, refer to as *irritability*. This includes both the ability to observe the conditions obtaining in the environment and to act accordingly, with orientation or movement. The more varied an organism's behavioural options, the greater its possibilities of movement, the more perfect observational skill it needs.

Botanists may observe how the lack of possibilities of motion seems to bother some plants; they attempt to spread their seeds as widely as possible, using the most remarkable methods, from a dandelion's parachute to the 'catapult' used by *Impatiens glandulifera* to the use of animal transport, as in the case of the burdock and the rowan. The parallel development of an organism's possibilities of observation and motion lead to a fundamental change in the dimensions and character of its environment. A bacteria's environment does not extend much further than its tiny body, while that of an eagle extends to thousands of square kilometres. For modern man, equipped with television, the Internet and aeroplanes, the environment consists of the entire surface of the Earth and a bit more besides.

Every living organism must thrive, and we could say of it, with only slight overstatement, that 'in his being, it is this being, what is at stake for him', as Heidegger says of human existence.[44] Opposed to this stands the seemingly incomprehensible strategy of limited life in time. The great majority of living things have no permanence; rather, they are born and after a certain amount of time they die.[45] Not only do they die from lack of light or water, but even if they have plenty of everything, after a while they will die anyway, by themselves. What kind of 'being' is this, that contains within itself the ticking time-bomb of its own mortality – the insurmountable limitation of its individual duration?

So the being of a living thing is, at first sight, not only fragile and precarious, but also strictly limited. Is this strategy not utterly suicidal? Perhaps not. For living things have also discovered something that seems to be straight out of a fairy tale: they can reproduce and multiply. Stop and think about this most everyday of events. Does it not almost defy belief? The finiteness of each individual life does not only imply limited duration but a certain *Zeitgestalt* in their ontogenesis; living things are born, they change, they grow, they age and they die. This process cannot be captured in a single image, but rather in a succession of what entomologists call *imagoes*, likenesses of their ontogenetic development. During

44 Heidegger, *Being and Time*, § 41.
45 The particular case of single-celled organisms marks a certain boundary: we may see cell division as a direct continuation, or like 'death' and rebirth in two.

their lives, they also reproduce, but not merely in the sense of producing a copy of an adult parent, worn down by time, but instead a new baby, a fresh start. Thanks to the wonder of reproduction, it is as though the living do not age, but are always new and fresh – as if they were (phyletically) immortal.

The power of reproduction more than balances out the precarious dependence, limitedness and sensitivity of the living; in fact, even the word *reproduction* is an understatement. This should be clear to anyone who has had to clear out moths from their wardrobe or ants from their pantry. If all these creatures did was reproduce, that would not be so bad; but they also multiply, and fill their new biotope at the slightest opportunity. Yeast will multiply in a sugar solution until it eventually kills itself with the alcohol it produces. Where on earth did it all come from? When our ancestors believed that fleas gave birth to themselves from sheer grease and dirt, they were not so far off the mark. It really does seem like that. The weeds in your garden and the mould on your bread really do seem to appear as from nowhere and to grow all by themselves; while on the other hand, maintaining a sterile environment requires the utmost effort. So, while individual life is indeed fragile, species and phyla are able to look after themselves, and to colonise any environment that is not outright hostile to them. This is far more than mere 'reproduction'; it is a (somewhat unsettling) demonstration of the 'selfish gene' in action.

So life, and living things, are characterised by an entirely different strategy of being. They do not place so much emphasis on the mere duration of individuals, caring for their own fragile, dependent and time-limited bodies; rather, they rely on the capability of reproduction and multiplication. This confers several considerable advantages: first and foremost an incredible dynamism and the ability to expand to fill an environment whenever an opportunity presents itself. There is most likely a link between this fact that each individual constructs itself anew, by itself, and the remarkable ability of organisms to repair accidental damage to their bodies.[46] Among plants this is almost unlimited; mown grass will always grow back again, and even a tree that has been cut down can throw up offshoots from its roots. If a lizard loses part of its tail, it can grow back in again later. Humans do not quite have this capability (although our hair grows back after being cut). We may admire the wonders of modern surgery, but we should not overlook the fact that surgeons 'merely' cut their patients up and sew them carefully back

---

46 Kirschner & Gerhart, *The Plausibility of Life*.

together again. Then the patients are given a bed to lie in, and the rest of the job – the real healing – is up to them.

These capabilities we have been speaking of – regeneration, the replacement of old and damaged exemplars with new and fresh ones – follow on from the strategy of growth and reproduction rather than from mere duration. The biological species and phylum (though admittedly not the individuals) appear to be collectively ageless – provided they do not die out altogether. Today's spruce trees, ravens and even people closely resemble their million-year-old predecessors, even if they are still babies with only a few decades of individual life before them.

The importance of reproduction is commensurate with the sheer amount of energy that organisms invest in it – from the incredible profusion of spores and pollen with which conifers can powder an entire landscape, through the luxurious apparatus of flowers and seeds, the thousands of roe and tadpoles, right up to the complex sequence of courtship, reproduction and the care of (scarce) offspring among humans.

And yet philosophers have given only scant attention to this most essential feature of living being. Moreover, what slight mentions there have been have often come from women: Diotima, with her slightly hedonistic remark in Plato's *Symposium*,[47] or the Queen of Sweden, who, in a letter to Descartes objects that, while his interpretation of the human body as mechanism is certainly ingenious, she is unable to imagine how two clockwork bodies, if they were put together, could succeed in bringing a third into the world. In Aristotle's careful description of life reproduction is often missing, while for Kant and Nietzsche the subject did not seem to exist at all. When Heidegger made the decision to pay closer attention to life and the living, still it eluded him.[48] And even Hans Jonas, in an essay devoted to evolution, makes no mention of it, even though reproduction – as we have seen – is the true key to understanding the amazing phenomenon of life.

It was the biologists who brought the subject of reproduction back into the discussion. It was clear to them that the focus of their study could not be the individual, but rather the phylum – the taxon of which each individual is a mere occurrence, or transmitter. It then became clear that phyla are characterised by their genetic equipment, which is passed down from generation to generation, and which controls not only the ap-

---

47 *Symposium* 206b–207a.

48 Heidegger, *Grundbegriffe der Metaphysik*, p. 63 ff. See also the contemporary American philosopher Ari Kohen, who looks to biological evolution itself for arguments for human dignity; he says nothing at all about reproduction (Kohen, *In Defense of Human Rights*).

pearance (*imago*) of the organism, but also its *Zeitgestalt*, or ontogenesis. This was all still palatable until it was man's turn for the same treatment. When it was demonstrated that even man developed from other living species, the hypothesis readily suggested itself that man too was no more than a transmitter of his species, of his genome, of his own 'selfish gene'.

This is the exact opposite of our modern idea of human autonomy as an absolute and as an end in itself. It is no surprise that it met with such a stormy reaction. In the neo-Darwinian conception, man has suddenly become no more than a medium for transmitting something which reproduces itself and continues independently of us and above our heads, leaving us with only the illusion that we are living for ourselves. Even the greatest drama of human existence – death – suddenly appears to be no more than a technical detail, only slightly more significant than the division of a cell. All the collectivist theories in the world cannot compete with this fundamental denial of our idea of ourselves. They only attempted to relativise human individuality, not to deny its very existence.[49]

The provocative neo-Darwinian conception of the individual as a mere transmitter of a genome certainly has some weaknesses, especially as it applies to human beings. It exaggerates the importance of genetic determination and ignores social and human culture.[50] Modern man is almost exactly the same, genetically, as he was several thousand years ago; and yet he is so profoundly different. He no longer lives in nature, but rather in a world that he has adapted to his needs, to such an extent that most of us could not survive in the wild. Thanks to this adaptation there are far more of us alive in the world than we would have thought possible not so long ago; and most of us earn our living in professions

---

49 This self-image of man is similar to that of archaic agricultural societies, which saw each individual as no more than a link in a chain, whose main purpose is the perpetuation of the lineage. This represents a quite unexpected return to ancient thought, from which otherwise we have preserved only the habit of our family names.

50 The already cited Richerson and Boyd have shown how in human societies cultural evolution overshadows genetic evolution because cultural changes can occur much faster. Cultural transmission is less demanding of energy and involves fewer mistakes. It also enables choice between established models ('biased selection' – something which has no biological equivalent). Precise imitation, in which children quickly become more adept than chimps, allows the transmission of even highly complex systems such as language, and also make culture cumulative ('guided variation'). Societies are more successful the more people in them can rely on each other; this is why groups must separate and 'close ranks' to a certain extent. Evolution supports rapid and approximate solutions, as life demands; but in successful societies people seek out large centres, where the freedom of choice is greater. Richerson – Boyd, *Not by Genes Alone*.

that did not even exist a hundred years ago. We do not merely live *in* society, but *thanks to* society – through thousands of largely anonymous ties and dependencies, mediated by complex organisations. A two-hour long power cut is a potential catastrophe in a modern city. How, then, would it cope with a genuine revolution that aimed to abolish all organisations and start again with a blank slate?

But let us return to our theme. The neo-Darwinian legacy has overturned a whole series of modern philosophical ideas. It represents a quite unexpected return of medieval realism – the conviction that only 'generalities' are real, and not concrete individual existences, as was almost unanimously supposed over the last few centuries. The reality, for biological science, is the group, species or phylum – albeit in the invisible form of its genetic inheritance. And 'real' does not mean unchanging, but rather the opposite: evolutionary, changing. While this change is transmitted by chance mutations, natural selection ruthlessly sorts it into systematic and irreversible evolution, all of which takes place above the heads of its unwitting agents. Life – all that lives – is the centre of attention for this science, life characterised by a curious history, without names and dates, and by an 'evaluating' selection of the fittest. This selection is not of our choosing, but neither is it accidental, and it therefore presupposes something like a 'better' and 'worse': some kind of evaluation.

Evolution and Evaluation

Here we must add a seventh characteristic to our original list of six characteristic features of life – namely, that of phylogenetic development, or, to put it more concisely, evolution. This, too, is the result of a fundamental strategy of living things, time-limited individuals and reproduction, which brings into the world not only new exemplars of the species but which also provides an opportunity for mutation. A fairly modest example of this mutation is sexual reproduction, through which is created not merely a copy of one parent, but an unforeseeable combination of two viable adult individuals – the mother and the father. Sexual reproduction, however, is itself a product of evolution, and so we must admit that we are unable to explain a large part of evolutionary change causally.[51]

---

51 See Wesson, *Beyond Natural Selection*, for examples. Contemporary biology seeks to explain this 'improbability of life' by referring to the complex dynamics of 'reading' and interpreting the genome in the construction of phenotypes. The statically observed genome needs to be

This reality, no doubt a troublesome one from the viewpoint of science, can be somewhat ambiguously described by the word *chance*. Chance may mean an honest admission that we cannot guess what the causes are, but also the scarcely provable assertion that there are no causes. The traces of evolution, as revealed by the surprisingly chaotic structure of the genome, with its myriad seeming dead-ends, suggest that evolution proceeded along the lines of trial and error, rather than some 'intelligent plan' people might consider it to be.

The theory of evolution has successfully combined research into living things as a whole, but Darwin applied it to man too, and it is this which will be of most interest to us here. The fundamental acceptance of the evolutionary view of life stems from the conviction that the reality in which we live is not divided, but rather forms a whole, one enormous 'event', with a beginning and – probably – an end.[52] This conviction is also the basis for establishing discussion between philosophy and the sciences; but it should not imply the acceptance of the reductionist concept of man as no more than a naked ape. And more problematic still is the attempt, by Herbert Spencer, to reduce all of human culture and society to a consequence of natural selection (an idea being further developed by contemporary sociobiology).[53] As Thomas Henry Huxley observed, Spencer overlooked one important thing: namely, that the evolutionary origin of certain features of man and society does not mean that we must accept them and reconcile ourselves with them. After all, if moral sentiment is an automatic consequence of natural selection, so are man's 'immoral' aspects. A substantial portion of cultural effort, then, rather than being governed by biological evolution, has gone directly against it.[54] To satisfy ourselves that this reductively biological view of life is mistaken, it suffices merely to observe that man owes his success

---

complemented by various processes of blocking and activating its individual components; so that evolution may also be primarily concerned with these dynamics of 'reading'. See also Kirschner & Gerhart, *The Plausibility of Life*.

52　Bergson (*Creative Evolution,* 1907) and Teilhard de Chardin (*The Human Phenomenon*, 1955) attempted a non-reductive account of evolution as a whole.

53　For example Ridley, *The Origins of Virtue*. This way of thinking also stems from Hume's primitive 'naturalism'.

54　Huxley, *Evolution and Ethics*. In: Bayertz, *Evolution und Ethik*. 'The influence of cosmic processes on the development of societies is the greater the less civilised they are.' Virtue and goodness are the opposite of that which, in the cosmic process, brought success: it demands, not self-assertion, but self-limitation and regard for others, and it is not concerned with the survival of the fittest. 'It demands that all who share in the benefits of community have in mind what they owe to those who founded it, and that no action of theirs should shake the building in which they have been permitted to live.'

as a species to such 'unnatural' inventions as language, law, morality or the monogamous family.[55] The attempt to make evolution a 'judge', as in social Darwinism or moral naturalism, lacks any scientific basis, but is rather an ideological defence of prevailing social conditions and human selfishness.

While we may agree with E.O. Wilson's ironic warning that 'ethical philosophy must not be left to the merely wise', we should emphasise the word *merely*.[56] The existing consequences of evolution give rich testimony to how they have played out in the past and we use them to learn about what we see around us.[57] But precisely because we take evolution seriously we cannot accept that our role in it should be limited to that of 'adaptation' as the reductionists would have it.[58] Even if we accept man as a result of evolution, we should not overlook the fact that this evolution has not simply followed a path of adaptation, but rather one of experimentation and innovation. With the arrival of man, it primarily takes the form of *cultural evolution*, in which people, with all their capabilities (including the 'wisdom' rather cheaply mocked by E. O. Wilson) have played an ever more active role. Reductionist naturalism is, in reality, the illusory abandonment of the idea of evolution and the denial of a large part of its dramatic content.

Of substantial importance to us is that the concept of evolution has *historicised* nature, that is to say, it has connected it to a sensible chronological whole; it considers the engine of this peculiar history to be competition and selection – and therefore evaluation. The criterion for this evaluation (which, in the Darwinian conception, is always retrospective) has changed somewhat in the development of evolutionary theories; instead of Darwin's *fitness* we now speak of *reproductive fitness*. The important thing is that this ruthless selection is not the work of any one individual, and yet neither is it arbitrary, for it manages to bring chaotic change into an evolutionary whole. And so something resembling evaluation has spread far beyond the boundaries of human life and even there it forms some kind of general orientation or polarisation, even if it is

---

55 The above-cited Richerson and Boyd illustrate this point with a pithy example: 'Right at this moment you are reading a book rather than concerning yourself with your progeny.' From the reductive viewpoint this is clearly a maladaptation, and yet very successful. (*Not By Genes Alone*, p. 149)

56 Wilson, *Biologie als Schicksal*.

57 This is the true remit of science, while all attempts at extrapolation belong to the realm of its applications and techniques; attempts at 'scientific' shaping of the future come dangerously close to ideology.

58 Calloused hands count as adaptation, while hammers or spears do not.

somewhat tautologically characterised as 'survival'. That which survives is that which was fit to survive, or rather, to reproduce.[59]

As soon as the word 'evaluation' is uttered, the question arises: who evaluates, and according to what criteria? But here we must be cautious. Darwin ducked the question elegantly by stating that evaluation is always retrospective and decided by competition and environmental conditions. The second question introduces the problem of 'values'. This modern term, borrowed from economics by Kant and developed by R. H. Lotze in the mid-nineteenth century, can only be defined circularly, as the result of valuation (or preference) and is thus rather problematic. The Czech philosopher Jan Patočka concluded that values are no more than the 'sediment of valuation', an auxiliary term to be used sparingly.[60] We will, in what follows, give preference to 'evaluation', something with which we have real experience, and we shall be more cautious about 'values'.

Understandably, evolution touches not only upon the biological aspects of man, but also – and even more noticeably – the development of his cultural, social, economic, technical and spiritual dimension.[61] Here, the part played by individual agents, either in their own decisions or in the overall 'evolution', cannot be denied. The phenomena of conscious imitation, adoption and purposive planning and seeking are all too evident. However hard biologists may try to resist this 'temptation' (which, probably mistakenly, has been attributed to J. B. Lamarck), the question concerning the boundary between the 'biological' and the 'cultural' (between *nurture* and *culture*) has not been satisfactorily resolved, and the contemporary consensus is that the question itself does not make much sense.[62] Many biologists think in terms of dimensions or levels

---

59 That more and more people are convinced that they should restrict themselves in the interest of survival is an interesting 'anti-natural' turning point in human culture.

60 Max Scheler, for example, considers values as 'ideal objects' (*Der Formalismus in der Ethik*, p. 43) in an eternally hierarchical order (*Ibid.* p. 261). The originally economical term of value also tempts us to see 'value' economically, as price.

61 It was first described as a three-stage development of civilisation by Giambattista Vico in his *Scienza Nuova* in 1725 – well over a century before Lamarck and Darwin. Montesquieu, Rousseau and Herder all drew inspiration from Vico, as did Hegel. Auguste Comte's 'three stages of development' and, consequently, a great deal of 19th century thought, owe a significant debt to Vico.

62 'It can be surprisingly difficult to determine in individual cases whether biological or cultural heredity is involved; often, the answer is both at once.' Zrzavý, *Proč se lidé zabíjejí* (*Why People Kill Each Other*), p. 20. 'Culture does not cancel out biological evolution, but significantly alters the context in which normal biological evolution takes place.' *Ibid.* p. 22.

of evolution, which Jablonka and Lamb refer to as genetic, epigenetic, behavioural and symbolic.[63]

Cultural evolution, which occurs primarily through the medium of language and human communication, is for the most part governed by the imitation of tried-and-tested models, as this demands the least energy and carries the slightest risk. Yet here also a decisive role is played by those creative people who have the courage to think and experiment, mostly at their own risk. Often these are people who no longer need to devote all their time to mere survival and reproduction. Thus man is no longer living 'for himself', as his deeds prove to be especially important for others, for those who come afterwards.

This juxtaposition of biological and cultural 'reproduction' is more than just an intellectual hobby-horse. For all the differences between them, there are also many common features, and these may help us to answer certain questions which have so far been answered only unclearly. One such parallel is the incredible care with which both biological and cultural reproduction seek to ensure the reliability and accuracy of succession. We have seen that the very continuance of life depends directly on its being passed on; among the more complex life-forms this is increasingly entrusted to its transmitters themselves. We have already remarked upon the extraordinary 'investment' that plants make in their reproductive organs – flowers, seeds or fruits – which simultaneously serve as a 'starter pack' for each emerging individual. And we have already observed the powerful sex drive of the animals, from which man is not immune – although, characteristically, in man it has become separated from reproduction; sexual intimacy can maintain partnerships and need not serve only the creation of new life.

The parallel in the cultural sphere is the care given to the reliable and accurate continuation of the social order (for example, marital laws and the family) and the reliable passing on of language. Traditional texts were often in verse, to prevent their being confused. They were repeated and memorised until a more reliable crutch was found in the form of the written word. Complex rituals held social structures together and reproduced their 'common spirit'. Obedience to these was enforced by powerful institutions and strict sanctions. Common custom was also handed down in the form of folk tales; the conservatism of folk tales is a source of wonder to the ethnologists of our own day. And finally, every school-

63 Jablonka & Lamb, *Evolution in Four Dimensions*; Wilson & Wilson, *Rethinking the Theoretical Foundation of Sociobiology*. See also Richerson & Boyd, *Not by Genes Alone* in relation to this entire passage.

teacher who has ever corrected a child's spelling has also played his (or her) part in ensuring the accurate reproduction of language, which each generation has to master anew.

These varied supports, which have helped to limit the risks involved in the passing on of life, have, in the last few centuries, come ever more under human control. The possibilities of life are changing rapidly, as are its forms. The supports provided by tradition, which have aided it and helped to prevent the loss of what has been achieved, have often come to be seen rather as barriers, and many of them have disappeared altogether.

However, as man has increasingly come to decide on the essential things of life, he has taken onto himself an ever greater responsibility for life *per se*. Rousseau was referring to this when he wrote that man is the first creature to be 'manumitted' from nature, although he may not have been speaking of life in its biological generality. Many people today ask whether man can afford this, and whether he has not gone too far. This holistic outlook on life may suggest to us that – in the same way that a caterpillar cannot remain a caterpillar, but must either pupate or die – phylogenetic development cannot stand still. Time will tell if man could afford to take this extra step, but it is becoming clear that he must at least be aware of the possibility and start to act accordingly.

This concerns not only the external conditions of human life but also the willingness and courage of human beings to continue in the adventure of living. This – as Teilhard de Chardin observed – is of a highly paradoxical nature.[64] As long as the majority of people are fully taken up with the 'struggle' for life, the effort is so natural and obvious to them that they would barely even understand any question of what life meant. The very capacity for reflection is completely bound up with this effort and serves it fully. It is only when some people manage to secure more than just day-to-day survival that the paradox of life – mortality – starts to dawn on them. And once this is realised, all their labour, no matter how successful, can be rendered meaningless by a simple reminder of what awaits us all in the end, no matter what we do.

People discovered this very early. The oldest surviving literary work – *The Epic of Gilgamesh* – shows us how people have tried to reconcile themselves with this fundamental reality. From the hedonism of the innkeeper Siduri, who rejoices in the pleasures of everyday life, to Gilgamesh's desperate and futile striving for immortality, symbolised by the construction

---

64   See, for example his essay *Le gout de vivre*.

of the indestructible city walls of Uruk, almost all of the ways in which man has tried to deal with (or rather, suppress) the spectre of mortality are presented here. Throughout antiquity and the Middle Ages, relative existential security was the preserve of elites, and so this radical scepticism only occurred in small circles of educated people.[65] The poor majority, on the other hand, either had no time for such thoughts or kept them at bay with various forms of religious hope.

It was only with the unprecedented success of the European emancipation movement that the masses were able to secure improved existential security and the secular hope for a better future that accompanied it. But, like the ghost at the feast, there arose the phenomenon of widespread scepticism and loss of faith. This led to a significant increase in suicide, which drew the attention of early sociologists such as Emile Durkheim and Thomas Masaryk. Although suicide never became a mass phenomenon, rich societies in the 20th century lost faith in the idea of progress and the reaction to this loss of faith was an everyday cynicism, for which the only remedy seemed to be ever-increasing consumption. Meanwhile, the flagrant abuse of people's 'hopes' by various totalitarian movements discredited very idea of hope, which is today understood as being almost synonymous with manipulation by the powerful and, on the other hand, as foolish naivety.

The phenomenon of nihilism, that 'uncanniest of all guests' at the door, appalled even its discoverers.[66] But, in the course of the 20th century, societies have become rather used to it, and proponents of radical emancipation have begun to discover its (seemingly) positive aspects – mainly tolerance.[67] Where nothing has any absolute significance, people have no reason to shoot each other. This way of thinking, which we will encounter again in the course of this book, is extremely widespread in modern societies, although it somewhat naively overlooks the phenomenon of need, which, as we have seen, will always be a source of conflict. Even human societies cannot be free of conflict, as the utopians have fondly supposed. Therefore, the question cannot be merely how to prevent conflict but rather how to manage it.

---

65   See the discussion on Epicureanism below (Ch. 3.2). Christ's thorough critique of 'riches' and praise of poverty points to the connection between achieving 'security' in life and the loss of hope. See for example Matthew 9:23, Luke 16:1–16 and Luke 18:23.

66   'Nihilism stands at the door: whence comes this uncanniest of all guests?' Aus dem Nachlass der achtziger Jahre, in *Friedrich Nietzsche Werke und Briefe* [27]. Digitale Bibliothek, Band 31: Nietzsche, p. 9500.

67   Here they part company with Nietzsche, who rejected this 'weak' or 'cowardly nihilism' (*Ibid*).

As the French philosopher Rémi Brague noted, modern nihilism seeks to suppress all evaluations and replace them, on the one hand, with formal prescriptions and, on the other, with purely personal 'preferences', to ensure that there can be no conflict in its name.[68] But such a complete eradication of good and bad, better and worse, also implies an abandoning of meaning. Schopenhauer understood this, and it led him to reject life – and reproduction – outright. This idea also has many followers in our own time, and is, in its most banal sense, a widespread approach to life – especially in rich societies, paradoxically enough.

The modernisation of life and society over the last century has brought radical new possibilities for intervening in the process of reproduction – to the passing on, the beginning and the ending of life. The extension of life through medicine, eugenics, prenatal diagnosis, genetic manipulation, euthanasia – all of these represent a profound intervention into life *per se*. They also raise new ethical problems, which we will not be able to solve by referring to familiar concepts of individual life or individual rights. Respect for each currently living person will need to be expanded to take in those who come after us. 'My life' also belongs to life as a whole and, in this regard, does not belong to me alone.

This brief philosophical overview of the broad realm of 'life' has pointed to several important things. Life and its evolution has been the focus of attention, not merely for science, but for the general public. The idea of evolution, as put forward by thinkers such as Vico, Herder, Hegel or Bergson, provides the interpretative framework for such diverse disciplines as biology, cosmology, sociology and anthropology. The seemingly insuperable barriers between man and the animals (and even between the living and the non-living) have been dramatically relativised as a consequence. The 'realism' of molecular biology constitutes, at the very least, a serious rebuttal of the nominalistic emphasis on the unique and the individual.[69] And the principle of life (with the aforementioned

---

68 Brague, *Les ancres dans le ciel.*

69 In the language of medieval philosophy, the word 'realism' means the belief that that which should be taken seriously as 'real' are 'universals' – that to which we give general names such as 'fox' or 'person'. Already in the late Middle Ages, however, there arose in opposition to this the 'nominalistic' belief that what is real are merely the individual 'occurrences', objects and men, whereas general designations are mere titles or names (Latin *nomina*). Nominalism went on to govern a large part of modern thought, focusing on the human soul and on individual existence. Science, of course, has always been interested primarily in that which is 'universally' valid, but only with the advent of evolutionary biology has it reached the stage of 'extreme realism'. It examines nothing other than populations and taxons characterised by a common genome, of which individuals are merely carriers or transmitters. Indeed Richard Dawkins

characteristics) brings to this entire sphere a certain orientation which allows even the simplest organism a non-arbitrary selection and, indeed, evaluation. Selection and evaluation are not exclusively human attributes, as supposed until recently. Indeed, the desire to face up seriously to this reality was one of the reasons for writing this book.

2.2 The Threefold Model of Freedom

If we return now to man and his actions, we must, in our attempt at conceptual clarity, begin with the term which probably causes more confusion than any other: *freedom*. Any discussion of ethics must presuppose that man acts and that this action differs from the mere *reaction* of Pavlov's dogs and behaviourist psychology, which are causally determined and therefore not amenable to moral evaluation. We must simply assume that which we know from immediate experience – namely, that while we cannot simply do whatever we want all the time, nonetheless we can very often choose and select, act or not act, do one thing or another. We also know that our past actions could have been different; and part of being human is that we sometimes agonise over such things.[70]

This looking back into the past, at concrete decisions and actions, demonstrates that, far from representing an 'absolute beginning', even free action is conditioned by some kind of impulse – a threat, a challenge, or an opportunity. This can put us into a complex situation that calls for thought and decision, but also simple situations which do not leave us with much choice. And because these situations can be urgent, we must learn to orient ourselves in them quickly and act almost spontaneously, without the luxury of thinking. And so it becomes all the more important that we acted correctly; the ancient notion of 'virtue' referred to this remarkable ability to act both well and quickly, without much deliberation.

The process of deciding and acting does not, as a rule, happen in a void, as there are various forces, both physical and non-physical, acting upon us. Philosophy makes a useful distinction between forces 'from behind' (*vis a tergo*) and forces, let us say, 'from in front'. The first of these, primarily physical, do not take into account our specific qualities,

---

considers the 'selfish gene' to be the true agent and 'subject' of evolution in its. Unfortunately for modern philosophy, it has no terms for this important distinction, and so must return to the old ones.

70 'No one deliberates about the invariable' (*NE* 1139a14).

but merely push us away. In this category belong wind and gravity – but also teargas and bulldozers. The second group, in contrast, luring and beckoning, act only on people and animals, and even then not all the time. The aroma of bratwurst is only attractive to the hungry; fresh grass may appeal to horses, but is of no great interest to people. But for all that, these forces 'from in front' can guide people (or horses) to exactly the right place, which, for the forces 'from behind', is a far more difficult task.

Despite all the efforts of philosophers, freedom has resisted precise definition; and a survey of the attempts to define it may put us in mind rather of a battlefield strewn with corpses. And, while the fighting is mostly over, we must take care that we do not join the casualty list. So we will avoid the centuries-long polemic surrounding 'free will'; it adds little to the subject at hand, it is difficult both to prove and refute, and therefore cannot escape Ockham's razor.[71] The term freedom, like most philosophical terms, is taken from common language, where it can mean many things ('is this chair free?', 'buy two get one free'). In common speech, this multiplicity of meaning is compensated for by context, but in theoretical discourse it can cause serious confusion and misunderstanding.

Nietzsche observed this, and made a provision distinction between freedom *from* something and freedom *to do* something.[72] The English philosopher Isaiah Berlin applied this distinction to freedom in general; he spoke of *negative* and *positive* freedom, a distinction which has found a ready audience, especially in political philosophy.[73] The weakness of this distinction, in my opinion, is that it understands 'freedom' as a state

---

71 The issue of free will first arose in Antiquity in connection with individualisation, freedom and the question of responsibility for one's actions. In the Christian tradition, man is eternally marked by the consequences of the original sin, which manifest themselves in a tendency to evil, and which man cannot free himself from on his own. Drawing on Paul of Tarsus, Augustine of Hippo (354–430 AD) emphasises that for good actions, God's mercy and a justification in the belief in Christ are a necessary condition. His contemporary Pelagius countered that if that were the case, man could not be responsible for his actions. This dispute was rekindled in the early 16th century by Martin Luther and Erasmus of Rotterdam, and it remained unsolvable as long as free will was regarded as a permanent human attribute. We will return to this topic in connection with the philosophers of the Enlightenment and Kant, who took a similar view to that of Pelagius. Hegel, on the other hand, refutes all attempts at apparent proof of free will, as 'it is given to us as a fact of consciousness.' (Hegel, *Philosophy of Right*, § 4)

72 'Free from what? What does that matter to Zarathustra! But your fiery eyes should tell me: free for what?' (Nietzsche, *Thus Spoke Zarathustra*, I.17)

73 Hegel speaks of 'negative freedom', 'empty freedom' which can lead to 'frenzies of destruction' as in the French Revolution. (Hegel, *Philosophy of Right*, § 4)

of isolated individuals – without regard to circumstances – and fails to mention that it only makes sense to speak of freedom when we are not alone, but living and acting among others. No one can stop a ship-wrecked sailor on an ice-flow from doing whatever he wants; according to Berlin, he would be 'negatively free'. But he is probably far worse off than the prisoner who does not enjoy such freedom but at least gets food and a warm bunk. It is undoubtedly true that all freedom is some kind of possibility, and not positive determination; and that there is something about it which is not quite 'negative', but empty.[74]

In order to avoid such misunderstandings, we will start from the more common understanding of the word freedom and attempt to illustrate its salient features with reference to concrete situations or 'ideally typical' experiences of freedom. Hopefully the reader will recognise him or herself in some of them, as no other form of 'argument' is available to us. It goes without saying that these are merely fragments from the far richer whole of free life. The aim here is not to say what freedom 'is', but rather to describe how – and in which circumstances – it presents itself to us, and in which forms we encounter it.[75]

As with so many other things, we first become aware of freedom when we feel that we do not have it. This tends to happen in puberty, when we start to chafe against having to be home by ten and telling our parents where we've been all this time. So the first idea of freedom is a fairly simple one: having our own key.[76] And this idea on its own is sufficient, until we eventually get the key and we realise that perhaps having our own key isn't the answer to all our problems after all. And it is not only keys and parents that limit our freedom, but also school, authority, and social mores: clothing, hairstyles, speech, music and dance – all the things that people in a given society do every day to demonstrate that they belong there. At a certain point young people come to see all these things as nothing but restrictions, to be done away with – or at least experimented with, to find out how serious society is about enforcing them.

Most of us have passed through this important phase of 'pubescent freedom', and it leaves its mark on us. For a great many people (philosophers among them) this notion of freedom is all they need. Many

74 Berlin's defence of 'negative freedom' is concerned with political freedom and is opposed to the temptation of depriving people of their freedom since they do not know what to do with it.

75 I apologise to readers of my other books who will already be familiar with the following account.

76 Or, for some, their own flat. You can't stop progress.

thinkers who have studied freedom consider it to be no more than the absence of compulsion, the removal of external barriers to my deciding and acting. The Oxford Dictionary defines it as 'the state of being...unrestricted ... absence of slave status ... not being controlled by fate or necessity'. Broken chains and handcuffs are the most popular imagery on monuments to freedom. To demonstrate that this idea is attractive to young people, we need only look at advertising. The people who create adverts have to know their 'target group' much better than any academic expert – after all, their livelihood depends on it. Just look and see for yourself. 'Free yourself!' shouts a sportswear advert. And billboards are populated largely by agile youths, lithe girls posing in inconceivable positions, or sun-bleached cowboys, lasso in hand, resting on a rock in the Arizona desert. Look around: not a fence or barrier or a parent or a teacher in sight. This is surely what freedom looks like.

There is no doubting, then, that the removal of barriers really is an experience of freedom. And, once we have tasted it, we will only want more of it, so we will search for more and more 'barriers' to break through. But there will always be one that we can't defeat: the gravity which holds us to the earth. So far, only astronauts have managed to escape gravity – but are they 'freer' for having done so? Hardly. The freedom of the astronaut, not unlike that of the solitary cowboy, has one major drawback. While they are free to move around wherever they want, this is of no help to them as it is the same everywhere. Nothing but waste and emptiness, not a soul anywhere. So while the removal of barriers (Berlin's negative freedom) is important, it is not enough. We also have to look elsewhere.

The second, more complex, form of freedom refers to the *freedom of choice* – freedom to choose between several possibilities, all different from each other. We are all familiar with the version of this freedom presented to us by supermarkets and department stores. A whole world at your fingertips – just choose what you want, and it's yours. The self-service grocery store is a psychologically perfect invention. The idea for it is said to have come from an immigrant in the USA who observed that the shopkeeper behind the counter of traditional shops represented an unpleasant barrier to non-English-speakers.[77] He started a shop of his own, with these barriers removed from it; it was an enormous success. This experience of freedom, in department stores and shopping malls, was perhaps the most effective argument in favour of Western capitalism

---

[77] The idea for a self-service store, with turnstiles, aisles and check-out counters, was patented by the American entrepreneur Clarence Saunders, but reportedly inspired by a German-speaking immigrant from the Czech town of Svitavy.

against communism. Once people had had their first taste of this, they decided it was something they wanted for themselves. And they vaguely (but perhaps correctly) guessed that choice on supermarket shelves was somehow connected to choice at the ballot box.

The experience of freedom – of choice and selection – is also one which people have wanted more and more of; and so grocery stores have grown ever bigger, turning into supermarkets and hypermarkets, where assistants cross the shop floor on roller skates and scooters. If you find yourself browsing aimlessly through one of these hypermarkets, they may seem to stretch on to infinity, with an inexhaustible supply of stock. But if you actually *need* something – a pair of shoes, say – you may go home empty-handed, complaining that they 'didn't have any'. Of course that is not strictly true – they probably had plenty. But maybe the soles were poor, or the colour was wrong, or they were too tight or cost too much. After a while, even the most gigantic hypermarket becomes familiar, and everything in it seems the same. This is why the shelves have to be moved around occasionally, and bold sigs declaring 'NEW!' or 'SALE!' have to be put up. But then, if we go in already knowing what we are after, we may not find it.[78] This also applies to politics – when an election is nearing, we often have the feeling that the thing we are after is not available: namely, a candidate we would happily vote for.

Freedom as a choice between given possibilities is not infinite; perhaps because we are choosing between options which are presented to us by others. It is as if our capabilities have not been put to their fullest use and have been left to lie dormant.[79] Is there a way round this? Couldn't he actively participate on creating the possibilities? In the case of shoes, probably not. But there are other situations where we all know how to do it. One of these is *play*.[80] Play is a remarkable phenomenon, which we must explore in detail. For simplicity's sake, we will restrict ourselves to amateur games, from which no one earns a living (although even professional sport has an aspect of pure play, and only provides a living to those who are exceptionally good at it).

---

78   The purpose of these bold signs is to persuade us into buying things we did not want to buy.

79   This is why Aristotle says that 'human good turns out to be activity of soul exhibiting virtue.' (*NE* 1098a17)

80   See for example Fink, *Spiel als Weltsymbol* (*Play as a symbol of the world*), or Caillois, *Man, Play and Games*. Günter Figal postulates that 'free spaces' do not form any fixed order which would require stereotypical actions, rather, 'they resemble a game'. Play as a model of acting within society is also proposed by the French sociologist Pierre Bourdieu. According to him, Plato's 'serious play' is a characteristic of cultural activities and he regards 'play' as a metaphor for purposeful activities regulated by rules. See *Practical Reason: on the Theory of Action*.

Characteristic of amateur games is that nothing comes of them, and no one profits from them. Throughout history, moralists have condemned all games as a waste of time; yet surprisingly enough, people have ignored all of these warnings and continue to play them with passion and relish – children and adults alike. Even the worst dictators have not dared to take this entertainment away; on the contrary, they have realised that apart from bread, it is the one thing necessary to keep the people docile. While it does seem difficult at a glance to find what links such activities, from children's games, to theatre, playing a musical instrument, sport, card games, and even gambling, there must be a link, for the language has good reasons for calling them by the same word. So let us put the question another way – what is the opposite of play? What is not play?

'This isn't a game, this is a matter of life and death.' Play differs from real life in that life itself is never at stake in it. But does this mean that there is nothing at stake? Only a person who has never played a game could think so. A player who does not approach a game with seriousness and commitment will only spoil it for others; a game played too casually is no game at all. There is a difference though. An actor who dies on stage can do so over and over again. The loser of a chess game will not be executed like a defeated general; the players will merely swap white for black and start another game.

So play is not 'life' and life is most likely not play, as the Romantics claimed, but there is still a connection between them. Theatre plays evolved from the religious mystery plays, which sought to show us the deepest secrets of life and the world. Perhaps play is, fundamentally, something that acts out real life, which presents a sort of artificial model of life and the world. Even playing music creates something of its own 'world', into which players and listeners alike enter for a while, in order to free themselves from the grey everyday world 'out there'. And this is even more emphatically the case with theatre or sport.

Every game is strictly limited, in both space and time, usually in advance. The clearly defined space and time are set apart from the rest of the world – by a white line, or a curtain, a whistle or a bell. While many of parallels can be drawn between the 'worlds' of play, there are no direct links. A sales person can play a queen, a president can play a brewery worker.[81] After the final curtain comes down, they will go back to being

---

81 The late Czech president Václav Havel did just this, in a one-off performance of *Audience*, an autobiographical play he wrote while working in a brewery.

what they were before. In ancient Greece, actors wore masks on their faces so that nobody could confuse them with real-life people, and even today actors and athletes alike still have to change out of their 'civilian' clothes. It was the advent of television, offering as it does a close-up of the actors' faces, which destroyed this important distance, so a TV actor remains 'the doctor' or 'the executive' from a TV series, even if we meet them in the street. If you beat your boss at tennis or chess, it does not mean that you will be able to order him or her about tomorrow; even the result remains in the realm of play and does not transfer into the outside world.

Play, then, is set apart from the rest of the world, and holds up a mirror to it. What do we see in that mirror? Even that which makes play different form 'life' clearly shows how we regard life, what we consider important and what we would like to change. The spatial and temporal separation of play stresses that everything will be different here – do not confuse play and life. There is no transition between the two; the obligations and duties we have in the world of play do not apply outside it (and *vice versa*).[82] Our positions and privileges are not transferable between the two worlds. They do not have anything in common. Those of play mean nothing in 'life' and the 'real' ones mean nothing in a game. This means that you must not be afraid to be free while at play. What you may do within a game, provided it is according to its rules, will have no bearing on your life.[83] Win or lose, there are no lasting consequences.[84]

Every type of game accentuates some aspect of life and provides the participants, and perhaps the spectators, with an opportunity to exercise these without worrying about the consequences, and in appropriately idealised conditions. Let us take an example which everyone is familiar with: competitive games such as football, tennis, or chess. All of these

---

82 The burden that we temporarily shed by playing is not merely worry about survival, but also about the 'good life' in the Aristotelian sense. No opprobrium attaches to an actor for playing a villain; but if he breaks his leg he will be excluded from the world of play for some time. Expressions such as 'playing with someone's feelings' and 'playing with fire' illustrate the danger of ignoring the difference between play and reality.

83 A similar situation is granted to children in schools: a schoolboy weak in arithmetic will not go bankrupt for this.

84 This is, of course, not the case in gambling 'games', which are more like a battle against fate and for 'happiness' – in the form of winnings. Because the participants are not playing against other people, but rather against 'blind fate' (as represented by, say, a fruit machine), they may have the feeling that everything is at stake. What started as play turns into a desperate battle, as the experience of those who lose them richly attests. The key features of play – detachment and separation from real life – are lost.

games simulate conflict or battle in its simplest form (one on one, the red team against the blue team). In this case the advantage of play is very obvious; few people leave a real battlefield in one piece. Of course the players have to put their body and soul into the fight, from the first whistle to the last; but when the 'battle' is over, it is as if nothing has happened. This is why 'fighting' games can afford the luxury of rules. In a real battle, the participants would no doubt also like to have rules, but who would adhere to them? The winner has no need for them and so they can be of little help to the loser. In games life itself is not at stake and so rules can apply and an unbiased referee can uphold them.

The presence of rules and referees sets play apart from real life. They restrict our options, making them clearer in the process. In chess, for example, the number of possible moves is finite (albeit vast). A superficial observer might think that such limitations would impair creativity, but in fact the opposite is true. Nothing spurs human creativity like good and firm restrictions. A violinist needs no more than four strings; my childhood attempts to expand the chessboard led nowhere. In music, this restricting function is fulfilled by the tonal system and the choice of instruments, and here, too, atonal music did not usher in a new era, rather a loss of clarity. The presence of a referee and rules stresses further the uncompromising desire for justice – another difference from real life. The simplified conditions stipulated by the rules of a game make such justice possible; and it is interesting to note just how important this is for play.

Different games demonstrate different ways of understanding justice. In a tennis match, the player who has lost a game loses all the points won in that game and whether the player lost the game closely, or to love, this will not in any way be reflected in the result of the match. The same also goes for winning a set and the match. Such a concept of 'justice' would surely be unacceptable to any rationalist, as it is blatantly unfair – a player who actually lost more points than his opponent can win the match. But this system has the virtue of maintaining suspense. In each and every game, everything is at stake. It is also very realistic and teaches the players something which is nearly enough a rule in real life. And it also bears a resemblance to the concept of 'justice' inherent in the 'first past the post' electoral system – which is perhaps no coincidence.

In every game, one of the players starts and the other responds. This regular turn-taking is most clearly seen in chess or bridge, but it is there in tennis and other games too. By incorporating it, play employs a typical aspect of human behaviour, something we might call 'demarcated freedom'. In tennis, the player serving has the freedom to choose how to hit the ball, and the receiving player has somehow to deal with this shot, which he himself did not choose.[85] Provided he can get to the ball, he then has a certain amount of choice – where to place the ball, how much spin to put on it, and so on. If you learned to play tennis by playing 'against the wall', you will know just how important a live opponent is. The opponent's shots can surprise you, while you very quickly come to know exactly where the ball will go when it bounces off the wall. It is as if the feeling of 'freedom' comes from facing a good opponent. You need a good partner if you want a good game; it is no fun playing with someone who doesn't know how to play.

Similarly in chess, white has the choice of the opening move; but every other move is influenced by what black chooses to do in response to this opening. Both players have their general plans and strategies, and these confront each other constantly on the chessboard, where one player's plan presents an obstacle for the other to overcome, and vice versa. So each player views the game as a continual alternation of moments of *choice* (within the given limits, and always restricted by the opponent's actions) and moments of *response* to the opponent's plan, as it gradually takes shape on the board. It is only white's first move which is entirely 'free'; all the following moves are partly necessitated by the opponent's previous moves.[86]

Having the first move therefore confers a certain advantage, obvious for example in tennis, where one player serves, and the rules applying to the serve are therefore markedly restrictive. The taking of turns on serve further dissipates this advantage. We have already discussed the confrontation of freedoms, about one person's desire to assert his or her freedom against the freedom of others, and to 'trump' theirs if necessary. It is this aspect of conflict and warfare that competitive games reflect – and their enduring popularity demonstrates their success in so doing. Using the benign circumstances of play (the provision of a fair environment and the absence of lasting consequences), people can repeatedly experience and practise one of the fundamental features of their life, namely the confrontation of freedoms which limit each other, but which also inspire improved performance. This is often more important than winning or losing. If we want a good game, we will choose an opponent at a similar

---

85 Some readers will be reminded of Heidegger's 'thrown projection' (*geworfener Entwurf – Sein und Zeit*, § 31, p. 148): the 'unlockedness' of being consists in understanding its possibilities and projecting into them.

86 Chess theory teaches us that, out of the twenty opening moves white can make, only two or three have any chance of success.

level of ability, not a beginner or an inept player that we can easily beat. If we want to win, we have to possess some skill, for sure, but we also need to have some luck; this element is particularly important in gambling games, where we are playing, not against each other, but against 'chance' or 'fate'.[87]

We have illustrated, on the basis of three characteristic experiences which we all know well, these three typical forms of freedom:

- freedom as the absence of barriers and therefore arbitrariness or licence;
- freedom as the possibility of choice;
- play as the encounter and collision of two freedoms, which mutually create and offer their possibilities.

We have seen the weaknesses of the first two; they exhaust themselves and, sooner or later, become wearisome to us. Notice that only in the first one are rules the same as impediments. In the first, other people appear as barriers, and so this is entirely individualistic. In the second they are out of sight, stacking shelves, and only present a barrier if there is a queue at the till. Only in the final form – play – does it become clear that 'my' freedom requires a competitor. Your approach to cultivating your freedom will depend on how you understand it. In the first case, you will aim to remove barriers and shackles; in the second, you will try to increase the choices open to you. But only the third grasps the fundamental difference between rules and obstacles: you cannot play without rules. The better the rules and the better the referee, the better the game. Without rules, games instantly degenerate; try to imagine a game of football without the handball rule. In this sense, genuine human freedom – that is, freedom among people and in society – is always 'limited' (or, more correctly, 'delimited') because it needs rules.[88]

The idea that good rules support, and indeed enable, practical freedom, may seem paradoxical;[89] but every driver knows it from everyday

---

87 See Caillois, *Man, Play and Games*. Chapter 'Mask and Vertigo'.

88 The neglect of this extremely important fact led the Epicureans and, after them, Spinoza and Engels to caricature freedom as 'acknowledged necessity'. Kant frequently identifies arbitrariness (*Willkür*) with freedom, which he conceives in purely individualistic terms. The difference between them is implicit in the definition of law as 'the sum of conditions under which the choice of one can be unified with the choice of another in accordance with a universal law of freedom' (*Metaphysik der Sitten*. AA VI, p. 230). Hegel considers the belief that 'freedom ... consists in doing what one likes' as being symptomatic of an 'utter lack of developed thought' (*Philosophy of Right*, § 15).

89 The American jurist Benjamin Cardozo talks of the 'paradox of freedom': freedom without rules is anarchy, but rules restrict freedom.

experience. Being ordered to drive on the right, for example, may strike beginners as a restriction on their freedom. But if these beginners decide to disobey that order and drive on the wrong side of the road, they will very quickly realise (provided they survive) that the compensation for this restriction is that they can (mostly) rely on others to drive on the right as well. Otherwise no sane person would ever set out on the roads. This is the case with many other well thought-out laws, and only a very naive concept of freedom could see a paradox in them.

This connection between play and freedom is not random, nor is it purely metaphorical. Play has taught people that good and strictly enforced rules allow them to play well, without mutilating each other. Thanks to the shared experience of 'fair play', they were able to take elements of play into the harder task of living: rules, an unbiased judge, and striving after justice. Where life is at stake, this is not at all easy, and societies can only be free when everyone understands this and endeavours to maintain these standards. Freedom is never perfect and needs to be worked on constantly. Every young person must learn afresh how to 'play' it. It is no coincidence that the playing of games passed on from the aristocracy to the English public schools, and that basketball is so important in American schools.[90] For they represent a practical training in freedom, at least in its competitive form. But because these are team sports, children also learn to co-operate, and to pool their resources, as human life has always demanded.

2.3 Freedom and Power

This model of freedom as a competitive game allows us to demonstrate another very important reality. The collision of two freedoms, in direct opposition to each other, is regulated by rules; and the most important demand to be made about rules is that they be fair. Every player knows that his or her opponent is competing under the same conditions and that they are in symmetrical situations. This of course does not mean that the opponent will evaluate the situation in the same way: quite the opposite. I experience every strike, or move, with which my opponent realises his or her freedom (or 'asserts his or her will') as a clear threat to my own goals, and as a challenge that I must face head on. Only if I am

---

90   Man 'is the plaything of the gods; therefore every man and every woman should live accordingly and play the noblest games' (Plato, *Laws*, 803).

able to reach a difficult ball can I try to use it as a resource towards my own, directly opposed, goals and put my opponent in difficulty.

We have compared the taking of turns, or the exchange of a ball, to Heidegger's characterisation of human being as 'thrown projection' (*geworfener Entwurf*); in some games, moments of 'thrown-ness' and 'projected-ness' regularly change places. That which I regard as an assertion of my freedom appears to my opponent as a threat to his or her freedom – namely, my power, which asserts itself against his or her will; and *vice versa*. And so play illustrates a fundamental connection between freedom and power: the freedom of one player will always necessarily appear to the other as an alien, if not outright hostile, power.

Naturally, this situation also occurs outside the realm of play, where it plays an even more critical role and where it can no longer be so strictly regulated. While my own claim to freedom aims to increase my possibilities, or power,[91] every acknowledgment of – and increase in – the freedom of others is a threat to my own. A simple thought experiment will demonstrate that this really is the case in society. Ask almost any group of people if they are in favour of freedom, they will give you the same answer, and the same incredulous look: of course they are in favour of freedom, why would you even ask such a question? You will get the same response if you ask people whether they agree with universal suffrage. Of course everyone should have the vote.

The difficulty only arises when we try to put these very general questions in more concrete terms. What about your neighbours? Should they have the same freedom of expression and voting rights as you? Consider all your neighbours one by one. If our respondents are honest, they will have to admit that the question is no longer so straightforward. And it will become even more complicated when we put the question in terms of the most important everyday 'freedoms', such as loud parties, graffiti or the use of your bin for their litter. Only now does the double-edged sword of universal rights and freedoms reveal itself in its full horror; while they increase our range of possibilities, they also do the same for everyone else. And suddenly we begin to see the dark side of something that, until now, had seemed to us to be only positive.[92]

---

91 'The Idea of Liberty, is the Idea of a Power in any Agent to do or forbear any particular Action, according to the determination or thought of the mind, whereby either of them is preferred to the other.' (Locke, *Essay concerning Human Understanding*)

92 This realisation is the basis of Thomas Hobbes' sceptical theory of society; people enter into a 'social contract' out of fear of others and they will gladly forego certain freedoms if the ruler – 'Leviathan' – eases this fear.

All of us know this double viewpoint from our own experience, as we have all found ourselves on one side or the other: we have all enjoyed being at parties, and we have all been the neighbour who can't sleep because of them. Inexperienced people for the most part do not see how their activities can possibly be a source of conflict and will, according to what the situation requires, defend their own rights and freedoms, complain about the inconsiderate behaviour of others or just go straight to the police.[93] Young people often go through a kind of double conversion; at a certain age they discover their freedoms and seek to assert them in their immediate environment. However, once they find themselves in the wider society, they realise that they tend to be on the losing side of unregulated conflicts, and as a result they become drawn to the idea of strict order. They change their clothes and hairstyle, and from budding anarchists they transform into budding skinheads. The Germans have an eloquent name for this group of young people: *Halbstarke*.

Whole societies go through a similar development, if they discover public and political freedom together at the same time. After an initial phase of relishing the new 'freedom', which they naively take to be that of the lone cowboy (or the shopper in the supermarket) there follows the phase of disenchantment, brought about by feelings of disappointment, defeat and impending danger. In stable societies, this natural development plays itself out among individuals, and is not too dangerous to social cohesion. But in the wake of social upheavals, where relations between people become, so to speak, synchronised, it brings about waves of 'anarchic' freedom on the one hand, and calls for a 'strong hand' to save us by drastically limiting the freedom of others.[94] Both of these are bound to affect us as well as our opponents; but for a person (and a voter) untrained in play, this realisation may only come when it is already too late.

These problems were unknown to traditional societies because freedom and power were not proportionately distributed there. Aristotle of course distinguishes between the free and the unfree; the first group must know both how to obey and command, the second only to obey. Even the eponymous grandmother in the classic 19th century Czech tale happily accepted that her place was in her little cottage and that she must obey the local lord, while the lady lived in the chateau and ruled

---

93 'He who is feared by others must also fear others' (*Tao Te Ching*).

94 The spontaneous wave of euphoria that swept across Czech society in November 1989 was replaced by just this kind of fear as a result of the presidential amnesties of the following January. This was a very important lesson for Czech society in the darker side of civic freedom – the freedom of others.

over her. 'It was ever thus'; and our task is to secure what happiness we can for ourselves in the prevailing conditions. This is why old societies, seen through the eyes of such grandmothers, often seem so idyllic. This apparent idyll was smashed by the burgesses of the late Middle Ages, who wanted to put themselves on an equal footing with the aristocracy. They cast into doubt the given order of the world, from which flowed the authority of the ruler and lord; and when the burgesses had secured this equality for themselves, they could scarcely deny it to the rest – the non-property-owning majority.

During the French Revolution, all these things seemed to happen at once. After the initial excitement came the terror. The Jacobins feared for the revolution and so started to liquidate its enemies, until no one could be sure of surviving the night and people began to call out for strong leadership. No matter if the strong leader limits our freedom, just as long as he limits the others' freedom too. The dictators of the 20th century followed the same path to uncontested power. Mussolini exploited the chaos and despair he found in Italy after WWI, and 'restored order', just as Hitler and Stalin did. And in the Czech context, the ruthless criticism that was meted out to the Czechoslovak parliamentary system after the Munich debacle in 1938 played into the hands of the authoritarian post-war government, and paved the way for the communists to seize power.

Today, the likes of Lukashenko in Belarus and Putin in Russia present a more modest form of the same phenomenon, rescuing their nations to the applause of those citizens who are terrified by the new-found freedom of others. However, the authoritarian regimes of the 20th century differed from their traditional forerunners in one very important respect: they could not justify their position by appealing to any higher authority, as this idea had been laughed to scorn and done away with by their predecessors. And so they replaced the appeal to higher authority with fear – and, when necessary, outright terror. But their leaders knew that, for terror to work, it had to be selective. Terrorising a minority – racial or political – ensures that the majority fall neatly and obediently in line. What lengths would we not go to, in order to avoid provoking suspicion that we were supporting a foreign enemy – or an 'enemy within'?[95]

---

95 Sebastian Haffner's memoir *Defying Hitler* (*Geschichte eines Deutschen*) provides a remarkable testimony of how a person could be swept along unwittingly by totalitarian propaganda. Haffner was a democrat but, in order not to lose his job as a court clerk, he took part in compulsory schooling and demonstrations. Eventually he realised that he himself was becoming an active part of this propaganda, and that people around him had started to fear him; he emigrated shortly after.

So, fear of the freedom of others – their power, if you like – paves the way for the elimination of freedom. How can we prevent this? One way is the division of powers, an area in which Europeans have been particularly inventive. If the power of the state is strictly divided and distributed, so that they stand in opposition to each other, then there emerges something akin to the situation of competitive play; and the rules can be regulated accordingly. The Americans refer to this as *checks and balances*. Another way of limiting power led to the declaration of civil and human rights; state power has firm boundaries, a minimum of rights or freedoms is guaranteed to each citizen, and even the power of the state may not cross these boundaries. A third way is to work to ease social tension and people's fear for their own wellbeing. This is the origin of the welfare state and the more sparing use of state violence (including the death penalty) which are characteristic of modern, affluent societies.

No matter how effective or successful these ingenious elements of modern political systems may be, still they could not resist the anger and panic of a frightened populace. This is especially true where demagogues were able to convince the people that the rules only exist to protect unjust power, or to guard unjustly-gained property. When everything is at stake, the rules are pushed to the side-lines – and once they have gone, the path to terror is wide open. Pleasant though freedom may have been, once it comes into conflict with security, it is mostly a looser. Of course my freedom matters to me – but my fear of the freedom of others is stronger.[96]

Let us try to look at the relationship between (my) freedom and (their) power in another light. Of course everyone values their own freedom, but why should they care for the freedom of others as well? We cannot easily concede our own 'will to power', simply by dint of being living creatures, driven by Spinoza's 'compulsive need to be' (*conatus essendi*). But why would we want freedom in a society, where we know that it will apply equally to everyone else? The answer to this question also states how we can (or cannot) defend such common freedom even though we know that it presents a greater risk to our own security.

Freedom – as we have seen – is no more than an arena of possibilities, the opportunity to act (or not act) in accordance with our own judgments and decisions. Because this arena allows for good and bad, for beneficial and harmful actions, we should ask which of these is more numerous. Is it, on balance, to my benefit that others are free, or to my

---

96   Terrorists play on just this fear; from the Baader-Meinhoff gang to the 9/11 attacks, the goal has been that free societies would take fright at their own freedom and abandon it.

detriment? And what view does the society as a whole take on this – can we even guess that? Good and bad, as we shall see, cannot even be defined without difficulty, let alone trying to measure them.[97]

Since we cannot avail ourselves of any reliable measurement but must nevertheless confront this question every day in one way or another, we tend to 'solve' the problem by practical judgment and choice. This is by no means the exception to the rule that it may appear to be for the rational thinker. This reality was most poignantly expressed by a writer from whom we would least expect it: Thomas Aquinas. In a passage concerning law and justice he states, with no further comment that 'good spreads itself more widely than evil'.[98] This is not just casual optimism; Aquinas does not presuppose that people are 'good' and nowhere does he promise us that such belief would pay off. However, it seems to me that only a person who shares this conviction can support freedom in society honestly and without ulterior motives.

This idea can be expressed in another way. People usually relate to others in their immediate environment with both affection and positive expectation, but also with their guards up. Nonetheless, whenever we speak of our relations with others, a peculiar paradox emerges; namely, that stories in which I did another person a good turn, or on the contrary, another person did me some wrong always dominate. If we were to sum up these individual cases, there would surely be a vast surplus of good turns which somehow went unnoticed by their beneficiaries, or, on the contrary, an enormous amount of meanness, for which no one seems to be responsible. This is perhaps the origin of the widespread conviction that while we do our best to help others, we can expect nothing but harm in return. A true defender of freedom for all would have to be someone who has been able to resist this idea and maintain their belief that 'good spreads itself more than evil' – despite daily reports of evidence to the contrary.

Competition, Rivalry and Enmity

The spectacular success of modern societies is usually attributed to freedom; this freedom has cleared the way for unfettered human effort, invention and creativity. Look closer, though, and we will see that there

---

97 Unless, that is, we content ourselves with quantitative data such as GDP or some other definable measure of 'quality of life'.

98 'Bonum est magis diffusivum sui quam malum,' quoted after Thomas Aquinas, *Summa Theologica*, ii. q.1, art. 81.2, sed contra.

might also be another cause. After all, even our peasant ancestors had a certain freedom of judgment and action, but this did not lead to an explosion of new ideas or innovation. The feverish dynamism of modern societies only became possible at the point when the work of individuals and organisations could be arranged in such a way that they could compare themselves with each other. This is the significance of the ancient institution of the public marketplace, although the principle of the marketplace took a long time to seep through into other areas. A symbolic milestone in this journey is the competition to design the bronze doors of the Baptistery of Florence, which was won by an unknown outsider, Filippo Brunelleschi. Previously, commissions had been awarded on the basis of a person's position or origins, or perhaps on the basis of experience with proven artisans, whose work was compared against acknowledged models. But here we see the beginnings of a new basis of evaluation: the measure of my performance is the performance of others. It is no coincidence that this event occurred in Florence, which was governed by the banker Medici, or that the construction of the Baptistery was led and financed by the draper's guild, where competition and evaluation on the basis of performance were regarded as givens.[99]

Competition has been part of human life from the beginning, and races were a part of great festivals in many places, not only at Olympia. But of course these competitions were ritualistic and playful, in disciplines which never crossed over into everyday life.[100] But already in the cities of Ancient Greece competition was flourishing not only between tradesmen and merchants, but also between individual cities – and perhaps rivalry is a more accurate term here. Competition can develop precisely in those places where there is no given hierarchy or accepted models, and where for that reason the comparison of results can take over. But comparing involves measuring, and that is not always as simple a matter as in a hundred-metre race. The system of comparison becomes more effective if measureable criteria can be found and agreed upon to decide what is good, better and best. It was only a matter of time until the universal criterion of success became money.

---

99 It could, of course, be countered here that great innovations can be discovered much further back in history. I have chosen the Brunelleschi story because we know a lot about it, that it presents the idea of open competition almost perfectly and that it has since become a norm. Not long before, an Italian textbook on painting had stated that, as a matter of course, the artist should begin by copying established models (Cennino Cennini, *Il Libro dell' Arte*).

100 The Greek *agon* was among the cultural-historical predecessors of competitive games. This originated as a competition in honour of the gods. Fair conditions for competitors were scrupulously adhered to and victory was considered a sign of favour from the gods.

Competitors are driven, on the one hand, by the given goal, and on the other hand by the measure of some criterion, ideally by one single measure, which enables the awarding of silver and bronze as well. All the competitors know that they are competing against others, but that they should not intervene in each other's actions in any way. This is the purpose of the lanes on a running track, of anonymous competition, sealed envelopes and so on. The competitors are competing, or literally running, alongside each other, and they are forbidden from interfering with each other in any way. Yet despite all the attempts to protect the objectivity of competition and the objectivity of its evaluation, we have never been able to entirely suppress the older and more primitive type of human relationship: rivalry or opposition. Here the participants stand openly against one another. One wins, the other loses. The law of first, second and third gives way to the law of 'I'll show you who's boss!' Whereas in competition only the results count, in opposition defence and attack come into play, and with them, a fundamental contradiction in evaluation: my opponent's success is my loss, and *vice versa*.

In this way opposition points to a relationship that is perhaps even more fundamental, and into which it can easily slide: enmity.[101] In opposition which is somewhat regulated by rules, the issue is whether we win or lose. But with animosity, everything is the issue. Enmity does not end with one collision, but rumbles on, and the only sure victory is the one after which no other conflicts can follow: the extermination of the enemy. The best enemy is a dead enemy. As long as such enmities were confined in one place or among individuals and families, they did not present a direct threat to wider society. But strong interpersonal bonds and familial ties enabled them to spread dangerously, in the form of family vendettas. And with the rise of larger societies they became the cause of wars. The dead enemy became the burned-out town and the ravaged land, as happened so recently in Bosnia.

In traditional societies it was sometimes possible to ritualise conflict, so that the clash of foes was understood, not as a test of force, but as divine judgment. And so battles could be decided in a personal duel between the two leaders, as happened until the late Middle Ages.[102] But naturally, in conflicts where lives are on the line, rules do not count for

---

101 Martin van Creveld sees a clear distinction between competition and conflict as 'a condition of civilised society'. *Die Zukunft des Krieges*.

102 When the already blind John of Bohemia besieged Krakow and king Casimir challenged him to a fight in a closed room, he sent back a message that he would gladly accept if the Polish king also allowed himself to be blinded. Charles IV, *Autobiography*, Ch. 18.

anything and there is no judge to enforce them even if they did. The combatants alone decide the outcome. As Martin van Creveld has observed, modern-day wars resemble civil wars, where it is not only knights and warriors who fight, but every citizen, and using every means available. In Europe from the 18th century on it seemed that wars could be 'tamed' to the level of a struggle between professional armies, and that their conduct could be regulated by rules.[103] But then during the Napoleonic wars there emerged 'partisans', irregular fighting outfits who could only resist the greater numbers of regular armies by rejecting all rules.[104] And the World Wars of the 20th century only served to confirm the old truth that when the stakes are high enough, the rules fall away. This asymmetry between regular armies and lone 'total' fighters has been taken to its logical extreme by modern-day terrorists, who are not fighting against armies but against entire societies where they are at their most vulnerable: in large cities.

The order in which we have presented competition, opposition and enmity is perhaps back to front in evolutionary terms, but hopefully having them this way round will serve to demonstrate the systematic regulation of conflicts and the limiting of violence that is so essential to civilisation. Human society cannot be free of conflict; what matters is how we deal with such conflict. Social and cultural regulation cannot entirely do away with violent conflicts, but only direct them towards milder and less dangerous forms. To be effective, this requires social authority and government which can monopolise violence and which can itself limit the use of force, provided it submits to public control. Even peaceful competition is only peaceful as long as it is presided over by the non-competitive authority of law and state.

Even the more cultivated forms of opposition and competition contain a more or less 'sublimated' element of conflict, which can, in the right situation, explode into outright hostility and enmity, as clashes between rival football supporters and 'economic warfare' between states continue to demonstrate.[105] Even free trade, and the global loosening of

---

103 For example a ban on looting, international treaties about the wounded, prisoners of war, the protection of civilians, or – in the 20th century – a ban on certain kinds of warfare.

104 According to Creveld, guerrilla fighters tend to incur ten times the losses of regular armies and yet they prove impossible to defeat in the end.

105 The very first step towards European integration was the now-forgotten European Coal and Steel Community, an international treaty on the regulation of coal mining and steel manufacturing. The participants knew all too well that both world wars were partly instigated by the desire for coal deposits and the steel industry, and the competition in their production. A curious example of 'Irenism' in the Hopi Indians is cited by Ruth Benedict: "The Hopis love

trade barriers demonstrate more than support for economic competition and efficiency; they also suggest the sharpening of conflicting interests. European countries have understood that they can only loosen economic barriers once they have established a political authority which is strong enough to prevent competition from slipping into rivalry, and rivalry from escalating into enmity. On the global scale, no such authority exists.

Happily, there is another way we can limit the potential for conflict in competition, one which human cultures have always known: namely, through consideration and courtesy.[106] If a crowd of people is trying to get through a door, they can either compete (perhaps with their elbows) or smile to each other and insist 'after you.' This second version requires training, and must be established in the society as something ubiquitous, not only in situations of conflict. This is the purpose of common greetings. The use of the polite form of address in many European languages (*you, vous, Sie, Usted*) can help to prevent unpleasantness; and indeed in all European languages people address each other as if speaking to someone 'above them'. The use of 'sir' and 'madam' is now largely a formula, and their meaning is largely lost, but nonetheless it is still a sign of a certain respect, and has a certain significance for the atmosphere in a society.[107] It is no coincidence that totalitarian regimes tried at all costs to eliminate this and replace it with the coarse, and equally insincere, 'equality' of 'comrades'.

Modern moralists are dismissive of courtesy, especially those who live in a courteous environment and can take it for granted. Cynical critics point out that total, 'categorical' courtesy in front of a door could lead to everyone left standing outside, smiling at each other like fools. But what looks like *aporia* in reality never happens; even courteous people can be decisive, and the crowd always ends up getting through the door. It would be far worse in the opposite case, if there were no courtesy at all; if people all try to barge through at once, they won't get anywhere, and if panic breaks out, they could all get trampled on.

This banal example is a good model for less trivial situations. Wherever competitors care too much about winning (for example, if the stakes

---

to race but anyone should win a race by too big a margin, they will be excluded from the next race lest he should 'spoil' it." (*Patterns of Culture*)

106 The word *courtesy* – like the French *courtoisie* and the German *Höflichkeit* – refer to the court and its fine manners. The concept itself, though, forms the backbone of all social manners and is not restricted to aristocratic courts.

107 The Spanish *usted*, nowadays used as the personal pronoun 'you', is a corruption of *vuestra merced*, your grace.

are high enough) then the rules fall by the wayside and the opinion that 'results are all that matter' takes hold. This is something which we all know about, in private and public life. In politics this is often masked by saying that 'everything is at stake' and in fact it means the declaration of war. Of course we can also come across instances of exaggerated courtesy, but these are harmless in comparison.

Modern rich societies, which perhaps devote too much energy to the prevention of conflict, can also be threatened by the opposite situation, in which nothing really matters and nothing is at stake.[108] Just as proponents of 'free competition' need to be reminded that competition requires rules, it is also necessary to criticise excessive striving for peace and harmony at all costs. You can find such peace in the graveyard; life means movement, tension and often conflict. People and societies exist, whether they want to or not, within the Aristotelian 'in-between' and living always demands seeking after and maintaining a balance between force and courtesy, between self-assertion and self-limitation. We are 'condemned' to this from the moment we take our first steps; even if we simply stand still, staying on our feet is an unending search for balance.[109]

2.4 Custom, Morality and Ethics

The realm of freedom, delimited by rules, is otherwise free. But it is not arbitrary – as shown by the fact that we *make decisions* rather than simply tossing a coin. We orient ourselves in this realm and, for the most part, we feel that we know why one decision or action is better than another. Even in this realm of possible action, it seems that not all actions are equally good; even here it seems our choices are governed by something.

The question of morality, of the Greek éthos and Latin *mos* is really the question of how our more or less conscious decisions and actions are governed. Even where they are free they are not random; they are directed to some goal, they have some aim. On the other hand, it is characteristic of man that he regulates his actions. Not all goals, and not all paths to them, are equally good; the surrounding society will not understand all our actions; some it will not even permit. So there is no simple answer to the question of what governs our actions, and if we wish to make prog-

---

108 'A desire for all things can easily turn into a desire for nothing, lethargy and apathy.' (Comenius, *De rerum humanarum emendatione*, p. 200)

109 This is why standing still is more exhausting than walking.

ress in this area, we will once again have to distinguish. For that matter, even in everyday speech we distinguish between what is impolite, what is immoral and what is outright repellent. As we do between the courteous, the honourable, the beautiful or even the heroic.

In the following, we will try to create a working distinction at least three levels of that which governs our behaviour, and show that there are significant differences between them. Indeed in some cases they may stand in contrast to each other. I will give the name *moral* to this whole realm of more or less voluntary self-regulation of behaviour, which practical philosophy must concern itself with. I will then distinguish between three levels, where we are governed by 'social custom', 'individual morality' or the seeking of better and best, which I will call 'ethics', in the narrow sense of the term. We will start with the first of these, social custom.

The situations we encounter most often are those in which we act unconsciously and automatically, like we were taught as children. When we wake up we need not think about what to do first, but rather we quite naturally head for the bathroom, then we get dressed, eat our breakfast and then leave home, taking our normal route to school or work – all of this without any real decision-making involved. Likewise we do not think overlong about what we will wear. When we meet neighbours and acquaintances we give the appropriate greeting or gesture.

This unusually rich level of learned cultural stereotypes may limit our behaviour, but it also simplifies it enormously – imagine if you had to say something original to everyone you met. For the most part, this has been handed down to us by parents or teachers and we adapt it to suit our peers. This process involves the exercise of authority ('what do you think you're doing?' 'You're not going out looking like that') which, for the most part, is supported by nothing more than the assertion that 'this is (or isn't) the way we do things'. Our behaviour and action is strongly homogenised by society, which enforces accepted models and punishes deviations.

Young people, when they are beginning to stand on their own two feet, often present a stern test for this social pressure and the accepted models behind it. They are keen to see just how serious their society is about these models, and how it will respond if they are blatantly flouted. And because every society, from New Guinea to New York, places great importance on certain very specific and similar things, the recipe is a simple one. All that is necessary is to dress oddly enough, or even better cut your hair oddly enough, and success is guaranteed – even in contemporary society with its relaxed 'customs'. An orange Mohican never fails.

So every human society enforces some degree of conformity, which is necessary for everyday intercourse: all of us, by our appearance, clothing, gestures and speech, make it clear to those around us whether we wish to belong to them, whether they can count on us, or whether they need to keep an eye on us. Social conformity creates in others a primary trust,[110] without which life in society would be unthinkable. Indeed, the significance of this conformity is best shown by cheats and conmen whose livelihoods depend on being able to display 'model behaviour'. Similarly to language, these models of action are a sign of belonging to a certain culture or society – and also of being different from 'others'. If a society did not tend to such things, it would cease to be a society.

This does not mean that social custom never changes. As we have seen, it depends on being handed down through the generations. That which is not handed down is lost, to be replaced by something else. Unlike language and law, which have been fixed in writing for a long time, the handing down of custom operates the same way in Prague as in the Upper Orinoco. It is hard to overestimate this ubiquitous phenomenon, especially since, for the most part, we do not even notice it. We only notice it when we are exposed to a different, foreign model of behaviour; and, naturally, we respond negatively. This is the natural foundation of all xenophobia. We should not delude ourselves that this is something secondary, of no importance. Enforced social custom primarily maintains the awareness of a certain community and a climate of basic trust; it simplifies everyday life tremendously, and can help to cultivate it. Courtesy, or manners, at the dinner table can make things much more pleasant for other people.

Social custom, then, is something like a summary of learned cultural models of action and behaviour, to which every society leads its members more or less forcefully. If we wanted to express it as a formula or rule, it would read like this: always do things the way they are supposed to be done, always act like others act. Not all of them, of course, but the good ones; even social custom is not amoral, but teaches us to choose the correct models and tells us how we should do things.

From this fundamental layer of 'social custom' or conformity, which we share to some extent with animals, comes everything else. Neverthe-

---

110 See Fukuyama, *Trust*. English makes a useful distinction between the basic *trust* (which for example allows us to ask a stranger for directions and take their answer seriously) and *confidence*, in the sense of strongly relying on someone or something. According to Richerson – Boyd the basic rule of behaviour in any society is: 'Be nice to those who speak, act and dress in a way similar to yours; beware of all the others' (*Not by Genes Alone*, p. 224).

less, it is important to introduce certain distinctions. If we were to confuse this conformity with the other layers of voluntary self-control, we would be unable to say anything reasonable about them. As there is – regrettably – no general consensus concerning how to name them, I have suggested a working distinction between

1. social *custom*;
2. individual *morality*, and
3. *ethics* as a 'search for what is best'.[111]

Social custom is extremely simple and effective, but fails at the moment of encounter between two 'customs'. Both are equally self-evident to those who 'transmit' them, they often emerge out of different experience and circumstances, but they have no argument to make against others, so the question which one is 'best' makes no sense. This is why inter-cultural conflicts are so frequent and so hopelessly unsolvable – no matter how petty and superficial they may seem to the outside world.[112]

At the very edges of social custom were to be found people who had in some way 'emancipated' themselves from their community and become individuals: individually acting people. This turning point is famously expressed by Socrates, when at his trial he told the Athenians: 'Wherever a man's place is ... there he ought to remain in the hour of danger, taking no account of death or of anything else in comparison with disgrace.' – 'Men of Athens, I honour and love you; but I shall obey God rather than you.'[113] The Bible provides us with an even more forceful expression of this: 'Thou shalt not follow a multitude to do evil.'[114]

The situation has suddenly changed: the consent of the majority, so essential for social custom and norms of correct action, is now rejected in the name of another authority. It is now possible that, when the multitude 'does evil' a person can be called upon to stand against them – and even more, to fear nothing else 'in comparison with disgrace'. But what

---

111 A similar distinction is introduced by Ricoeur, *Oneself as Another*, and after him Cornu, *La confiance dans tous ses états*, e.g. pp. 11, 38. Cf. also Ogien, *L'éthique aujourd'hui*, p. 16.

112 This is the view of moral critics, such as Jonathan Swift: in his Lilliput, people argue over which end to crack a boiled egg. The problems that arise daily in 'multicultural' neighbourhoods perhaps suggest that Swift underestimated the importance of such seemingly petty differences of custom. It is worth noting that some 'impossible' manners were still common in our part of the world at the beginning of the 20th century: the almost mandatory head cover for married women, corporal punishment in schools, different notions of baring body parts, personal hygiene, or waste disposal.

113 Plato, *Defence of Socrates*, 28e, 29d. 'We must not consider at all what the many will say of us, but what he who knows about right and wrong, the one man, and truth herself will say.' (*Crito*, 48a)

114 Exodus 23:2.

should a person rely on in this situation? How are we to recognise evil when it is done by a multitude? Socrates appeals to the 'inner voice' of his daemon, which always alerts him if he is about to do something bad. And the Old Testament goes further than this. A few pages before the sentence quoted above, it offers a brief overview of the main 'evils', which the acting person ought to be especially wary of: the Ten Commandments.[115]

The Law of Moses – like other ancient codices – stands at the border of religious morality and law.[116] In common with legal texts, it presents an exhaustive list of prohibitions and obligations, which are to apply to everyone, everywhere, at all times.[117] The Ten Commandments differ from modern law in that they formulate the prohibitions and obligations in the *singular* ('Thou shalt not kill'), and in that they do not indicate any sanctions.[118] The remaining text of the Torah, like the Code of Hammurabi, contains a great deal of detailed legal regulations and sanctions; but here, at the very start, are only these few terse commands, summing up the main content of individual morality. Morality as voluntary self-restriction, regardless of the actions of the majority, or the state of a given society.

These exhaustive lists of proscribed (or prescribed) action are the source of law. And law takes all its fundamental features from them: authority, the sense of obligation, universality and unwritten sanctions. Here we can see clearly the normative (or, as Luhmann says, 'counterfactual') character of law:[119] the job of law is to prescribe, and it does not base itself upon how people act.[120] Even if the majority of people acted differently, it would still be valid. For this reason the demand it makes of us must be clear, and clearly formulated.

---

115 Exodus 20:2–17 and, in a slight variation, Deuteronomy 5:6–21.

116 Especially the Indian *Laws of Manu*, a traditional Brahmin codex which makes no distinction between what we would nowadays call legal and religious. In the *Chamurappi Codex* on the other hand, these terms are separated but the validity of the legal matter is based on religious authority, as is stated both in the foreword and the final summary.

117 To begin with, this would have applied exclusively to the members of the tribe of Israel, the participants of the treaty (Exodus 24:7n) but elsewhere a concept of 'universal' applicability of the law as such appears (e.g. Isaiah 63:20).

118 The motivation should not be fear of a punishment but rather gratitude for what the Lord has already done for Israel (Exodus 20:1), in one case 'a long life upon the Earth' (Exodus 20:12).

119 A norm is 'a counterfactually stabilised and expected behaviour' (Luhmann, *Das Recht der Gesellschaft*, p. 134).

120 'Valid' in the sense of normative theory: on the other hand, R. von Jhering, and sociologists of law, stress the importance of the 'lived' law. That is not to say that law could be guided by empirical reality but that it cannot do with mere normative validity, that it must impose itself on life.

With the expansion of state power, a large portion of human action passed over from the realm of (individual) morality to the realm of law. This certainly helped to strengthen these regulations, and also to strengthen the expectation that all the other members in a society will obey them. But something fundamental had changed. Unlike the moral language of the Ten Commandments – which addresses each individual and which urges him or her to act in a certain way – legal language deals in generalities. Distinguishing between acceptable and unacceptable action is a task for third parties, evidentiary hearings and 'forensic' (i.e. public) procedure.[121] This is why law cannot cover the whole realm of moral action. Legal proscription and punishment can only deal with demonstrable action, distinguished correctly by third persons. Despite all the successes of law, certain socially dangerous actions (such as lying, for example) remain beyond its reach and firmly within the realm of individual morality and voluntary self-restriction.[122]

The highly developed, technically rich area of law covers a very important part of what governs human action in society. Alongside the guaranteeing of subjective rights, the punishing of wrongdoers and the checking of state power, it strengthens a certain expectation among citizens. Law cannot guarantee that no one will suffer a wrong or an injury, or that all wrongdoers will be punished; but it does offer some support to those who avoid crime, and affords them some security that others will also avoid it. The existence of such security is extremely important for life in society. And yet all legal protection is by its very nature incomplete; many important areas of human action and expectation remain outside of it.

No general regulations and rules can precisely surmise the complexity of human actions and situations, and so even a correctly applied law can cause injustice: *summum jus, summa injuria*.[123] Older legal traditions paid particularly close attention to this problem, taking their lead from Aristotle, who frequently observed it and who warned against reliance on mere lawfulness or *legality*.[124] This is why current law leaves a certain freedom

---

121 Hegel draws attention to the considerable difference between morality and law. *Philosophy of Right*, § 94, Addition.

122 Only in exceptional circumstances can formalised lies, such as perjury or fraud be legally prosecuted, and even then, proving 'intent' is a difficult task.

123 'The apex of law, the height of injustice.' According to Livy, 'The laws are a deaf affair, unable to be moved by entreaty.' (*Ab Urbe Condita*, 2.3)

124 'For among statements about conduct those which are general apply more widely, but those which are particular are more true.' (Aristotle, *NE* 1107a) In contrast to Plato who wanted just decisions to be entrusted to 'a man of kingly knowledge' (*Republic*, 294a), Aristotle devotes

of decision-making to the courts, and uses words like 'proportionately', 'in good faith', and so on. This is where general legal awareness, as embodied by judges, becomes involved.

Human action, where it is truly free, does not only look to what is permitted, but to what is *better*, or *best*. The search for something better is characteristic, not only of the merchant bargaining over prices, but of every acting person; and here neither morality nor law can help us. We cannot approach this realm of excelling – of seeking what is better and best – merely by obeying the rules, but rather by going after a goal or an ideal, or comparing ourselves against the performance of others.[125] The neglecting of this difference and the reduction of the whole of moral thought to morality of rules is the target of Nietzsche's passionate critique of morality – his 'immoralism'. If we content ourselves with just obeying rules, we are giving up on the best we are capable of: 'creation'. Merely obeying the rules brings happiness and 'good digestion' only to those who are capable of nothing better; and worse, it gives them a weapon with which to terrorise the 'best'. According to Nietzsche such morality schools us in fear, envy and vengefulness, the worst which he could imagine – in short, nihilism.[126]

A more balanced viewpoint is proposed by Czech philosopher Pavel Barša, who distinguishes between the closed 'morality of justice, which allows us to live peacefully in situations of competition over inadequate resources and the struggle for recognition, and the ethics of love, which turns us toward other people, and allows us to forget about this competition and struggle'. At the same time, he acknowledges that humans

---

the tenth chapter of *The Nicomachean Ethics* to the term EPIEIKEIA, EPIEIKÉS (*aequitas* in Latin, *equity* in English) – 'all law is universal but about some things it is not possible to make a universal statement which shall be correct.' Ibid. 'The equitable is just, but not the legally just but a correction of legal justice.' (Ibid., 1137b) 'For when the thing is indefinite, the rule is also indefinite.' (Ibid., 1138a), citing the example of flexible (lead) measure allegedly used on the island of Lesbos.

125 As a finite physical being, man cannot only search but must also at some point begin to act. Brentano consistently speaks of 'the best of the achievable' and everybody with some experience behind them knows that the best can be the enemy of good.

126 It is a part of his provocative 'revenge on the world' that Nietzsche, stricken by poor health and an unhappy fate, sought a remedy in the admiration of ruthless power (e.g. in *On the Genealogy of Morals*). He philosophises with a hammer in order to see if anything survives the wreckage. An attentive reader cannot fail to observe though that the sensitive Nietzsche, fairly obsessed with the categorical demand of 'truthfulness' and 'honesty' fought against this 'big lie' not just around him but within himself, too. In that, he is radically different from his epigons who only saw his immoralism as justification of thoughtless brutality towards 'the weak', with appalling consequences.

are not perfect and that 'the closed morality of justice is a necessary condition for the protection of life in peace and dignity. It is not, however, a sufficient condition, but requires completion and grounding in the open ethics of love'.[127]

This is why it is so important to distinguish this realm of free searching after what is better and best from the preceding two, and to give it a separate name so they do not become confused. Independently acting people – in politics, business or any other endeavour – allow themselves to be limited by law, morality and other considerations, but only so that they can pursue their goals. In the realm of trade (in the broadest sense of the word) these goals are called 'interests', and are often understood as the highest possible profit. In life, where even profit can be at most means to an end, the word 'interests' is perhaps misleading. But it is clear that any person who seeks to excel must search and invent, compare and choose, and not only according to the rules but... well, what exactly? This is a question which should be examined by ethics – that part of practical philosophy which asks what is good, better and best.[128]

2.5 Relative, Relativity and Relativism

These terms play a significant role in contemporary discussions of practical philosophy. They all have their root in the Latin *relatio*, which originally meant *carrying back*, then later came to mean *narration* or *recital* and finally came to mean relationship or ratio. Ratio, or difference, is something which we can easily test. We may not agree on what is light and what is heavy; but it is plain that objects are either lighter or heavier than other objects, and that the scales we use to demonstrate the ratio (or relativity) of these objects are themselves not relative.[129] It is for this reason that they can serve as a symbol of justice.

---

127 Barša, *Imanence a sociální pouto*, pp. 54, 65.

128 The term 'ethics' is commonly used as a synonym of practical philosophy, and aforementioned distinction introduces a certain ambiguity. But as I wish to demonstrate that morality, as well as social custom, should at the end of the day serve 'the search for the better and the best', that they are in a way based on this search and that they stem from it (and not the other way round), it is hopefully not unacceptable.

129 The 'relativity' of weights and measures is an interesting issue. While they were created by convention, all modern societies strive to rid them of any relativity. Otherwise what would be the point in them after all? Even Einstein's relativity theory is based on the speed of light in a vacuum, which is not relative.

The same applies to other human judgments. The modern stress on the relativity of these judgments, as being conditioned and limited is usually a protest against efforts to deny this relativity. But it can also take on a more radical form, calling into question the general validity of any and all judgments. Not only is there nothing that can be called 'absolutely' light or heavy, but there are not even any scales we can use to tell the difference. But if everything is merely relative, there is no basis for evaluation or judgment. In reality, this means that all we have left is the trial of strength and, in modern societies, economic evaluation. Money is, after all, still valid. This position is sometimes called relativism, but the word is mostly used pejoratively by those who oppose relativism.

We have already seen that social custom is culturally conditioned, and that customs are varied among different societies. It is in the collision of these customs, which seem so natural and beyond doubt, or 'absolute' for each society, that their different evaluations, their conditionality and relativity become clear: one show itself to be relative compared to another, one 'relativises' the other. Already in antiquity, there were signs of societies reacting dynamically and openly to this significant reality; and European societies in the early modern period discovered it again. But for ordinary life in homogenous societies, accustomed to relying on their own custom to lead the way, it was a hard blow, and a new reality, to which they had to somehow reconcile themselves. The first and most obvious reaction of a homogenous society to another custom is of course an unfriendly one: this is nothing but wickedness, which must be suppressed and eliminated. There is no need to go into the countless examples from history and even the present day. But we should remind ourselves that this reaction stems from the very definition of society. A society which does not guard against deviations ceases to be a society, and dissolves like a sugar cube. The question is to what extent a given society is able and willing to tolerate differences, without endangering its very existence.

Ancient and modern societies sought ways of dealing with this difficulty, with some success. The first step in this journey can be considered the discovery of individual morality, which seems to stand above relativised customs. It began to weigh them up on the scales of individual conscience, and in so doing contributed towards their relativisation.[130] Against the monolithic custom, which determined everything from hairstyle through human relationships all the way to holidays and festivals,

---

130 See Plato, *Euthyphro.*

individual morality began to distinguish between the *substantial* and the *superficial*. Even the Ten Commandments attempt to name the essential obligations and prohibitions, without which a society cannot function, and distinguish them from everything which could be different. In debates over what is and what is not necessarily binding, Christianity separated from Judaism and moved the boundary between obligation and freedom even further; for example, it dramatically relativised language, origin and social status.[131] The fact that this generous programme of universal religion was unable to fulfil its promise, collapsing into myriad particularisms, does not change this crucial fact. For that matter, historians and sociologists would be able to find good reasons why, in the given conditions, it could not have been otherwise.

Unlike monotheistic religions, which base their universal programmes on the idea of divine revelation, the early Greek philosophers were embarking on an even more radical path. Plato's Socrates, inspired by Pythagoras' discovery of geometry, wants to find the key to the good life in unaided reason; and not arbitrary individual reason, but a reason guided by geometry and its very particular lawfulness. A reason capable of reflecting on its own life can never come into conflict with itself.[132] Thought, 'the talk that the soul has with itself on any subject it considers'[133] can arrive at dangerous knowledge – and not only in geometry. If it is successful in this venture, it can afford to relativise many more things; and it is for this that Socrates was condemned to death.

Socrates' wisdom has one very unpleasant condition: it must never suppose that it knows something that it does not know, or it ceases to be wisdom.[134] By insisting on this condition, Socrates laid an explosive charge in the very foundations of his own philosophy, and all consequent philosophy: only they who doubt things, and not those who know things, can be free of the charge of being 'unwise'. It now requires only a small step of logic – like the ones Socrates performs over and over again in his dialogues – for us to wonder if wisdom consists in anything at all other than doubting. And there are good reasons for wondering this; after all, what does it really mean to 'know something', other than in the realm of geometrical proofs?

---

131 'There is neither Jew nor Greek, there is neither bond nor free, there is neither male nor female: for ye are all one in Christ Jesus.' (Galatians 3:28)

132 'I would rather have ... any number of people disagreeing with me and contradicting me than I should have internal discord and contradiction within my own single self.' (*Gorgias* 482b)

133 Plato, *Theaetetus*, 189e.

134 Plato, *Defence of Socrates*, 21d.

Once we are over this thin line, however, we will encounter a standpoint which could not be more different from Socrates' own: namely radical scepticism, or, to give it its modern name, relativism. Socrates says of himself that his role among his fellow Athenians is that of a 'gadfly'. Now such flies of course require a herd; and perhaps an overly peaceful herd also requires them, although in a different sense. When the flies become too numerous, and the herd becomes overly agitated, then they are nothing but a pest. For Socrates to succeed in his invaluable role as a gadfly, there needs to be someone to pester and something to pester people about. In a society where everyone is a Socrates, the role is redundant. So relativising is itself by its very nature also 'relative' – dependent on the contemporary character of human life and society, in which people cannot merely examine and doubt, but must also evaluate, decide and act. This takes us to the profoundly true core of Nietzsche's protest against Platonism and the whole Apollinian tradition, which must, according to Nietzsche, necessarily end in nihilism. Life is not primarily about knowing wisdom, but about life itself, in all its unconditional and unsecured fragility. Nietzsche's objections do not concern Socrates himself. Plato's Socrates is not a logical machine but a living man, himself hounded by doubts and worries about the future of his endangered community. Nietzsche's targets are those who have made a profession out of 'relativistic' scepticism, who no longer take an interest in the fates and concerns of the surrounding herd, and who have settled comfortably into the role of doubters.

But relativism is problematic from another viewpoint as well. As we have seen, different cultures and customs relativise each other. Socratic philosophers can of course make this *relative-ness* clear and even relativise themselves, that is, place themselves into mutual relationships. But, should they forget that relativity is by its nature a relationship, and start to insist that 'everything is relative', they could be suspected of relativising 'everything' as it relates to them. That they see themselves as omnipotent judges, whereas everything they encounter seems somehow inadequate and 'merely relative'. But this is not an accusation we could ever level at Socrates himself.

Practical philosophy came into being precisely because of the need to overcome conflicts between cultures and customs; and it went about this task by relativising the differences between them. It showed that these differences were mostly superficial and that they hid more fundamental things we all have in common. It has millennia of experience with relativity and has no reason to fear it. It must not only accept this relative-ness, this dependence on the social conditions of the time, but carefully guard it. It must not allow itself to adopt a 'divine' overview from the position of the absolute, assuming for itself the right to judge and condemn; but neither must it allow itself to degenerate into the pandering pose of those who only say what the society wants to hear. Incidentally, the modern era has found that it is possible to combine both of these positions; this is what the tabloid press does, for example.

It is possible to view the real situations of acting people, and their relativity, from yet another angle. We have mentioned that people usually follow goals. But when they achieve those goals, they usually realise that this achievement has not brought them more happiness; and so they set out after other goals.[135] This experience may have been at the root of Plato's idea of the Good – the idea of one common goal of all rational action; whereas opponents of this idea find in it reason for their own belief in the relativity of all human aims. Acting people, of course, do not and cannot see any absolute goal. But they can find a certain common direction in all their actions and endeavours, which, surprisingly, does not change. In this they are perhaps like mountaineers who, while they cannot see the peak in front of them, they can nevertheless tell which way goes up and which way goes down.

2.6 Decision and Responsibility

Every action takes place in time; and man is characterised by the fact that actions concern him in a threefold chronological relation, Heidegger's 'ecstasy' of time:
- when he prepares himself for action and decides concerning the future;
- when he acts in the present, and
- when he evaluates retrospectively, as if in the past.

Elementary human experience teaches us that these three views are fundamentally different from each other.[136] In the first, everything is still open and uncertain. The second follows how an idea becomes reality, and the third has behind it a *fait accompli* which can no longer be changed in any way.

---

135 See Rosenzweig, *The New Thinking.*
136 According to Greek mythology each of these is governed by one of the Fates: *Lachesis* (from *lachos*, condition), *Clotho* (weaving) and *Atropos* (unswerving) (Plato, *Republic*, 617c).

The first phase, prior consideration which will eventually turn into decision, is characterised by uncertainty and unknowing.[137] To begin with, we need to clarify our ends, so that we can find the means towards them. In organisations this takes the form of written mission statements and 'feasibility studies'. In this phase we reduce complexity by breaking big questions down into smaller ones, and we reduce uncertainty by availing ourselves of experience or scientific prediction. In this way we reach a decision, which, though conditioned in various ways, is still more or less free in that we could have decided otherwise. This is why Kant's practical philosophy, for example, limits itself only to this phase, while others also take into consideration the foreseeable consequences of our decisions.

Of course, this is a highly idealised notion of the process. It is also possible for our decisions to be immediate and instinctive, if circumstances force us to decide and to act swiftly; we saw this in the case of ball games. There may also be something much more important than a game of tennis at stake, and the ancient notion of virtue refers to the admirable quality some people have to act spontaneously, almost without thinking – but still do the right thing. It is in fact one of the jobs of social custom and the rules of morality to support this ability; and they do this job by reducing the complexity of decision-making, or even rendering it unnecessary.

The second view must give its attention to what is happening at that exact moment – to the individual phases of action, the deployment of means, the way the situation develops, and other somewhat technical affairs, and is, by its nature, a closer view. In military terminology we could speak of tactics, and, as far as we know, other animals share this with us. On the contrary, in the first and (especially) the third views, we are trying to see our actions as a whole, and how they relate to a goal we have set; we will be careful to maintain a certain distance here to ensure that we do not miss anything in the more complex whole. In the first phase, we may put off instrumental and technical questions, and in the third they need not trouble us – provided our action does not founder because of them.

But at this point the planning view ahead and the evaluating view backwards can be very different. The unwitting Oedipus strikes down a stranger in the woods, only to find out much later that it was his father. But we know this from entirely banal situations too; a man argues with

---

137 If we knew, we would not need to decide. Derrida says in this regard that the impression of *undecidability* is a necessary condition of all decisions (*Hospitality, Justice and Responsibility*, p. 66).

a surly official, bangs the door shut and then, out in the corridor, remembers that he does not have the stamp that he went there for. The planning view forward of a person who is only now making a decision to act is, by its nature, working with incomplete information.[138] It is only after the event that it is easy to be wise – when all the results are in. This is why people have, since time immemorial, tried to limit the uncertainty of the future, whether through palm-reading or modern science, the practicality of which lies in its ability to find and exploit lawful patterns and to calculate the future. And once this can be done, as in the construction of aeroplanes, then action can move to a level lower and concern itself only with obeying the requirements of the design engineer. But even design engineers need to sign their name under their drawings; what if they made a mistake?

The difference between projections into the future and retrospective evaluations most likely becomes clear to us in cases when our action has not reached its target; by which time nothing can be done. The strength of humans is in their ability to analyse what went wrong and learn lessons for next time – in other words, to gain experience. Trial and error is an often-used method in the empirical sciences, even if it is always informed by the previous experience of others. But it can also happen that everything goes according to plan and yet we are unhappy with the result. Where was the mistake? Who is to blame for it?

Action – or inaction – where there is something at stake will have brought something about, and the results would have affected someone. There is nothing we can do about this. But where the consequences cause damage to other people there is also the problem of responsibility and guilt:[139] who is responsible? Who needs to go up before the victim, or even the court? Those who are in the process of deciding should think carefully about what their action may cause; and in modern societies they have to expect that they will 'bear responsibility' for it. This collocation can mean different things, though in every case it means something more than just the direct consequences of action. While consequences are what they are, the important thing is to know to whom they should

---

138 This is why many people think that games in which we have to make decisions with incomplete information, such as most card games, are closer to reality than games with complete information. But even in chess, where the positions of all the pieces are visible, the most important piece of 'information' – the thoughts of our opponent – is not available to us.

139 This is the standpoint of 'moral minimalism', whereas 'maximalists' judge that even harm to ourselves constitutes a moral problem. See for example Ogien, *L'ehtique aujourd'hui. Maximalistes et minimalistes.*

be attributed – who is guilty, and to what extent. A man who cuts his finger off will of course bear the consequences – a missing finger. But if it was his fault, he will also bear responsibility for it: in front of himself, his family, his colleagues, or perhaps his health insurance company or even the state. So responsibility can mean three things: demanding that we reconcile ourselves to our share of the consequences, that we answer the questions of other people, and, finally, the possibility that we will have to answer for them to a court – in the knowledge that we may have to compensate for the damage caused or accept punishment.

This third component – legal and penal responsibility – is clearly indispensible for the functioning of societies where people have to be able to rely on each other. While it cannot guarantee us that we won't be robbed, or that bricks won't ever fall on our heads, it at least offers the comfort that we need not be afraid of walking down the street. In this sense legal, or forensic, responsibility has long been separated from custom and morality (from which it came) and is entrusted to an 'operationally closed' organisation or societal mechanism, and we will not concern ourselves with it here. But we will, in what follows, give our attention to that responsibility which is not enforced – and, for the most part, cannot be enforced – by legal systems, because our share of responsibility, and especially our intention to hurt someone, cannot be proven and distinguished from 'unhappy accidents'. If you admonish a waiter that the sum to pay is too high, he would probably apologize for the slip, but is this true?

Karl Jaspers, in his famous post-war book about responsibility for Nazism, distinguished three levels of guilt beyond criminal guilt:
- political (and therefore to a large extent public) guilt, which is borne not only by those who asserted and supported Nazism, but also those who did not do enough to stop it;
- moral guilt, which everyone must attribute to him or herself, and
- metaphysical guilt, which is to be borne before God.[140]

In the area which concerns practical philosophy, the surrounding society has always acted as a sort of 'judge'; but today we place more emphasis on each person who has decided and acted (or not acted) judging his or her own guilt. Man probably discovered this ability to look from at a distance at himself and his actions at the same time as his 'soul'; this ability is traditionally given the name of 'conscience'. Plato considers it from that side which is most important for living among people, as the

140 Jaspers, *The Question of German Guilt* (*Die Schuldfrage*).

capacity to feel shame.[141] In the biblical story of David and Nathan we are told that sometimes someone else has to 'awaken' this capacity in us.[142] In Christianity, the conscience is regarded as the voice of God, the highest authority, but nonetheless a voice which must be 'awoken' or cultivated in each individual. For Heidegger, it is the 'silent voice' which confronts existence with being. Freud reduced this confrontation and guilt to a mere 'feeling of guilt' which he regarded as a neurotic symptom requiring treatment. In doing so, he discredited the terms 'guilt' and 'conscience', paradoxically at the very time when they were most needed – as Jaspers demonstrated. Although philosophical literature uses these terms rarely, they are still the foundation of everyday moral life.

The 'incomplete information' referred to above means that even judging our own degree of guilt in our own conscience is not a simple task, especially if we want to look at action in its 'three-phase' whole, which includes all sorts of random accompanying phenomena and circumstances that we can hardly influence. The endeavour to make moral judgments more efficient and 'operative' and bring it closer to the function of law gave rise, in the later 18th century, to the development of two significant traditions of moral thought which split this whole right down the middle. On the one side stands the deontological tradition founded by Kant, which limits responsibility to our own decisions; and on the other stands utilitarianism and the whole 'consequentialist' tradition,[143] which evaluates actions purely according to their consequences, which it also tries to measure. We shall return to both of these later.

* * *

Decisions are always *somebody's* decisions, but not necessarily decisions of a private person for him or herself. In many instances, for example where we lack specialist knowledge, we entrust decisions to doctors, lawyers, brokers and others. They then act in the interest of their patients or clients, to whom they have a greater or lesser responsibility.

In modern societies and their organisations, the decision of the entrusted occurs ever more frequently. This flows from their accreditation in a function or role. The decisions of managers, master workers, bureaucrats and generals belong in this category. Unlike decisions for ourselves,

---

141 For example, Plato, *Protagoras*, 322d. 'Shamelessness' is 'for all, both privately and publicly, a very great evil'.

142 II Samuel, 11–12.

143 From the word *consequence*.

which are limited only by our possibilities, by laws and by morality, and guided by goals we set for ourselves, these people are making decisions mostly about others, and are strictly limited by the scope of the mandate entrusted to them and by the commands of their superiors. The goal has also been set for them by someone else. This is why, on the one hand, their responsibility is usually limited only to what they decide from their own volition and, on the other, their guarantee of results is also limited. We will return to these important questions in Part 4.1.

Responsibility is not a straightforward relationship, as it may seem from studying simplified models of it. It includes at least three elements, namely *who* is responsible *for what* and *to whom* (or *before whom*); and, in the legal realm we can add some further literal delimitations of responsibility and the level of guarantee. In the case of the bearer of responsibility, or the 'responsible person', we can distinguish an undivided responsibility of the individual person and the delimited contractual responsibility, say, of an employee towards his or her employer, which in turn often blurs into the responsibility of experts. This is different in that experts – doctors or lawyers – must answer not only to their patient or client for the help they have given them, but also for their expertise, whether they acted *lege artis*, to their professional chambers or associations. We have already mentioned collective responsibility, but I would just like to mention one further responsibility; we can call it human responsibility. Not in the unfortunate sense that 'we are all guilty', but instead in the sense that some of our responsibilities seem to lack counterparts – those before whom we should feel responsible. And yet they could be the most fundamental and most important responsibilities of all.

2.7 Justice

While custom and morality regulate action from the viewpoint of the agent, we can also look at it from the viewpoint of a disinterested 'third person'; here we encounter the important term justice, which we met earlier in our discussion of play. Although we now connect it more readily with law, it has a far wider significance and evidently precedes law. A commentary on the Roman Digests states that 'law (*jus*) comes from justice (*justitia*) as from her mother; justice existed before law'.[144] Just as

---

144 Gloss of 1.1 pr. D. 1.1 quoted in Radbruch, *Rechtsphilosophie*, p. 34.

the notion of justice is a kind of substratum upon which law grows, it is also a norm, which law is always measured against; critics of law often object that it is a long way removed from justice.[145]

The experience of injustice is often the first experience that teaches us the notion of justice. By this is meant the kind of experience which affects me personally, and which I regard as a grievous wrongdoing. Very young children experience this; and, according to some ethologists, so do animals.[146] To the extent that moral theory mentions this, it is in connection with politics; whereas the writings of social critics and revolutionaries are awash with injustices. This is perhaps because there are an endless number of injustices, and only the idea of justice can give the impression that there is only one. Injustices can also mobilise people against those who commit them, whereas the feeling of injustice often does not survive an objective analysis; it is just my feeling, and in the eyes of other people things may look different. Among practical philosophers, injustice was studied carefully by Cicero, who concluded that people allow injustice in two ways: either by directly committing it or by not preventing it even though they can. There is also a big difference between an injustice committed 'in a momentary distraction' and premeditated injustice which is far worse.[147]

In the whole Western tradition, justice is regarded as the fundamental necessity for action among other people, as the 'queen of virtues'; it is so important that even robbers cannot do without it,[148] and according to Aristotle it is 'the good of others'.[149] According to Augustine it is the basic requirement of political power, for 'what is a kingdom without justice? It is just a gang of bandits'.[150] Cicero says that 'the foundation of justice is fidelity, i.e. constancy and truthfulness of what is spoken and agreed ... what is said should also happen.'[151]

---

145 'The height of law is the height of injustice' (*Summum jus, summum injuria*), as Cicero was fond of saying (*De officiis*, 1.33).

146 Frans de Waal describes how a group of chimpanzees approve a 'punishment' for breach of rules, demonstrating an apparent sense of social predictability (*Good Natured*, p. 95).

147 Cicero, *De officiis*, 1.27. Plato calls the first 'unwise' and the second 'untrustworthy' (*Laws*, 730d). According to Plato the duty to prevent injustice and punish killing is more important than not to commit injustice ourselves. (*Laws*, 870.)

148 *Justitia una virtus omnium est domina et regina virtutum* (Cicero, *De Officis*, 3.28).

149 *Allotrion agathon* (Aristotle, *NE* 1130a, 1134b). In Plato's *Republic* Socrates rejects Thrasymachus' idea that 'justice is good for someone else, a loss to oneself' (*Republic*, 343c, 392b).

150 *Sine justitia, quid sunt regna nisi magna latrocinia* (Augustine, *De Civitate Dei*, 4.4).

151 *Fundamentum autem est iustitae fides, id est dictorum conventorumque constantia et veritas ... fit quod dicitur* (*De Officis*, 1.23). The final part, 'what is said should also happen', is an inversion of the classical definition of truth as the 'harmony of thought and reality'.

While even small children can protest when they feel an action to be unjust, the term itself is somewhat complex and ambiguous, and it is useful to try and analyse it more precisely. The classical distinction of the main types of justice comes from Aristotle.[152] He distinguishes two different meanings of justice, namely retributive justice and the more complex distributive justice.

Retributive justice evaluates the relationship between two parties and seeks to find a balance in this relationship. If this balance is upset it should be renewed as soon as possible, for example by enforcing fulfilment of an unfulfilled obligation, by compensation or by punishment. Retributive justice is the basis of civic and criminal law, which must correct a wrong which has already happened; this is why retributive justice is sometimes called corrective justice. But it is also the basis of 'fair' exchanges or prices, which actions should be governed by.[153] Retributive justice is symbolised by a blindfold lady – she should be 'blind' to the identity and social position of the parties before her – with scales in one hand to measure the sought-after balance, and a sword in the other, with which the public authority of justice will be asserted. 'Justice without strength is powerless, strength without justice tyrannical.'[154]

Significantly more complex than retributive justice is *distributive* justice. It applies in different situations; it should guide the action of those who distribute benefits or responsibilities.[155] In this sense, a parent should divide a bar of chocolate justly among his or her children and the state should divide tax burdens justly among its citizens. But what exactly does the word *justly* mean in this regard? A bar of chocolate can be broken up into pieces that are all the same size, but should everyone pay the same taxes? Should everyone have the same opportunity to become scientists, artists or athletes? Should everyone have the same pay, or even the same amount of property?

The simplest solution, which Aristotle calls arithmetical equality, is in practice the most common, but it is not enough. Employees are unlikely to be motivated by unified wages and the ancient head tax placed an incomparably greater burden on the poor than on the rich. The mistake is perhaps in the 'blindness' of justice, not seeing the dif-

---

152 Aristotle, *NE* 1131f.

153 The German philosopher Ottfried Höffe has attempted to create, on the basis of the idea of exchange justice (expanded to 'transcendental exchange') an idea of mutual bonds and duties, including human rights.

154 Blaise Pascal, *Pensées*, fr. 298.

155 John Rawls' *Theory of Justice* is devoted to this problem.

ferences among people and distributing everything accordingly. Aristotle, therefore, introduces another notion, 'geometrical equality', which takes merit into consideration; the best artisan deserves the best pay, and wealthier citizens, who have easier access to government offices and who benefit more from the safety of the community, should also pay higher taxes. This is what actually happens everywhere today; but there is still discussion as to whether the percentage of tax should be the same for everyone, or whether tax should be progressive, rising in line with income.

But 'geometric equality' can also be understood the other way round: as a need or responsibility to compensate for various disadvantages or handicaps. Various forms of social support can be understood as indispensible for societal peace, as an expression of human solidarity, or even as a requirement of justice; people are not to blame for the fact that they are disabled, or were born poor, or have other difficulties. As long as this support was understood as solidarity, it was entrusted to civic or religious charities; as soon as it came to be seen as a political necessity or a requirement of justice, it became the role of the state to support various groups of people from public funds. Of course, these funds are finite, and so state support for the needy has become the subject of endless parliamentary debates, lobbying, and expert discussion on the need to rein in the 'nanny state'.[156]

For the sake of completeness, we must also mention the modern conception of *procedural* justice, which plays a significant role in law. It demands only that the state, and the state's justice, decide similarly in similar cases and differently in different cases: in short, that it decides coherently. Though even procedural justice may be difficult to maintain, it is far removed from real justice; even the vilest regimes and organisations have been able to decide coherently.

For all the justified emphasis on justice as the basic condition of a decent society, we must recognise that it is not everything. Justice is a necessary but not a sufficient condition for good relationships between people to arise. Aristotle tells us that justice according to general rules is indispensible, but that in certain cases it demands a correction that cannot be governed merely by rules. 'How much wider is the realm of duty than that of laws, how much more necessary honour, humanity, generosity, justice and trust, all of which stand outside of written laws,' says the

---

156 The aforementioned Pascal has this to say: 'Civil wars are the greatest of evils. They are inevitable, if we wish to reward desert; for all will say they deserve.' (Pascal, *Pensées*, fr. 313)

Stoic Seneca;[157] and Cicero also names generosity, or largeness of spirit, in the same breath as justice. For the German philosopher Axel Honneth, the indispensible requirement of the 'good life' is the threefold recognition which comes to people in civic society: in the first place affection or love, from which we build self-regard and which then formulates itself as legal recognition and which realises itself in practice as solidarity.[158]

Aristotle, on the other hand, says that among friends justice is not necessary; he is thinking here of justice as a principle for settling conflicts, the likes of which could never arise among friends. For Emmanuel Lévinas justice is something provisional: 'Justice summons me to go beyond the straight line of justice ... beyond the straight line of the law the land of goodness extends infinite and unexplored, requiring all the resources of the unique present'.[159] This to some extent corresponds to our distinction between morality and ethics.

157 *Quanto latius officiorum quam juris patet regula, quam multa pietas, humanitas, liberalitas, justitia, fides exigent, quae omnia extra publicas tabulas sunt* (Seneca, Ad Novatium de ira, ll 28.2).

158 Honneth, *The I in We: Studies in the Theory of Recognition*.

159 Lévinas, *Totality and Infinity*, III. C 5.

3. Main Ideas of Practical Philosophy

It is one thing to list and describe the opinions of philosophers. It is quite another thing to speak with them about what they say, or rather, what they say it about.[160]

Even practical philosophy has to be philosophy, and shares with all other philosophy one fundamental restriction; it cannot permit any absolute authority and is therefore limited to that which it can expound and defend as being persuasive. This is both its strength and its weakness – strength to the extent that what is persuasive to one thinking being could be universal, persuasive to everyone; and weakness inasmuch as it must always be seeking arguments and will always appear like Baron Munchhausen, trying to pull himself out of the mud by his own hair. It must always be asking 'why', of itself more than anything else. But, as we mentioned earlier, we are today in the slightly happier position of having at our disposal at least two other fields of knowledge, both of which have their own claims to universal credibility: namely, historical experience and the findings of science.

It is not our aim in this chapter to conduct a whistle-stop tour of the history of practical philosophy, appealing though that may be. The chief virtue of such an approach – the accumulation of historical material – is also its limitation. It presents to the reader a gallery of thinkers and leaves it up to him or her, what to do with the information. Our goal is both more modest and more demanding. We will be engaging with the main concepts and guiding thoughts, rather than with individual thinkers and schools. These should not serve as authorities but as examples, or as reminders of something we might have forgotten about. For this

---

160 Heidegger, *What is Philosophy?*

reason we cannot avoid repetition, as long it is called for in relation to this account.

Of course attempts at providing a persuasive rationale for moral and ethical evaluations, which practical philosophy also concerns itself with, are based on many different starting points and presuppositions. To separate the discussion of these from 'material' attempts at establishing moral rules *per se*, this area of practical philosophy is sometimes referred to as *metaethics*.[161] In the following summary we will be setting out on a different path, because we cannot accept the prerequisite of this school: that we can reduce moral evaluations to utterances and then simply test their truthfulness.

Moral theories are often opposed to each other and their emergence was commonly accompanied by adversarial polemics. Despite this, however, we will not consider them to be mutually exclusive, but rather complementary – one completing and correcting the other. Even human action is not monocausal, but rather has its springs in many different impulses and must also consider the entirety of a given situation.[162]

Before we throw ourselves into conscious and reflected efforts with which people have tried (and continue to try) to rationally explain their choices and evaluations, we should not overlook what preceded them: how hard even the oldest and simplest human groups worked at 'humanising' themselves. It is only recently that ethnologists and anthropologists have noted one of the oldest motifs on which human culture is based: namely, the attempt to differentiate ourselves from our animal cousins. This is also an illustration of the paradoxical situation of mankind pulling himself out of the mud by his own hair.

The need to differentiate and separate (ourselves) from animals appears only infrequently in written human history. One such example is Descartes' distinction between 'extended things' and 'thinking things', which places man and the animals into two opposed categories of existence. Unlike the Aristotelian tradition, which characterises all living things as having something like a soul, and so places them all in the

---

161 The chief limitation of contemporary metaethics is its method: it stems from the belief that the moral realm is created by utterances, and evaluation is replaced by asking how truthful these utterances are. We can, therefore, only agree with Bernard Williams' highly sceptical evaluation of the possibilities of such philosophy.

162 Ulrich Beck – referring to an old article by Wassily Kandinsky – regards the move away from the 'either –or' schema which defined much of the 19th century, to the 'also – and' schema (this and that, connection, uncertainty) as one of the characteristics of our time. (*The Reinvention of Politics*). John Rawls' concept of 'overlapping consensus,' as a 'consensus of reasonable comprehensive doctrines', has its roots in the same thinking.

same 'camp', Descartes ascribes a soul only to man and attempts to interpret all other life mechanically or causally. We have already described as 'aesthetic' the shock caused by Darwin's *Origin of Man*. A closer look shows us that it was a direct challenge to, and in sharp conflict with, this stubborn human striving after differentiation and separation which has accompanied humankind from the very beginning. While Aristotle's contemporaries were seemingly untroubled in their humanity by his teachings which attributed (different) souls also to animals and plants, the response of Darwin's own era was considerably more hostile – perhaps because it did not feel so certain of its own humanity.[163]

Only recently, in the light of deeper studies of 'primitive nations',[164] has it become clear exactly how much energy our ancestors devoted to the task of distinguishing themselves from animals. There is no point in wondering to what extent the transition to an upright stance and bipedalism was 'cultural'; it is almost certain that it was not conscious. Nonetheless, all human cultures place great emphasis on it, and connect to it a whole range of cultural notions. Bowing, kneeling and genuflecting, in which we concede at least part of the 'privilege' of being human, have always been expressions of deep respect. Slight bows, and nodding of the head, are an almost reflexive aspect of social greetings.[165] It is characteristic of comical figures that they fall to the ground, and boxers try to get each other onto the canvas or the ropes, that is, to deprive them, at least for a short while, of their humanity.[166]

---

163 David Hume's insistence that there is no significant division between man and animals represents an important departure from most modern philosophy. I am not certain to what extent this was a legacy of omnipresent Aristotelianism, an attempt at a naturalistic reduction of man, or simply a desire to provoke. For Hegel, too, 'every living thing of any sort is a subject' (*Philosophy of Right*, § 35, addition).

164 Especially those conducted under the influence of Levi-Strauss and Garfinkel which have attempted to understand the unusual and surprising features of their seeming 'primitiveness.'

165 On the other hand, prostration – the gesture of lying on the ground, face down – is the expression of profound submission to God or ruler. The comfort of sitting or lying down – positions from which it is difficult for people to defend themselves – was in the past possible only in the safety of the home. The traditional gentlemanly gesture of offering a seat to a lady was an expression of the man's willingness to defend her if necessary.

According to Elias Canetti, sitting on a raised throne has the exact opposite meaning as it is derived from sitting on horseback: the sovereign can rule with a glance or a gesture. The longing to sit in the presence of others is, to Nietzsche, a characteristic of 'servants' The contemporary rejection of these 'barbaric', 'sexist' customs belongs, in this context, to the rejection of the 'merely natural'.

166 There are several other metaphors and expressions that use the dual images of standing and falling. So, for example, you have to 'stand for something' in life, or 'stand up for your rights'; or you may win a debate with a 'knock-down argument'.

To the extent that we can believe the (rare) reports of children who were 'raised by wolves', it seems that these children have all managed, albeit with some difficulty, and despite the lack of support in their environment, to walk upright.[167] We can, therefore, consider upright stance to be a component of biological speciation. And humanity has taken many further steps in its attempt to differentiate itself permanently and irreversibly from the animal kingdom; these, however, have a cultural, not biological, character. Among the first and most effective of these belongs clothing, which in the case of many 'primitive nations' is hardly necessary for practical purposes, and which is everywhere frequently 'symbolic'.[168] For all that, however, we do not know of any society where adults have been able to forego clothing entirely. The widespread use of tattooing in such 'primitive' communities is a marked attempt at cultural differentiation, and, as demonstrated by Pierre Clastres, people regard it as such.[169] It is only with the arrival of 'civilised' society that individuals are able to avoid this extremely painful procedure – which of course signifies the end of their native culture.

The widespread practice of circumcision – the attempt to give a cultural meaning to human sexuality – also belongs in this category. And one of the most widespread means of asserting cultural difference is the myriad ways in which people treat the remains of their fur. From tearing it out, through brushing and decorating it and shaving (or not shaving) all the way to wearing wigs, these models of behaviour (which are otherwise scarcely comprehensible) are culturally determined and enforced in every society, and form an important part of its cultural – or subcultural – identity.[170] Even in our modern and tolerant societies, which have long since forgotten about this connection, a provocative hairstyle is a sure way of provoking shock and outrage.

These almost ubiquitous social phenomena, while they do not belong to the realm of practical philosophy, are an important corrective against naive naturalism; man comes from nature and carries within himself significant traces of his primate origins, but also stands in opposition to it. Animal behaviour may of course illuminate much of human behaviour, but it cannot be used to justify it, let alone become a norm for us. The

---

167 See, for example, the thorough study of French doctor E. M. Itard, 'Victor from Aveyron', available at http://www.feralchildren.com/en/pager.php?df=phillips1802.

168 For example the 'penis sheath' used in the Pacific island region.

169 Clastres, *Chronique des Indiens Guayaki*.

170 Of all the significant reforms of Peter the Great (1672–1725) in Russia, perhaps none aroused more obstinate opposition than the ban on facial hair.

examples shown above demonstrate how human societies have begun to seek their own cultural regulation of life, and how they have articulated their goals in forms which are not written, but which are nonetheless socially binding and enforced norms. This should warn us against underestimating the pre-conscious and pre-reflective foundations on which human cultures stand.

3.1 The world in balance

One of the oldest extant philosophical texts, Anaximander's fragment, expresses an idea which we also encounter in many other cultures:

> Whence things have their origin, there they must also pass away according to necessity; for they must pay penalty and be judged for their injustice, according to the ordinance of time.[171]

The world is order[172] precisely because it is balance; and every birth or origin entails a disruption to this balance. This must in turn be followed by retribution, perhaps not immediately, but 'according to the ordinance of time', namely destruction and with it, the restoration of justice as eternal balance. This is not a commandment, and does not lead to any moral conclusions. It is merely an explanation of the real state of things and a way of rebutting people's complaints about 'unjust' death or other loss. Everything which is, and which we could ever have, is from the beginning burdened by the 'injustice' of its creation and must eventually pay the price for it. Balance, or justice, will sooner or later renew itself, and the peculiar game of creation and destruction will continue.

On the one hand, Anaximander's 'physiological' view of the world as being of the same eternal nature[173] has a markedly moralising character (using terms like *judgment, injustice* and *penalty*) but, on the other hand, it leaves precious little room for the luxury of human freedom – and no one

---

171 Anaximander, fr. DK 12 B 1: *Ex hón de hé genesis tois úsi, / kai tén fthoran eis tauta ginesthai / kata to chreón. / Didonai kai auta dikén kai tisin allélois tés adikias / kata tén tú chronú taxin.*

172 As the Greek word *kosmos* so strongly stresses: its primary meaning is 'jewel, ornament', in a slightly metaphorical sense 'ordering'. Our 'cosmetics' stems from it.

173 It is perhaps unnecessary to add that nature (*physis*) does not mean here the subject of the natural sciences, but rather the given and living reality of the world into which we are born, and which we cannot alter. In this sense, Anaximander is also a 'physiologist' – a thinker who tries to understand the human condition against the background of this given and 'natural' reality.

seems to need it. Eternal balance, though endlessly disrupted by minor episodes of creation and destruction, maintains itself like the level of the sea; to be aware of this, and to reckon with it, is a sign of wisdom. The wise do not bewail death or mortality; they understand them as necessary components of the living world, the symmetrical counterpart to creation and birth.

This is, of course, the ancient conception of 'nature' as the unalterable totality of everything that is, was and will be. It is where 'things have their origin' and also where they meet their destruction according to the remorseless 'ordinance of time,' or fate, as it seems to us. And yet even in this all-powerful whole, characterised by the ancients as 'elements', there are to be found tiny islands which can choose for themselves. Even the tiniest organism, once it has separated itself from the surrounding environment and created its own interior where it can maintain conditions different to those outside, starts to behave as a discrete whole. We can, with a certain amount of licence, say that it begins to defy fate, to look after itself and to follow certain goals. This may seem to us, with our grounding in modern science, to be unacceptable anthropomorphism, like the 'animism' of the primitives, which ascribed souls and intentions to all things. And yet, if we truly wish to observe the reality of life *per se*, we will find it difficult to avoid using the kind of terms we use to describe ourselves. When we say of a stone that it 'defies the vicissitudes of time' this is a metaphor, and if we say it of an old tree, it is perhaps still largely a metaphor; but if we say it of the behaviour of an animal seeking water and safety, it is a fairly accurate description.

But let us return to Anaximander. Although he knew nothing of bacteria, he characterised the automatic and neutral course of the 'elements' with typically 'anthropomorphic' and evaluative terms. This is no physical balance of forces which instantly neutralise each other; it also involves a memory which enables it to mete out its retribution 'according to the ordinance of time'. It is closer to a system of book-keeping, with debts and 'fines', than to the blind collision of bodies. It is the view of a man who is speaking to other people. He had no need to instruct the waves upon the sea whence they come and go; but he did want to tell his listeners and readers something important, which would influence their earthly labours. In a way that is characteristic of the future development of philosophical and scientific thought, this message is both sceptical and consoling. All that is born must also die – the order of the world (and therefore its justice) is built upon this. True wisdom, therefore, rests in freeing ourselves from the obsessive concern with survival and reproduction; in becoming detached; in shedding our dependence on our own lives; and, as a result, losing our fear of death. Plato means something similar when he has Socrates say that philosophy should teach us how to die; although Plato had in mind an entirely different perspective, encompassing the idea of Good.

However, the world is full of living beings, not only the waves upon the sea which emerge and disappear with so little fuss; and that complicates things somewhat. A being which takes care of itself, and which 'lives for-itself in-itself', must face not only the vicissitudes of fate and the elements, but also other beings similar to itself. A man may die of hunger if the harvest fails and he has nothing in the pot; but he may also die in a dungeon. If a man dies in an earthquake, his loved ones may console themselves with the wisdom of Anaximander; but what if someone kills him? There is clearly a difference between these two cases, and practical philosophy concerns itself with precisely this difference.

If creation and destruction are themselves no more than waves on the surface, what are human actions, interests, passions – and crimes? Can we content ourselves with the stance of the disinterested, 'wise' observer, which has been the aim of centuries of 'stoical' philosophy and even science? Can we even look upon murder as part of the natural circle of life?[174]

Anaximander was not concerned with this side of things, but crime cannot be overlooked – at least, not by those who are affected by it. The wrong which has been committed upon them and their loved ones is not merely a neutral fact, which we need only observe and register in the 'ordinance of time'. It is, to a greater or lesser extent, also someone's action, behind which stand an aim and a decision. It was not caused by 'nature' but by people, who are also responsible for it; it cannot therefore be passed over in silence in human society. And so human freedom comes into play, bound as it must always be with responsibility. Something must be done about it, or, more accurately, we are bound to do something about it.

Justice is not acted out among 'things' which cannot pay for any 'injustice', but rather among people. And it does not concern creation and destruction, but rather the spilling of blood, which 'cries out for vengeance'. It concerns wrongdoing, crime and villainy, which separates

174 I have found only one document that attests to this attitude: certain passages in the aforementioned *Chronicle of the Guayaki Indians* by Pierre Clastres (the chapter entitled *Murder*). However unique and difficult to understand, it would be mere speculation to regard this as 'archaism'.

people into clear categories of perpetrator and victim, from the will and decision of the first group. On one side stand the perpetrators and their crimes and on the other side stand the unwilling victims of their actions. Even the beguiling metaphor of scales as a purely mechanical instrument of justice should not blind us to the reality that scales, while they measure the physical properties of things, are in fact human, cultural inventions, and that their first use was in the service of 'just' exchange and commerce, before they were used by science.

Almost all known human cultures have looked at justice in this way; and, according to ethologists, something similar can be observed among animals. It is possible that children are born with an embryonic conception of justice; and it is clear that they identify with it from a very early age. We may not need to know how things are with inanimate objects and natural forces, where waves and winds are born and die; but we all take an active interest in how people behave among each other and towards us. Moreover, it was characteristic of the thought of ancient people and societies to personalise natural forces, seeing them as acting beings. The contrasting viewpoint of scientists and philosophers, who see even in people nothing but mechanisms and forces, is the achievement of a highly abstracting mode of thought, which only began to assert itself in the recent past.

Retribution and Compensation

Retribution and revenge are, in all known cases, the forerunner to (criminal) law. The victim's relatives must avenge the death of their loved one, and even in Aeschylus' *Oresteia* the choir sings:

'For a word of hate let a word of hate be said,
Justice cries out as she exacts the debt,
and for a murderous stroke let a murderous stroke be paid.
Let it be done to him as he does, so says the age-old wisdom.'[175]

It took a very long time until it became clear to people (in some parts of the world) that they could not allow themselves this form of justice and retribution. One of the most important acts of the semi-mythic Athenian lawmaker Dracon was evidently the distinction between murder and

---

175 *Oresteia, Libation Bearers*, v. 308.

(unpremeditated) killing, which he attempted to exempt from the law of obligatory revenge. Among the utterances of the Seven Sages, this interesting pronouncement is attributed to Chilon of Sparta: 'When you suffer a wrong, reconcile yourself: when you suffer a disgrace, avenge yourself'.[176] Here too a line is being drawn between that harm which one can and should tolerate and that which one must avenge: slander and dishonour.[177] Solon was the first to forbid this kind of payback entirely, and he had little success. Even in parts of Europe, blood feuds were still common until the 20th century; so strong is the idea of order and justice as the balancing out of deviations.

Vengeance and retaliation, as a way of balancing out injustice, appears in all archaic societies, but also among groups of people, and among states, to this day; and every teacher encounters it among children. It is problematic because victims have a natural urge to 'up the ante' and then their retaliation can seem like an injustice to the original perpetrator. Moreover, group solidarity is highly developed among humans, so the circle of the 'victim' can expand almost without limit – to encompass extended family, village, or the entire tribe. The Trojan wars were started by the kidnapping of a man's wife; and throughout history there have been cases where the murder of one person divided an entire society, causing a civil war.

And so the principle of revenge has frequently led to endless cycles of killings and violence; and it is interesting to observe how archaic societies have struggled with this. Ethnologists and legal anthropologists have described a whole range of more or less successful attempts at regulating revenge, such as the strict terminological distinction of crime and legitimate retaliation (the institution of socially-controlled blood feuds or vendettas), the principle of proportionate retaliation ('an eye for an eye and a tooth for a tooth', *Exodus* 21:24) or the institution of places of asylum, where perpetrators could hide themselves for a while, thus enabling negotiations with the injured parties. But the one definitively successful solution proved to be the prohibition on taking punishment into one's own hands,[178] and the reserving of the right to inflict punishment

---

176 Ibid., p. 68.

177 The ancient custom of duelling, widespread among herdsmen and warriors, and practiced by army officers until the early 20th century in spite of all secular and religious proscriptions, is part of this tradition. Duels were originally regarded as 'divine judgment'; later it was claimed that the duelling parties considered their honour more important than their lives. See Stewart, *Honor*.

178 'Vengeance is mine, and retribution' says the Lord in Deuteronomy 32:35.

for an independent third party – a judge. Only when this function was assumed by the state, and backed up by the state's monopoly of violence, did the principle of revenge cease to threaten societal peace and security.

Although societies have had to take measures to prevent the worst consequences of tribal revenge, it should not be overlooked that the principle of revenge was evidently the first attempted method of societal restriction of violence and wrongdoing; and a reasonably effective method at that. The 'punishment' which followed also had a preventive aspect, and criminals had to expect that their crimes could have very unpleasant consequences for them. And even when the duties of retributive punishment were taken over by judges and the state, its guiding principle continued to be that of proportionate punishment and compensation. While modern theories of law emphasise the correctional, deterring effects of punishment on the individual perpetrator, the principle of a public 'reckoning' with crime remains very important, legitimising punishment in the eyes of the public. On the other hand, unpunished crimes have a damaging effect on public confidence in the justice system and, by extension, on the whole moral climate of a society.[179] As the *Laws of Manu* tersely expresses it: 'One quarter of an unpunished injustice falls on him who committed the crime, one quarter on the witness, one quarter on all the judges, one quarter on the king.'[180]

The principle of compensation is precisely formulated in Roman Law: by committing a crime the perpetrator brings upon himself the responsibility both to compensate for the damage done – similarly to returning borrowed money or goods – and, additionally, to accept punishment. This duty to the victim arises automatically, but because (unlike in the case of a loan) it has come about without the victim's consent; the perpetrator has also breached civic peace and deserves the proportionate punishment. For this reason the oldest legal codices command that the perpetrator should pay back in double or fulfil compensation through some further punishment. Crime is certainly not the same as debt, but there is a certain common ground between them; and for that matter, unpaid debts were severely punished in ancient law. In both cases, the emphasis is on the responsibility of the perpetrator to remove or make good his crime.

So the principle of compensation remains to this day an important interpretative and legitimising method, but one which, for our pur-

---

179 Compare this with the repeated calls from sections of Czech society for 'a reckoning with the Communist past'.
180 *The Laws of Manu*, book 8.18.

poses, requires some further clarification. If we do not accept Anaximander's view of compensation as an almost physical process in which we are merely passive objects (or at most observers); if instead we see it as a social balancing out between people, then we must remember that there are two sides to it: perpetrators and victims, debtors and creditors – or, in modern legal terminology, liable and authorised persons. That which may strike the disinterested third-person view as 'imbalance' has, for each of these parties a very different, indeed directly opposite character; one is in debt or under compulsion, the other has a claim or is entitled.

For this reason, 'compensatory' measures will necessarily have a different character when seen from either side, and if a third party seeks to try the case, he or she will be obliged – in consideration of the disrupted balance – to act asymmetrically or even one-sidedly. In modern societies we encounter this problem whenever we try to compensate for something, or address an imbalance. For example, positive discrimination, which was intended to compensate for past injustices, may strike others as unjust and may, in some cases, even bring about fresh injustice. Because it does not occur before a judge and one case at a time, it is open to abuse, while for many it simply remains out of reach.

Older societies were in no doubt as to the requirement and the justification for punishment:

Neither anarchy nor tyranny, my people.
Worship the Mean, I urge you,
Shore it up with reverence and never
Banish terror from the gates, not outright.
Where is the righteous man who knows no fear?[181]

The Chinese sage Shang-Yang even regarded punishment as a father of virtue:

Punishment breeds coercion, coercion breeds strength, strength breeds honour and honour breeds virtue. So virtue comes from coercion.[182]

Even Kant regarded criminal sentences – including the death sentence – as the right of the criminals, as an obligatory acknowledgment

---

181 Aeschylus, *Oresteia*. Cited in Höffe, *Lesebuch*, p. 70.
182 Cited in Höffe, *Lesebuch*, p. 55.

of their human autonomy and responsibility.[183] On the contrary, Pascal expresses doubts as to the effectiveness or even the sense of violent punishment, and Nietzsche points to the human weakness of criminals in his radical critique of violent punishment as a form of revenge.[184]

If crimes 'cry out for vengeance', what do gifts or acts of kindness 'cry out' for? Despite a certain symmetry between the two cases, legal theory has a simple explanation why rewards are not a subject for the law: the potential giver has acted freely and 'to a willing person no injury is done,'[185] so there is no threat of conflict. Nonetheless, the social custom of ancient societies rigidly enforced the 'paying back' of gifts; and perhaps they were even founded on the mutual bonds brought about by such exchanges of gifts. We will return to this idea later.

The Golden Rule

No human society is able to avoid all injustice and wrongdoing; but implicit in the very term *society* is the idea that society is able in one way or another to prevent them. First and foremost it achieves this by distinguishing them, naming them as such and condemning them. Secondly, it institutes certain procedures for the compensation of individual injustices and it takes care to prevent further injustices from being committed. However, even the best-devised system of compensation, punishment and repayment remains merely an attempt at remedy after the event, which in many cases can be of no use to anyone. Hanging a murderer cannot help his victims, and, as Pascal reminds us, instead of one corpse there will be two.[186]

The methodical, systematic use of condemnation and punishment does not only have an impact on the direct participants (the perpetrator and the victim), but also has a preventative impact on the whole society. Provided that it applied evenly across the board, and guided by meaningful principles, it also shows everyone else what they should avoid and what they can expect if they do not take a telling. And this desirable

---

183 Kant, *Metaphysik der Sitten* Akademie Ausgabe V, p. 333.

184 *Thus Spake Zarahtustra*, I. 6. "The Pale Criminal." – This characteristic combination of profound scepticism and ineffective sentimentality evidently begins in Greek tragedy; it is also to be found in Pascal, in Romanticism, and even in Nietzsche. In our own time, it is the default position of the tabloid press.

185 Volenti non fit injuria.

186 Pascal, *Pensées*, fr. 911.

effect would be felt all the stronger if such principles could be easily formulated, put into circulation and confirmed as binding in practice.

One of the oldest and most widespread principles of this kind is the so-called 'golden rule'. Its expression in the (deuterocanonical) Book of Tobit is perhaps the most significant for western culture: 'Do that to no man which thou hatest.'[187] The following pronouncements all express the same idea:

'Do not do to your neighbour what you would take ill from them.' (Pittacus of Mytilene)

'Do not do unto others what you do not want them to do to you.' (Confucius, *Analects* 15:23)

'One should never behave towards others in a way disagreeable to oneself. This is the essence of all morality.' (Mahabharata, Anusasana Parva 113:8)

'What I disapprove of in the actions of my neighbour, that – as best I can – I will not do.' (Maeandrius of Samos, according to the *Histories* of Herodotus, III 142)

'Do not do unto others what is injurious to oneself.' (Zoroastrian text *Shayast-na-Shayast* 13:29)

'What is hateful to you, do not do to your friend. This is the whole Torah. All the rest is commentary.' (Talmud, *Shabbat* 31a)[188]

The idea of the golden rule is so simple and clear that it does not require any particular interpretation, and the very fact of its being so widespread attests to its obviousness to man. It has its roots in the everyday experience of people recognising others as people, and this encounter – provided it is not distorted by enmity or fear – arouses a certain emotional interest or even sympathy. And, because others are in a similar position – *ceteris paribus* – these meetings can naturally lead to fellow-feeling and mutual recognition.

This experience, which was later developed and systematised by Martin Buber and Emmanuel Lévinas ('the encounter with the face') is by no means negligible for practical philosophy, and it gives the golden rule its practical persuasiveness. This rule presupposes that people are enough alike that the most effective regulation of our behaviour toward others is to imagine ourselves in their place.[189] In order to do this, we must have

---

187 Tobit 4:15, King James Version.

188 Cited in Höffe, *Lesebuch.*

189 Contemporary debate makes frequent reference to the 'role-reversal test' that should precede any action. (Williams, *Ethics and the Limits of Philosophy*, p. 82)

a certain detachment from our own actions, enough that we would even think of wanting to control them. But this requirement is not entirely unrealistic. While we often encounter truly selfish action, this is the exception rather than the rule and even the most thoughtless wrongdoers try to avoid direct contact with their victims.[190]

Because we can more easily distinguish the wrongs done to us than the good done to us, and bad action more easily than good, the golden rule does not try to tell us how we should act, but rather what we should *avoid doing*. While some critics have maintained that the golden rule does not help us in all cases,[191] the fact is that it can be applied successfully to human actions towards others. The Talmud and the Mahabharat rightly consider it to be the core of all morality or law.

The New Testament, however, formulates the golden rule differently, and this difference is important: 'And as ye would that men should do to you, do ye also to them likewise' (Luke 6:31). A similar formulation comes from the 9th century Muslim lawyer and theologian Ahmad Ibn Hanbal: 'What you wish for yourself, wish also for others; and what you do not wish, wish not for others'. While the basic sentiment, and the assumption of human similarity and mutual recognition, is the same, the content of this formulation is stronger. This is mostly because it is *positive* – it says how people should act – but also because it, in fact, commands action. This seemingly slight difference may have significant practical consequences, and it challenged Adam Smith's incisive observation: 'We may often fulfil the rules of justice by sitting still and doing nothing'.[192]

Kant and the Categorical Imperative

Immanuel Kant provides us with a characteristic critique and development of the golden rule. Kant was critical of several aspects of it, but

---

190 Neither Hitler nor Stalin ever directly killed anyone. Hitler would not even allow the technical details of the extermination camps to be discussed in his presence. Today's politicians entrust their dirty work to various agencies; in modern warfare, soldiers often see their targets only on a screen. This inhibits our natural scruples and drastically weakens the possibility of both personal and legal responsibility.

191 So, for example, Eberhard Wesche objects that it would be impossible for a policeman to give anyone a fine since he does not want to be given one himself. (http://www.ethik-werkstatt.de /Goldene_Regel.htm) This is, of course, a misunderstanding – the golden rule relates to our own freely chosen action, not to the performance of a public function, where there can be no 'role-reversal' (see Ch. 4).

192 Adam Smith, *Theory of Moral Sentiments*, II.2.1. Metalibri 2005, p. 73.

especially the way in which it seeks to deduce moral judgments from the unreflected feelings – *preferences*, in modern parlance – of each individual person. Such a judgment could be based on nothing but contingent individual experience. Each person's experience is different, and changes so much throughout life, that experience cannot possibly be a reliable, universal guide to moral evaluation and decision-making. Only reason, which argues from indisputable foundations and which is common to all people, can do this. Kant doubts that all people are similar (the foundation of the golden rule) and instead postulates impersonal equality as the rational conclusion of individual freedom – a fundamental prerequisite of his theory.[193]

Kant's fears have their origin in his acquaintance with the British tradition of 'moral sentiment', scarcely accessible to reason, which led first of all to sentimentalism before reaching its peak with Hume's radical scepticism.[194] Kant's aim is to construct a firm and unshakable dam against this – a rational and formal dam. He was inspired in this task by the idea of moral sentiment, as distinct from knowledge; but unlike the British proponents of moral sentiment, he refused to accept that it could elude rational control. While moral judgment may differ from scientific argumentation and knowledge generally, it can be rationally investigated, and can even be founded on reason. Kant was not interested in a description or explanation of how people make moral decisions, however; his goal was the establishment of the highest moral principle *a priori* – a principle that must necessarily guide every decision.[195] It is for this reason that he distinguished between the 'kingdom of necessity', to which belong scientific enquiry on the basis of natural laws, and the 'kingdom of ends' or freedom, in which human decisions and actions play out. This also corresponds with the twofold nature of reason – the-

---

193 Our own freedom, the recognition that this freedom is the origin of our acts, is conceivable only as a universal law. All genuinely free people must recognise each other as such. See Kant, *Groundwork*.

194 In his effort to demonstrate that the origin of all morality lies in the individualistic concern for the protection of property (*Treatise of Human Nature*, III.2.2.), Hume reached the conclusion that the idea of freedom is 'fantastical' and 'absurd', and that human action is governed by the same necessity as natural phenomena. 'When we consider how aptly natural and moral evidence cement together, and form only one chain of argument betwixt them, we shall not scruple to allow, that they are of the same nature, and deriv'd from the same principles.' (*Treatise*, II.3.1.)

For this reason Hume reduces morality to useful rules, primarily those concerning property. This is probably the only reason why Hume – a radical denier of freedom – enjoys such popularity among contemporary neoliberals; they are not particularly interested in freedom either.

195 Kant, *Groundwork*. AA IV., p. 388.

oretical and practical – which arises out of the postulate of freedom and is therefore immune from the onslaught of philosophical determinism which in Kant's day was already threatening to undermine the notion of freedom. Kant's practical reason is founded on this freedom; and yet it remains reason, and therefore cannot be satisfied with mere experience and sentiment.

Kant's most important discovery, which to this day determines a significant part of practical philosophy, is the categorical imperative. It is a fundamental principle and does not serve the discovery of truth or natural laws, but rather it commands us. Kant chose the term 'imperative'; his successors speak of 'prescriptive' or 'counterfactual' utterances. Unlike the common hypothetical imperatives, which are conditioned or dictated by certain ends – 'if you want x, do y' – the categorical imperative is unconditional; it must be equally valid for everyone, everywhere, all the time, and entirely independent of all other considerations. In his *Groundwork for the Metaphysics of Morals* Kant formulates it in these terms:

> Act only according to that maxim by which you can at the same time will that it should become a universal law.

From this he deduces this conclusion:

> Act so that you treat humanity, whether in your own person or in that of another, always as an end and never as a means only.

Finally, he stresses again the axiomatic nature of this imperative and places it on the plane of rationally understood rules of nature:

> Act as though the maxim of your action were to become by your will a universal law of nature.[196]

In order to understand Kant properly, it is necessary to explain the character of his 'maxim' and its relationship to (moral) rules. In a paper published after his death, Kant explains it in this way: 'The character of man demands that he first set himself maxims and only then rules. Rules, if they are not restricted by maxims, are mere pedantry... they are mere walking frames (*Gangelwägen*) for children. Maxims must deter-

---

196 The word *Naturgesetz* (natural law) is for Kant a philosophical term, not an empirical, scientific one; and it refers to something that is beyond human control. This differentiates it from the similar-sounding utterances of Hume.

mine which case falls under the rule'.[197] Maxims, therefore, are not rules but general principles to guide the selection of rules.

The categorical imperative ties in with the idea of balance; but instead of the reciprocity of the golden rule, here the criterion is 'universal law'. This has the effect of objectifying, and universalising morality,[198] so that moral judgments can be made, on this basis, by everyone, and not only by agents in their own consciences; such judgments then come to resemble law. However, in this attempt to dismiss anything that is in any way dependent on experience, the subject of morality must become markedly narrower; moral evaluation concerns only the 'will', or the decision itself. These maxims have the appearance of limiting rules for decisions and they therefore belong to the realm of individual morality, and not that of ethics, in the sense of the setting of goals and searching for what is best.

With this foundational act, Kant opened up the possibility of the rational exploration of a morality which did not appeal to religious authority but which was built upon the foundations of independently thinking, rational and responsible individuals, from whose freedom is deduced the principle of human equality. The categorical imperative, in both its forms, is a necessary consequence of the acknowledgment of other people as being equally free and responsible beings; and it corresponds exactly to the Enlightenment idea of human society as an association of equals, in which the only authority is voluntarily acknowledged authority, and in which no privilege is acceptable.

Kant rejects the idea that people should submit to the laws and rules of external authority. Such heteronomy would be a denial of human freedom. On the other hand, free and responsible individuals should submit to rules which are dictated to them by their own reason, as in the case of the categorical imperative, or in the acknowledgment of socially beneficial authority of the ruler. Rational beings must submit to the 'dictates' of their own reason, which alone is capable of guiding their decisions and taming those inclinations and passions which must not be allowed to influence decisions. According to Kant, morality (*Sittlichkeit*) only rules when 'the mere legislative force of maxim is alone the sufficient determining basis (*Bestimmungsgrund*) of a will'.[199] The dictate of reason is, in Kant's conception, justified by it being *my* reason; the rules

---

197 Kant, *Lose Blätter*, Nr. 1164, AA, XV, p. 514.

198 The term *universalisability*, as used by R. M. Hare, is an attempt at a different formulation of the categorical imperative.

199 *Critique of Practical Reason*. We will return to the problem of autonomy and heteronomy in Ch. 3.3.

it enforces are those which rational beings set themselves. Although we must submit to the dictate of reason in all our decisions, we nonetheless remain autonomous, in the original, literal sense of the word: we are our own lawmakers. Following this new conception of agents leads Kant to conclude that 'good' decisions must be decisions guided exclusively by obedience to these rationally grounded laws, and therefore decisions which we are *compelled* to make (albeit by ourselves). Of course, Kant also includes the responsibility to obey rationally founded and accepted authority, especially that of rulers and their laws. A remarkable, and surprisingly pathetic, sentence about duty in the *Critique of Practical Reason* demonstrates how much importance Kant ascribed to this.[200] In the light of the French Revolution, which took place a year after the *Critique* was published, this emphasis on the authority of rulers could have been read as a prophetic warning, and not only in Germany.

Kant's systematic rationalisation ushered in a new chapter in practical philosophy, but also moved it distinctly in the direction of jurisprudence. It is no coincidence that the greater part of the *Metaphysics of Morals* is taken up by the 'Metaphysical foundations of jurisprudence' and that, at the end of the book, Kant delimits ethics as the 'pure practical philosophy of internal legislation'.[201] But this, of course, is not how morality appears to the acting person; and perhaps the growing gulf between the abstract thinking of philosophers and situations of real decision and action is an unintended consequence of Kant's achievement. Removed from the traditional, and dramatically vivid, categories of good and evil, the task of 'practical philosophy' is to probe ever deeper into general laws and abstract notions of equality, none of which says a great deal to the acting person.

The strict exclusion of 'moral sentiments' removed from philosophy's purview our undoubted (if also unexplained) moral motivation, the almost 'natural' need we have to act 'well' and, on the other hand, the feelings of spontaneous horror and revulsion we feel when faced with cruelty or crime; and it also removed common and traditional moral ex-

---

200 'Duty (*Pflicht*)! Thou sublime and mighty name that dost embrace nothing charming or insinuating, but requires submission, and yet sleekest not to move the will by threatening aught that would arouse natural aversion or terror, but merely holdest forth a law...' (*Critique of Practical Reason*, A 154f.)

201 *Metaphysik der Sitten*, II.2 AA VI, p. 491. Axel Honneth speaks of the 'separation of morality and ethics', as Kant had supposed that the conditions of the good life are beyond the control of general determination and must therefore be eradicated from practical philosophy. According to P. Koller the entire Kantian tradition seeks to define what is 'correct', and therefore our duty, regardless of any conception of the good.

perience, which has had the effect of weakening its power, especially among educated people.[202] This theme is taken up by Kant's first critics, among them Moses Mendelssohn, who felt that Kant is also demolishing a great deal (he called Kant '*Alleszermalmer*' – 'all-destroyer'). And even Nietzsche, while accepting and admiring the results of this 'demolition' (and gleefully continuing with it) sees in Kant the origins of how the supposed 'real world' was turned, in the hands of this 'fanatic of morality' into a 'cold, northern, Königsbergian' mist.[203]

One of the most significant and serious criticisms of the shortcomings of Kant's practical philosophy came out of bitter experience. In the desperate aftermath of the German defeat and the collapse of the defeated states, in 1919 the German sociologist Max Weber attempted to dampen the revolutionary fervour of young Austrian officers with his lecture *Politics as Vocation*.[204] Towards the end of the lecture Weber introduces a distinction between the 'ethics of conviction', which he ascribed to Kant, and the 'ethics of responsibility', which must be governed by the foreseeable consequences of every decision and action.[205] Weber may have been speaking only of politicians when he spoke of the moral responsibility to consider the consequences of decisions, and for all evaluation to include this forward-looking consideration; nonetheless, he was expressing something which Kant's practical philosophy had, in the interests of rationality and flexibility, undoubtedly overlooked. And in this regard, Kant's conception has stayed far behind the ordinary human conception of good decision.

An even more thorough critique of Kant's practical philosophy was given by another sociologist, Georg Simmel.[206] Simmel acknowledges Kant's contribution in considering morality, for the first time, as something entirely independent and based purely on the principles of freedom and equality. However he criticises what he sees as a somewhat mechanical quality in Kant: the desire to reduce life to a sequence of individual 'actions' devoid of context. Kant has almost no interest in the real motives, and more remote consequences, of action. He is not an

---

202 All 'movements of the heart' were literally excluded from philosophy by the reformer Philipp Melanchthon (*Philosophiae moralis libri duo*, 1961, p. 176; cited in Ritter & Gründer, *Historisches Wörterbuch*, ii, Col. 772.)

203 Nietzsche, Götzen-Dämmerung, p. 258, (*Nietzsches Werke*, x.).

204 *Politics as a Vocation*.

205 Perhaps Weber wanted to say that this enchantment with the idea of 'ethics of conviction' among the German leaders, which had led to the declaration of war with Serbia, was one of the reasons for Germany's defeat. No historian could subscribe to this.

206 Simmel, *Kant*, pp. 142–167.

optimist like Rousseau and does not believe that it is sufficient for people to 'obey themselves', but he does presuppose that the 'real', deep ego is moral. However, according to Simmel, a morally-minded man knows that his badness and depravity have their roots in the same depths as his moral sense, and therefore he cannot blame them on sensuousness and passion. Kant does not see this, and that is why he can place duty and obedience in opposition to sensuousness, which lies in the realm of sin.

Kant is not, according to Simmel, an ascetic, and the seeming contradiction between duty and happiness comes from the fact that we can only be certain of the morality of an action if it has run counter to our desire for happiness. Nonetheless, the attempt to set happiness in opposition to the categorical imperative has led to 'happiness' being regarded, in the Kantian tradition, as a parody of selfish indulgence. While a scientific success, for example, may bring satisfaction, that most certainly was not its motive; true love, too, brings happiness, but that does not make it selfish. Simmel's chief criticism of Kant is not the excessively narrow conception of morality, but rather the *absolutisation* of morality; everything else – happiness, beauty, creativity or love – is not only secondary to morality but can only be justified by it. Simmel sees in this an 'unprecedented suppression of our real evaluations by the rigidity of an abstract term'.[207]

But of course, with Kant the issue is not that these motives have been overlooked or neglected; Kant is trying to provide human judgment with a firm, unbreakable guide. Coming from the rationalist tradition, which sought to transfer the attributes of permanence and eternity that in Christianity were the preserve of the Creator, to the created, in the form of exact and unchanging laws of nature. Kant claims the same generality, precision and cogency for human reason, from which he deduces the categorical imperative, which should be a 'rule of nature'. This is why he needs to exclude accidental experience from moral thinking (hence his criticism of the golden rule) – and especially subsequent experience. The evaluation of a correct decision, which was necessarily governed by duty and not by inclination, obviously cannot depend on the consequences of that decision. With the categorical imperative, evaluation becomes operational and objective to such a degree, that anyone can perform it, as in legal thinking.

Kant paid a heavy price for this operationality. If the whole problem of the acting person were to be reduced to correctness of decision,

207 Ibid., p. 165.

we would be like viewers at a horse race, who place our bets and then simply look on, incapable of influencing the outcome. How could any decision be good if it automatically absolved us of any further responsibility? What would the autonomy of the will mean, if it was restricted to individual decisions, which we could instantly judge either good or bad, meaning we would never have any reason to regret anything? And if we also factor in the extremely high value placed on duty mentioned above, we are left with something like a caricature of action, something which the exceptionally honourable and scrupulous Kant could never have imagined.[208]

3.2 Happiness and Wellbeing

The motif of balance – from Anaximander through Kant to Rawls – draws the attention of the acting person to certain rules (or even lawfulness) which should not be overlooked. Whether it formulates itself as a balanced circle of emergence and destruction, as the balance of justice or in the form of a demand to see our action through the eyes of others, it is always a call for caution and prudence, or a warning against licentiousness, the Greek *hubris*, which must always, by its very nature, lead to catastrophe. According to the distinction we have drawn up, this belongs in the field of morality, which regulates and restricts human action.

As Paul Ricoeur[209] has observed, however, it leaves untouched the question of the positive motivations of action – those things that the acting person is really concerned about. Ricoeur criticises Kant and emphasises the primacy, in practical philosophy, of the human focus (*visée*) on living a full, rounded, successful life, a 'good life with others and for them in just institutions'.[210] In life, people want things, they care about things, they long for things – these are all motives which compel us to act, whether we are seeking to excel at something, or whether we are just hungry. Morality – the attempt to articulate rules and norms – is certainly important, but can play only a supportive, auxiliary role. People are

---

208 A shocking example of this kind of abuse was presented by Nazi war criminal Adolf Eichmann, who defended himself in court by appealing precisely to Kant's 'duty'. See Arendt, *Eichmann in Jerusalem*. See below, Ch. 4.4.

209 Ricoeur, *Soi-meme comme un autre*, Paris 1990, p. 200.

210 Ibid., p. 202. The British philosopher Henry Sidgwick also complained that, while the ethics of the ancients was 'attractive', modern ethics were 'imperative' (*The Methods of Ethics*, 1907, cited in Ogien, *L'ethique aujourd'hui*, p. 61, note 5).

primarily focused on their own ends and will select (and retrospectively evaluate) their actions according to whether these actions helped them achieve their ends or not: according to their desirable or undesirable outcomes.[211] We have identified this layer of moral distinction, guided by our focus on ends, as ethics (in the narrow sense of the term) and we have characterised it, with Aristotle, as a search for what is best.

For this evaluation and selection of better over worse humans are equipped by nature: they feel pleasure and pain, joy and sorry, they have their spontaneous inclinations and aversions. For that matter, all morality presupposes these, although it may regard them with incredulity. Morality stresses that these inclinations – or passions – can overtake us, as they do with irrational animals. Unlike other creatures, however, man is able to think, learn from experience, predict consequences and even evaluate himself; and it is the task of morality to help him in this. This is why the older traditions of practical philosophy are full of warnings about the baleful consequences of succumbing to blind passions, which may promise momentary pleasure, but will, in the end, destroy happiness.[212]

Aristotle and Eudaimonia

The question of positive motives and the final ends of action (or, for that matter, all of life) are explored by Aristotle in the *Nicomachean Ethics*. He starts by stating that all people aim for some good, which he then, in a circular definition, calls 'that at which everyone aims'. Like all other living creatures, man is determined by a particular perfection, *entelechy*,[213] which is part of his nature and which it is his task to cultivate. As the young of animals must pursue that particular perfection of their species, so man must also first mature and then pursue the 'perfection' that is designated to him. Unlike an animal, whose whole life is governed by this designation, man's *entelechy* is his soul, and especially the highest part of it – reason, which is to guide him through life.

---

211 Hence the name *consequentialism*.

212 This sceptical position is taken to extremes in Buddhism, which sees the solution in the extinguishing of all passions and the suppression of the 'thirst of life'. Unlike many ascetic movements, which see the extinguishing of these passions as a means to a better life, in Buddhism this is the end in itself.

213 The etymology of this word, apparently a neologism of Aristotle's, is debatable. In one account it is derived from *entelés* ('fully developed') while in another it comes from *en-telos-echein* ('having its end in itself'). See Ritter-Gründer, *Historisches Wörterbuch*, art. 'Entelechie', ii, col. 506.

Every person has his specific task or vocation, which he has to perform properly.[214] But an individual can also excel in this task, and it is precisely in this that our difference from animals is to be observed. Aristotle presents the example of a guitarist who may be able to play, but who may also excel in this area, going beyond mere accomplishment. This excelling, or 'surplus' is seen in individual excellent acts and, if it is repeated, it can form what is called *habitus* (*hexis*), which is what Aristotle means by virtue.[215] And so human perfection is not determined in terms of its content, but seen rather as a way of living. Aristotle therefore defines human good as the excellent performance of the best capabilities of the mind 'in a complete life. For one swallow does not make a summer'.[216] This is why Aristotle's ethics do not lead to any moral commands, but rather concentrate on seeking ways to ends, to excelling and to virtue.

People, according to Aristotle, choose between three types of life, depending on whether they seek pleasure (the 'merchant life'), honour (the 'political life') or knowledge (the 'philosophical life'). Pleasure, honour and knowledge are not important to us for their own sake, however, but because of the happiness or wellbeing they can bring us. No one asks 'why' a person wants to be happy; so it would seem to be the highest end. Aristotle's *eudaimonia*[217] is not, however, simply a self-contented feeling or state of mind. It also has an active component; and if it did not have it, it would cease to be happiness. As a 'search for the best' it will always lead further, beyond the point that a person has already reached; and for Aristotle this means that it can be achieved only in a free society of equals – in a *polis*.[218]

---

214 The Greek *ergon* may mean that which man procures as his work; but in many proverbs it takes on the meaning of that which each person ought to do properly, what belongs to him as his own task. H. Rackham translates this as *function*.

215 The word *areté* combines with the word *areion* – better, stronger, more accomplished: it can be translated as 'prowess' or 'excellence'.

216 '... *tés psychés energeia kat' aretén, ei de pleiús tai aretai, kata tén aristén kai teleiotatén*' (*NE* 1098a).

217 H. Rackham translates this as 'happiness', but remarks that it could also mean the state of a person who is living a good life (*prosperity, well-being*).

218 Aristotle's ethics are not as individualistic as that of the Epicureans, and for him the *polis* is 'a partnership of families and clans, aiming at a perfect living in itself' (*Politics*, 1280b 30–35). The *polis* does not emerge from the contract of its citizens: on the contrary, it is the *polis* which offers its citizens the opportunity to achieve their goals and give their lives meaning. It does not consist of individuals but rather of 'families and clans', although these are of course represented in assemblies by their husbands and fathers. The condemned Socrates considers himself too the son (or slave) of the law of his community, which he cannot escape. (*Crito*, 50d)

The positive or 'eudaimonistic' character of Aristotle's ethics manifests itself in that, while it may also warn against passion and imprudence, it is entirely founded upon virtues as being the characteristic features of the 'good life'. Virtue, to Aristotle, is the same as excellence: 'the habit (*hexis*) of a man which makes him good and which enables him to do his own work well'.[219] Virtues tend to lie 'in between' two undesirable extremes, 'between' insufficiency and excess; but they are most certainly not an intermediate point between them. Generosity lies 'between' miserliness and extravagance, and courage 'between' cowardice and rashness: but only in their content. On the other hand, as far as perfection is concerned, virtue is the highest and cannot be compared at all to these extremes. And so the common conception of Aristotelian virtue as something like a 'golden mean' is somewhat misleading.

* * *

Aristotle's ideal of the good life in a free community of equals started to break up within his own lifetime, largely due to the collapse, first internal and then external, of the Athenian *polis*. In place of a well-ordered community where everyone seeks to excel in the sight of others and where they would be ashamed to commit wrongdoing, there emerged the populous and confused societies of Late Antiquity, not unlike modern states. The notion of searching for the best in the sense of excellent acts in the eyes of others necessarily became an illusion. There is no community before which everyone would feel shame, or in whose eyes everyone would wish to excel and write themselves into its memory.[220]

The realm of 'political' action, ceasing to be public – that is, available to all citizens –becomes 'politics' in the modern sense: an arena of governing powers, the domain of rulers and warriors. Individual excellence, or virtue, which was meant to become manifest in public life and which, according to the ancient Greeks, is the starting point of justice and courage, loses its meaning. Where, now, ought we to look for guidance to the 'good life'? What should be the goal of free people, who care about

---

219 *NE* 1106a22.

220 The Scottish philosopher Alasdair MacIntyre shares a similar vision and critique of the contemporary situation in affluent Western society (*After Virtue*). It is, however, questionable to what extent his idea of 'traditional' society corresponds to the historical reality and to what extent it is an idealisation. The same can be said of the Athenian *polis*; the admiring depiction of 'Athenian democracy', as presented e.g. by J. Bleicken in his book of that name, is pretty far from Thucydides or Plato.

more than merely their own lives, but who either cannot share in public affairs at all, or have almost no chance of success in such an endeavour? It is almost certain that they will come into conflict with powers overwhelmingly greater than them, which they cannot control and which will almost certainly condemn them to defeat – the fate suffered by Socrates, and described by Plato in his 'Seventh letter'.

This is a fundamental question, and one which we are grappling with to this day. Greek thought offered two very different answers to it and, in so doing, created two traditions that are still with us today – the Stoic tradition and the Epicurean tradition. Both come from the realisation that individuals are now alone, dependent upon themselves, or at most, on a small group of like-minded friends.[221] Only among such people can we find support for our criticism of, our evaluations and decisions. On a superficial reading of the preserved fragments there may not seem to be much difference between these two traditions: both abandon the hope of finding widespread public agreement and both make occasional use of the term 'virtue'. Both emphasise the importance of individual reflection and experience; but they differ fundamentally on how the humanity of the individual is displayed in them.

In the Stoic tradition, which probably stems from Pythagoreanism, man is characterised by the ability to 'see', and be aware of, that which both transcends and binds him: Pythagoras' 'cosmic order' and Socrates' 'care of the soul'. Man understands himself as the only being which can glimpse something 'above' him – something which others may not see but what is nonetheless valid for everyone everywhere – from the remarkable and exact laws of geometry, through the Stoic virtue to Plato's 'idea of the good'. But this places it into a different context, which we will examine below.

Epicureanism and Hedonism

The second direction, traditionally known as hedonism and connected with the name of Epicurus, seems to have drawn entirely different conclusions from the common experience of the mass societies of Late Antiquity. Perhaps because its originators were people of more modest

---

221 The very high value placed on friendship by Epicurus and many others in Western practical philosophy attests to the fact that many of them have abandoned the idea of the *agora* as a public community of 'equals'; perhaps many of them never experienced it.

social origin,[222] Epicureanism sets itself much more limited and 'realistic' goals. Epicureans regard man as a complete and self-sufficient being, who should abandon unattainable hopes and arrange his life so that such things do not spoil his enjoyment of it. He should, above all, rid himself of all his fears – primarily the fear of dying and of the gods – and should work only to achieve the most satisfactory life possible.

Although tradition has presented Epicurus as a proponent of pure self-indulgence (he himself complained of this) he also regarded self-control and self-restriction as part of the road to happiness.[223] Like a true Greek, he had enough experience and wisdom to know that any surrender to passion, and any excess, would come back to haunt him. So while the aim of life is happiness, here it is individual and present happiness, in the voluntary company of friends. The substantial difference between this practical philosophy and that of Plato's Socrates is that Epicurean individualism is more radical; it rejects everything that would transcend or bind everyday life, and in consequence withdraws from public life. It is a philosophy of private life, which does not entirely reject public concerns but does not ascribe great importance to them and would willingly renounce them should they prove a barrier to individual happiness.[224] The wise man knows that he is not even lord and master of his own short life, let alone of the world, and if he seeks to be happy in this life, he must respect its finite nature. He cannot allow himself to imagine that his actions would influence his community or the overall conditions of his own life, and must seek happiness where it can be found: at home, or among like-minded friends.

Epicurean individualism represents a radical resignation and is a philosophy of that scepticism which often accompanies periods of peace and contentment. Such happiness as can realistically be gained from life is by necessity limited and cannot rely on anything which transcends this life – with the single exception of close personal friendship. Instead of following high-minded ideals, we should enjoy what life has to offer and our happiness should be based on ridding ourselves of fear and pain, avoiding all worries and sorrows. If we can manage this, then we have all the happiness we need. We should, however, be on our guard against certain pleasures, as they can cause subsequent pain and suffering. Epicurus called his school the 'garden' and the sign above its entry

---

222 However, in his *Last Will*, Epicurus freed four of his slaves. (Diogenes Laertius. X. 21).

223 Diogenes, *Lives of Eminent Philosophers*, X. 131.

224 From the fragments that have come down to us it seems that the Epicureans regularly avoided even their own families, and married only "exceptionally".

gate reportedly said: 'Stranger, here you will do well to tarry ... a kindly host will welcome you with bread and water in abundance ... here your appetites will not be whetted, but quenched.' Epicurus' garden may be detached, but it welcomes all strangers equally, promising them that, if they restrict their demands to that which is necessary, he will teach them to live without fear and will offer them modest happiness in the company of like-minded people.

Happiness, the aim of every life, is for Epicurus the vivid feeling of the present moment; and we must not allow this to be spoiled by fear of the future – especially of death – or any of the other sorrows which normally stem from failure to master passions and indulgence. 'Everything that we do, we do to free ourselves of pain and fear. When we achieve this, the storm in our soul is calmed. Nothing else, and nothing more, is required for us to feel perfectly content in soul and body'.[225] A certain parallel with the Epicurean tradition can be found in the more radical teaching of Buddha: 'Birth is suffering; old age is suffering; sickness is suffering; death is suffering; sorrow, lamentation, pain, grief and despair are suffering; association with what is unpleasant is suffering; dissociation from what is pleasant is suffering; not to get what one wants is suffering'. 'Happy is seclusion to him who is contented, to him who has heard the teaching ... to overcome self-awareness is the greatest happiness'.[226]

The attractiveness of the Epicurean ideal of modest, private happiness lies in its emphasis on the present moment; it does not have any expectations or desires, it fears nothing and demands nothing exceptional from us. Who would not be tempted by this unhurried life in the 'garden', among friends, so close to the old idea of paradise? The only problem is that, from the viewpoint of the 'strategy of life' that we discussed earlier, this approach entails a distinct withdrawal and resignation, which could never become a rule: a society of Epicureans would soon collapse because no one in it would be concerned with its future. Who would supply them with bread? This is why Epicureanism was the preserve of people living in favourable conditions of peace and prosperity, and people from those strata of society which did not have to bear any responsibility for that society. They were therefore able to live only for themselves and, from a certain viewpoint, to 'parasitise' on an environment that was created and maintained by others.

---

225 Quotations from Diogenes, *Lives of Eminent Philosophers*, X. 126.

226 Buddha, *The Sermon at Benares*, 1.3.

This Epicurean scepticism has a further paradoxical consequence, this time individual; the attempt to limit suffering and to overcome the fear of death must significantly relativise life as such. As Epicurus says: 'The wise man does not deprecate life, nor does he fear the cessation of life'. But if the sole aim of life is to live it pleasantly and painlessly, the question arises during every suffering whether it would not be better to end life voluntarily. And if we do manage to live with peace in our souls and without suffering, then feelings of aimlessness and boredom start to haunt us. As Pascal says:

> Nothing is so insufferable to man as to be completely at rest, without passions, without business, without diversion, without study. He then feels his nothingness, his forlornness, his insufficiency, his dependence, his weakness, his emptiness. There will immediately arise from the depth of his heart weariness, gloom, sadness, fretfulness, vexation, despair.[227]

In times of strife, when life is a constant battle for survival, Epicureanism cannot take hold; and even in the most peaceful and prosperous times, it has usually been the preserve of a narrow group. It was fundamentally at odds with (and unacceptable to) Christianity, and only re-emerged at the start of the modern era, among the privileged classes and in times of peace. Only in our modern, affluent societies, saturated with consumption and possibilities, does the 'Epicurean' life seem to be on offer to the majority of people – either in the primitive sense of simply 'enjoying life' or the more enlightened sense of voluntary seclusion and withdrawal. Of course, this is only possible to the point where this illusory existence begins to threaten the favourable conditions in the society at large, which enabled this life, and which those who enjoy it mistakenly regard as a given.[228]

Christianity and Morality

In this context of ethics as a search for happiness and beatitude it is worth looking at the ethics of Christianity, which also speaks to us of

---

227 Pascal, *Pensées*, fr. 131.

228 The same holds true today for the widespread 'apolitical' attitude among intellectuals. The scientists, writers and artists who proudly proclaim this stance are overlooking the fact that they belong to a minority in the society, which urgently needs the public space of freedom, whereas the majority can live without it and if necessary will content itself with security and comfort.

possible salvation and beatitude, albeit not a happiness and wellbeing which is in our hands, which we could achieve by our own efforts alone. In this regard it is fundamentally different from other ethics based on *eudaimonia* and its entire history can be viewed as a struggle over this difference.

The European understanding of morality as the free responsibility of each person is founded on Christianity, but Christianity in turn takes its morality, as expressed in the Ten Commandments, from Judaism. The biblical formulation of the Ten Commandments is original and unique, but we can find individual prohibitions of killing, sexual abuse, stealing, lying and coveting in almost all cultures,[229] along with commands to care for parents. Judaism transformed this universally human foundation of morality by binding it to religious faith – as demonstrated by the first three Commandments. The Israelites have a duty to obey these commands, not because they are socially beneficial or necessary, but out of gratitude to the Lord, the creator of the world, who rescued them from their captivity and who, in the covenant with Abraham, promised them a great future.[230] In later Judaism, this originally collective hope of the tribe is projected into the fate of individual lives and into peoples' own souls.[231]

The teaching of Jesus presupposes this twofold founding of morality on gratitude and hope, but also radicalises it.[232] On the one hand, Jesus follows on from Jeremiah: 'I will plead with thee, because thou sayest, thou hast not sinned'.[233] And he interprets the Ten Commandments so radically that no one could obey them: 'Ye have heard that it was said by

---

229 Kant is of the same opinion: 'Common human reason knows very well how to distinguish between what is good and what is evil ... we do not need science and philosophy to know what we should do in order to be honest and good, and even wise and virtuous' (*Groundwork*, AA IV., p. 404).

230 Exodus 20:2, Deuteronomy 5:1, Genesis 22:15.

231 See for example Ezekiel 20:2 and the end of the book, Ch. 36; Job 19:25. The content of this hope is described as in dream images and the Christian tradition has resisted the natural tendency to 'concretise' or objectify 'eternal life'. 'Eye hath not seen, nor ear heard, neither have entered into the heart of man, the things which God hath prepared for them that love Him.'

232 See Mark 10:19. Criticising the morality of modern Christianity, Remi Brague emphasises that 'Jesus did not preach morality, he preached forgiveness. He did not have to say what was to be done, the law of Moses was well known'. The main question for him is: 'Why, when we all know what we should do, do we not do it?' The Christian answer comes in two parts: into the past there leads the prospect of possible forgiveness, into the future the promise of grace. 'The Christian revelation does not consist in the prophecy of law but of charity and grace.' (Brague, *Du Dieu des Chrétiens*. Paris 2008)

233 Jeremiah 2:35.

them of old time, Thou shalt not kill; and whosoever shall kill shall be in danger of the judgment. But I say unto you, that whosoever is angry with his brother without a cause shall be in danger of judgment'.[234] The idea that virtuosic obedience to the law makes a person just therefore turns out to be a dangerous illusion. This does not, of course, mean that we should not try to obey the law;[235] but we must first admit our own weakness and depend upon forgiveness that God alone can grant. If we genuinely accept this forgiveness – so that we are also able to forgive – we need have no further fear for our soul, and even death ceases to torment us. This radical 'reversal'[236] entirely upsets the common concepts of 'happiness' and 'wellbeing', replacing them with the so-called 'Beatitudes', the nine fold blessing of the Sermon on the Mount.[237] They are not intended as new commandments, but they change the very idea of what is better and best. Not the happy and the wealthy, but rather the poor and the meek can find favour with God and hope in his salvation – precisely because they evidently cannot be expected to rely on themselves.

Jesus' teaching is plain and can be understood by anyone; but it is also religious teaching, and therefore paradoxical. It does not belong to any system, and any attempt at a purely rational interpretation of it is bound to distort it.[238] But it has a place in our discussion of practical philosophy because it addresses a very serious and seemingly unsolvable problem. All systems of morality try to advise people how they should act, and also tell them why. But what about a person who understands the advice well, but who has not acted accordingly? Can such a person only choose between dishonourable excuses or cynical denials, and the honourable, but despairing, idea that he must live the rest of his days in the same skin as a criminal, as Socrates says?

Philosophy has not found an answer to this simple and basic question – if it has even asked it – and it cannot give a rational explanation for the religious answer. It can only see that the root of the wrongdoing, which lies in the soul of the perpetrator, cannot be eliminated by external

---

234 Matthew 5:21.

235 Matthew 5:18. See also Luke 18:10–14.

236 The Greek *metanoein* appears in Plato and it means 'to change one's mind consequently', or 're-gret something'. The New Testament *metanoia* is usually translated as 'repentance' but literally it means 'turning around' – similar to the Nietzschian 're-evaluation of values'.

237 Matthew 5:3–11, a shorter version Luke 6:20–26. There is no exact equivalent for the Greek *makarioi* in the modern languages. They are 'blessed', i.e. they enjoy divine grace, even if they might be considered miserable.

238 If some of Jesus' teachings were to be generalised, they could lead to socially unacceptable behaviour: see for example John 8:3 or Luke 16:1–8.

judgment and punishment, but only by a fundamental reversal in his own evaluation – put simply, by confession and remorse. This, however, is only bearable if he can hope for a commensurate acceptance in the wider society, or to put it another way, for forgiveness and the chance to start over again.[239] In smaller communities – in families or among friends – this kind of forgiveness is quite common, as it would be impossible to live together without it. The Christian attempt to expand this forgiveness to cover larger communities had a formative influence on European societies for many centuries, until it met with resistance and outright rejection from the 18th century on.[240]

One reason for this rejection is that the idea of forgiveness and of hope has been so open to abuse. Dietrich Bonhoeffer spoke of 'cheap grace', which he thought made light of the seriousness of crimes, and even of death itself. We may deny the paradoxes of human existence, but we can scarcely explain them. The importance of the chronology of action is thrown into sharp relief against the background of the problem of human weakness and failure. While society must insist that lying, stealing and killing have always been and always will be contemptible, from the viewpoint of the agents there is a huge difference between something they are merely contemplating and something they have already done.

* * *

Jesus' teaching of 'conversion' and hope was addressed to his listeners, who had grown up in a Jewish environment. The Christian church, which emerged from it, had to somehow formulate this teaching as Christianity began to spread throughout the world. Already in the letters of Paul we see an attempt being made to recreate it for a new environment, and to show Christians how they should act in a society which does not share their beliefs. These letters stress the necessity of morality, and, where they speak of universal vices and virtues, the influence of the Stoics – and perhaps even the Cynics – can be felt. Other writers of Christian antiquity, educated in the Greek environment, created various syntheses

---

239 An extreme example of this arrival of hope at the last minute is Jesus' words to one of the criminals crucified alongside him: 'This day you will be with me in heaven' (Luke 23:43).

240 In his early polemic with 'Hitlerism' Emmanuel Lévinas saw its 'terrifying danger' in that it denies one of the central pillars of Judeo-Christian civilisation, namely the possibility of remorse and forgiveness, and the chance to start again. It returns man to the fateful 'grip of the past', as in Greek tragedy, and it knows only the 'voice of blood', which in turn necessarily means war and expansion. (Lévinas, *Quelques réflexions sur la philosophie d'hitlérisme*, 1934.)

of the Gospel and Stoicism, and especially Platonism, which offered itself naturally.[241] In this way the traditional Christian morality – with its characteristic features of restraint and asceticism – was created.

This tendency, hinted at in the New Testament, was already radicalised in antiquity and it peaked, in the teachings of Marcion of Sinope († cca. 160), for example, in the dualistic conception that it is necessary to reject this world altogether, as it is the result of the struggle between good and evil, and with it the entire Jewish tradition (and especially the idea of creation). The Christian church did not accept this, but nonetheless the focal-point of Christianity switched to 'the hereafter'. This led to a weakening of the binding character of 'earthly' life, and the hope of the Gospels was restricted to the expectation of life after death. This idea was to some degree borne out by the crises of the Late Middle Ages and early modern era, so it came to govern (at least Western) Christianity for the entire modern era and even to this day.

The sober yet rich thought of Aristotle reappeared in the history of Western thought in the High Middle Ages and turned the attention of thinkers to the possibilities of independent human experience, based on observation. Medieval scholasticism incorporated Aristotle into the Christian worldview in a way that transformed both. In the context of practical philosophy, Aristotle's importance to scholasticism is in his logic – the attention given to correct thinking and rational language – and in the idea of natural law, which is given to people and societies as an indispensable guide to the 'good life' and the 'good society'.[242] And so the whole of the Late Middle Ages is characterised by the tension between the sovereign authority of biblical revelation, on the one hand, and the attractiveness and authority of well-captured experience and correct argument on the other.

It was the threat posed by this 'secularisation' of the idea of man and the 'good life', along with the wealth and political power of the church, which sparked the protests of the reformers. Luther's resistance to Aristotle can be understood as *pars pro toto* also as resistance to the growing self-awareness of man, as illustrated by the Italian humanism which was

---

241 In this they could be following on from Alexandrian Jewry, especially in Philon. Clement of Alexandria went further and produced a highly detailed guide to life for Christians, including dress and other everyday matters (*Stromateis*).

242 The Latin *lex naturalis* can be translated as 'natural', though of course only in the pre-scientific conception of 'nature'. From Kant on, this usage would lead to misunderstandings; unlike the technically exploitable 'laws of nature', as the kingdom of necessity, *lex naturalis* leads somewhere else: It is a law which restricts human license.

inspired by antiquity. According to Mirandola's famous *Oration on the Dignity of Man*,[243] God placed man above all other creatures and placed his fate in his own hands. It is from this point that humanists began to create a new theory of the power of rulers, not founded upon the sacred authority of the ruler, but rather on the consent of the ruled, and on contract (H. Grotius).

Against this, Luther emphasised the paradoxical nature of Christ's teaching, suppressed by scholasticism's attempt at rational understanding; and he rejected the attempts of philosophy to depend on unaided reason. In this he was following on from the teaching of Augustine, who said that human nature was so tainted by original sin that it cannot be relied upon. Man has also long ago lost that free will which the Creator once gifted him with, and must therefore be guided by the word of God, and by earthly rulers. In the spirit of late medieval inward piety, Luther set himself against the humanistic search for happiness in the world, and instead emphasised the entirely different character of Christian 'happiness', which man cannot earn by himself. The logical extreme of this viewpoint was the doctrine of 'predestination': our salvation, or damnation, is decided by God in advance. But then how are we meant to bear any responsibility for our actions?

On the contrary, the Catholic church stressed the importance of human decision and action and, without undermining the authority of Augustine, it reached the boundary of the opposed viewpoint, the so-called Pelagianism.[244] The polemic surrounding 'free will' and the role of man in seeking his own salvation thus became theological ammunition in the twofold conception of man, society and state power. This divided the whole European continent and brought about a number of cruel conflicts, in which theological questions were sidelined. Thus the Reformation's emphasis on man's dependence on God's grace, leading all the way to the fatalistic doctrine of 'predestination', paradoxically created the 'Protestant morality' of personal responsibility and prepared the way for modern democracy, while on the contrary, the Catholic emphasis on human reason and the freedom of the will strengthened the position of

---

243 Mirandola, *Oration on the Dignity of Man* (1496). See also below, especially 'Autonomy and Heteronomy'.

244 Pelagius (c. 250–420) was an English ascetic monk, preacher and theologian, who lived in Rome, where he argued with Augustine. He objected to Augustine's pessimism and fatalism, and countered these with an emphasis on free will and the responsibility of man. Augustine and his pupils had Pelagius condemned; however, modern scholars believe that Pelagius did not defend the condemned teachings, which were in fact created by his pupils.

absolutist rulers and also a less melancholy approach to life. The traces of both traditions can be clearly seen to this day, along with the 'retreat from the world', still present in both of them.

Utilitarianism

The reformation took a different path in England, which never entirely abandoned the legacy of the Middle Ages. Instead of polemics around free will and human dessert, in England there begin to emerge ideas which see the task of man as being primarily the 'pursuit of happiness' in *this* world. John Locke circumnavigated the thorny question of 'free will' with the consideration that freedom is not an attribute of a will, but of a person. It is 'a Power in any agent to do or forbear any particular Action, according to the determination or thought of the mind, whereby either of them is preferred to the other'.[245] Although he is at all times under the pressure of his own needs, man is a rational being, and should always act with regard to the ends that have been naturally given to him. He needs freedom so he can follow his own idea of happiness and salvation. Locke was, for this reason, a defender of religious tolerance, no matter how limited.

Throughout the entire modern period, thinking on happiness has been marked by individualism, which, although it has its roots in Christianity, has far outgrown its original, religious limits. The Scottish Enlightenment recognised this insufficiency and began thinking about happiness as a social quantity. And, because it grew out of ground prepared by Calvinism, its ideas were radically different to Epicurean ideas, especially in their *activism* – their emphasis on the duty to act effectively in society. What creates the happiness of man? We can say, with a certain simplification that man desires life, security, health and at least some property to live from. These interests are common to all people and can be quantified and measured.

Francis Hutcheson (1694–1746)[246] concluded that, while the motives of action can be varied, action should be retrospectively evaluated according to its consequences, and that these should be measured by what was later referred to as the principle of the 'greatest happiness'. The best action is that which produces the greatest happiness for the greatest

---

245 Locke, *An Essay concerning Human Understanding*. Book II., Ch. XXI, 8.

246 *Encyclopedia Britannica* 1911, http://1911encyclopedia.org/Francis_Hutcheson. We will return to Hutcheson later in relation to the theory of 'moral sense' (see below, Ch. 3.5).

number. Hutcheson, in the nominalist tradition, viewed society as a sum of individuals, and went so far as to consider whether the morality of action could be precisely calculated.[247] Adam Smith was also attracted to this idea, and later it was fully developed by the English reformer Jeremy Bentham, the founder of utilitarianism.

Utilitarianism – which continues to influence practical philosophy to this day – posits that human action should be evaluated according to its consequences, and that these consequences can be objectivised, delimited along the same parameters for everyone, and even quantified, summarised and measured. This is the main strength of utilitarianism: it offers – albeit at the cost of considerable simplification – a flexible instrument for measuring and evaluating 'happiness' and, by extension, all human action. The many current systems for measuring, not only economic output (GDP), but also 'quality of life' (*quality of life index,* QOLI), 'human development' (HDI) or the 'physical quality of life' (PQLI) are all descendants of this idea.

However, despite the apparent simplicity and directness of utilitarian thought, there are many questions. Utilitarians must assume that all human action has a purpose, and that the fulfilment of this purpose can somehow be measured. The consequences of action (or of inaction) can to some extent be evaluated retrospectively, even if the question remains as to when the evaluation should be made, and what needs to be considered in such an evaluation. However, at the moment of decision, this is all mere guesswork and expectation, entirely dependent on the model we choose for the contemplated act. The apparent 'objectivity' of utilitarian criteria in reality leaves the door open for all sorts of dreams and wishes, no matter how unrealistic, which can then be used to 'justify' evident harm of seemingly smaller scale. Everything depends on how we set the parameters for evaluating utility or harm. The danger is all the greater because of the impression of scientifically founded objectivity which this procedure can give.

Another significant weakness is the vague definition of 'happiness' or 'welfare'. What should be included in it and from what viewpoint should it be evaluated? Does welfare mean quality or length of life, or such 'subjective' quantities as the happiness of survey respondents? And what about situations in which all possible action will most likely result in loss or harm? Should we 'measure' the limited loss or the harm inflicted? Should the sum of individual losses be the deciding factor, or the gain

---

247 Hutcheson, *Inquiry concerning Moral Good and Evil* (1725), Ch. 3.

or loss to the whole, which individuals cannot evaluate?[248] And at whose expense is 'greatest happiness for the greatest number' to be achieved?[249]

One of the questions that have divided utilitarians is whether the criterion of maximum utility should be applied to every individual act, or – following the Kantian model – only to the principles of action.[250] Bentham's pupil John Stuart Mill (1806–1873) attempted to give utilitarianism a more philosophically coherent form. He distinguished between happiness and pleasure, and insisted that what mattered was the maximisation of happiness and not pleasure. 'It is better to be a human being dissatisfied than a pig satisfied: better to be Socrates dissatisfied than a fool satisfied.'[251] Others have added that happiness is to be understood as the experience or the 'feeling' of happiness. This may be a more satisfactory explanation, but it comes at the expense of objectivity and operationality, the chief advantages of the utilitarian approach.

In the second half of the 19th century, as philosophy found itself increasingly under the pressure of the triumphant idea of progress and the positivist critique, which sought to reduce all knowledge to demonstrable experiential facts,[252] many thinkers tried to accept for philosophy the same principle which had proven so effective in the sciences. The German philosopher Franz Brentano (1838 – 1917) was convinced that practical philosophy was founded on indubitable principles which could be understood and from which it was possible to develop practical philosophy as a science. Brentano flatly rejected all relativism and was convinced of the universal validity of the 'natural moral law' – the moral order of the world. Already Descartes distinguished three types of mental activity, namely ideas, logical judgments and evaluations or preferences. As our judgments can be evaluated as to their truthfulness and untruthfulness,

---

248 For example, the *Happy Planet* project compares the life expectancy and feelings of happiness of respondents, divided by the ecological demands made by the given society. These quantities are scarcely commensurable, as most people have no idea what their 'ecological footprint' is. The sequence that results is entirely the opposite of that which comes from other polls. Top of the list are Cuba, Vietnam and China, while the USA and Luxembourg are at the bottom alongside Sudan and Ethiopia. The question of why people continue to flee in their droves in the opposite direction, away from these 'happy' countries, has escaped the notice of the pollsters. See http://en.wikipedia.org/wiki/Happy_Planet_Index.

249 For a systematic philosophical critique of utilitarianism, see Williams, *Ethics and the Limits of Philosophy*, p. 85.

250 In the contemporary terminology, *act utilitarianism* and *rule utilitarianism*.

251 Mill, *Utilitarianism*, Ch. II.

252 Compare the 'law of three stages' – teleological, metaphysical and scientific (or positive) of French philosopher, Auguste Comte (1798 – 1857), first published in his *Systeme de philosophie positive* in 1824.

so we can also evaluate our inclination or rejection, love or hate, on the basis of some internal correctness. That to which it is correct to adhere, that which it is correct to love, is therefore good. In addition, Brentano adopted Aristotle's distinction between means and ends – between that which is good 'for something' and that which is good 'in itself', or which has intrinsic value. He held, as a kind of categorical imperative, that we should choose the best available option, not only for ourselves but for our family, our state, the whole world and for the future. In other words, always do that which will give the highest possible intrinsic value to the overall state of the universe. A necessary and sufficient condition for calling any act 'good', in the normal sense of the word, is that it is a means to exactly this end.[253]

Brentano's account is not the clearest, and it mixes Platonic and Aristotelian ideas together, but his formulation of the final end is avowedly utilitarian, albeit in its augmented version. The Cambridge philosopher George Edward Moore (1873 – 1958) developed a similar theory, and formulated it more precisely, in his influential book *Principia Ethica*, published in 1903.[254] Moore also wanted to develop ethics as an independent science and he took Brentano's generalised utilitarianism, founded upon the absolute validity of the moral order of the world, to be a self-evident premise. But he went along a slightly different path. Moore was primarily interested in evaluative judgments as utterances or statements which could be investigated using the methods of logic. Like Brentano he distinguishes between the 'extrinsic' value of a thing as a means and the 'intrinsic' value of a thing as an end, between assertoric and evaluative judgments (Brentano had used the term 'preference'). He also places emphasis on the whole, which is greater than the sum of its parts.

Moore shared the conviction of his teacher, Henry Sidgwick, that the foundation must be the term 'good', and that analysis could go no further than this term. He regarded any attempt to deduce criteria for moral judgment from natural or other givens a 'naturalistic fallacy'. To demonstrate that the term 'good' cannot be interpreted or defined with the use of any other terms, Moore introduces the open question argument: if we think that some other attribute, say 'happiness' or 'pleasure', could be a definition of 'good', we may ask 'you may be experiencing pleasure, but is it good?' The question is worth asking, as the two are not

---

253 Brentano, *Vom Ursprung der sittlichen Erkenntnis*, 1889.

254 In the same year Moore published an enthusiastic review of an English translation of Brentano's *Vom Ursprung der sittlichen Erkenntnis*. *International Journal of Ethics*, vol. 14, No. 1 (October 1903), pp. 115–123.

synonymous. We may adopt an evaluative stance in response to every evaluative utterance.[255] It is for this reason that the idea of 'good' cannot be deduced from anything other than the label of 'good' and it means, according to Moore, 'the sum of all good things'. Against naturalism, Moore emphasised the autonomy of ethics and evaluative judgments founded exclusively on intuition. Of course, not all intuition is correct, but nonetheless our evident moral intuitions can be relied upon.[256]

Moore reduced practical philosophy to the logical examination of evaluative utterances, and in so doing placed it in the framework of what was later called analytic philosophy, where his theme was taken up by other 'intuitionists'. The focus of debate then shifted to whether evaluative judgments are knowledge (as Brentano and Moore had supposed), whether they have the character of commands (prescriptivism) or whether they are, on the contrary, an expression of emotion, as the emotivists have it. Quite apart from these discussions stands American pragmatism, which rejects all considerations of presuppositions, and states that the entire sense of action lies exclusively in its consequences. Pragmatism begins with Charles S. Peirce (1839–1914) who doubted that we have anything at our disposal beyond our own experience; with his successors (William James, John Dewey and, later, Richard Rorty) this doubt assumes a radical form, leading eventually to the outright rejection of all theoretical ethics. Nonetheless, pragmatism also belongs in the common framework of consequentialism: the belief that action must be evaluated according to its (foreseeable) consequences, and according to utilitarian methods of measurement. The term consequentialism – and its definition – come from the English analytic philosopher G. E. M. Anscombe (1919–2001), who allowed that other criteria than happiness could be used as evaluative criteria. The problematic nature of this approach is that it could be summed up as 'the end justifies the means'.

Another version – supported by Karl Popper among others – is negative utilitarianism: instead of maximising happiness we should aim to minimise suffering, which is not so far removed from Epicurus.[257] The rigorous application of this principle would, however, demand a rather radical solution; humans can only be relieved of all suffering if they

---

255 Moore, *Principia Ethica*, § 13. See also Ricken, *Allgemeine Ethik*, p. 47.

256 See also Scheler, *Der Formalismus in der Ethik*.

257 Thomas Henry Huxley countered this by saying that 'hopes for lessening evil in the world are only possible when we cease to believe that the true aim of life is flight from pain and suffering.' Cited in Bayertz, *Evolution und Ethik*, p. 200.

were (painlessly) killed. The newer versions of negative utilitarianism, therefore, demand only that we limit suffering which is caused by the impossibility of carrying through our choices or preferences, or from limits to our freedom. But even this – as we have seen – is a rather problematic idea.

Utilitarianism correctly supposes that the acting person desires happiness; unlike Aristotle, however, it is mistaken in that it has turned happiness into an object. In so doing it gave significant support to the Enlightenment hope that human beings could solve their own affairs through their own efforts; but the problem is that happiness – like unhappiness – is not something that we can directly bring about by our actions. It is not in our hands; which is perhaps why people seek for it in games of chance. Although happiness may be the true, ultimate motive of human action, it cannot be planned for and cannot, for that reason, be its direct aim. As the French philosopher Émile Chartier (Alain) puts it: 'Happiness is the reward of those who do not seek it'. [258]

3.3 The Discovery of the Soul

At approximately the midway point of the 1st milenium BC, as the surviving literature of that period attests, a quite remarkable turning point was reached. Bruno Snell calls this 'the discovery of the soul'– the discovery of the individual ego, reflecting upon its own inner life.[259] In the context of Greek literature, this marks the end of the Homeric world of great deeds and heroes – many of whom bear no responsibility for these deeds as they were brought about, one way or another, by the gods. The later poets, the tragedians Sophocles and Aeschylus, and finally, Socrates and Plato, all present us with an entirely different image of themselves. In Scripture, the most famous examples of this new way of seeing are Abraham or the Book of Job; and in Asian literature, Gautama Buddha and Chinese lyric poetry. Karl Jaspers, who observed this remarkable chronological convergence, speaks of this period as an 'axial age' (*Achsenzeit*).[260] And although it can be countered that this 'discovery' of our own inner

---

258 Alain, *Propos sur le bonheur*, p. 200.

259 Snell, *The Discovery of the Mind*. See especially the first study. The German title of Snell's book is *Die Entdeckung des Geistes*. *Geist* can be translated as both *soul* and *spirit*. The same is true of the Czech word *duše* which is used in the original version of the present book. There is no individual word in English that contains this overlap of meaning.

260 Jaspers, *The Origin and Goal of History*.

life – or rather, our own mortality – is already on display in the much older *Epic of Gilgamesh*, the term is nonetheless helpful, as something fundamental really did change at this epoch.

It would be easy for a contemporary reader to underestimate the significance and consequences of this turning 'inside', to the reflection upon individual actions and persons. After all, the 'individual' understanding of moral terms is as obvious to us today as it was incomprehensible to ancient cultures. Once our evaluation of our own action ceases to be governed by how others view them, and becomes internalised, the whole character of moral evaluation changes.[261] Social custom loses its moral force; people come to regard it as something akin to etiquette or courtesy, if not mere formality – something of no moral significance. Moral evaluation, in its entirety, is transferred to the realm of individual conscience, becoming invisible to everyone else in the process. The moral life of mankind becomes 'first-person ethics'; its intimate and scarcely communicable mystery evades all external control.[262]

In order that at least some socially binding action could be commonly evaluated (and, if necessary, enforced) the new and autonomous area of law was indispensable. Law, of course, grows out of morality and is based upon it. But, in our modern conception, law differs radically from morality in its methods of forensic examination, proof and the public force of its evaluation. So right away a dangerous division is created between morality and law, which must limit its morally significant content to that which can be proved. One consequence of this enforced separation is that defendants can lie with impunity in court, since lies cannot be proved beyond doubt (that is, distinguished from mere error) by external means. This undesirable 'moral nihilism' of court procedure significantly undermines the credibility of law.[263] It is hard for the public, who continue to regard law as an instrument of justice (a view enforced by the use of the title 'Ministry of Justice'), to understand how these two things go together; the blame is placed on the cynicism of lawyers and lawmakers. But in reality this is simply a consequence of the acknowl-

---

261 Immanuel Kant provides a terse expression of this difference: 'If everyone in a nation has his own character, the nation has none; if no one has his own character, the nation has it' (*Lose Blätter*, Nr. 1163, *AA* XIV, p. 514).

262 Pascal observes the problematic nature of internal self-evaluation and its various criteria: 'there are only two types of people: the just, who believe themselves sinners, and sinners, who believe themselves just.' (*Pensées*, fragment 534).

263 Consider the ancient cynical proverb: 'the first principle of law: deny what you have done' (*Prima regula juris: quid fecisti nega*) European law punishes 'crooked' witnesses. In American penal law, defendants can either tell the truth or remain silent, but they can never lie.

edgment of human freedom and the primacy of that internalised moral evaluation into which others cannot see.

Honour and Conscience

The ancient notion of honour, which was known already to Homer's heroes, can be seen as a forerunner of this 'turning inside', the reflection upon the self, which, in moral evaluation, gradually comes to overshadow the phenomenal aspect of human acts. Until recently, and in some cases even today, 'honour' can mean the external expression of recognition or esteem, for example in such titles as 'honorary function'. *Lèse-majesté* was until recently strictly punished, and the defamation of heads of State is still a punishable offence in some countries today. This meaning of societal recognition and prestige was clearly dominant in ancient 'heroic' societies, where soldiers could lose their honour through cowardice, the breaking of promises, or unwillingness to stake their lives whenever their honour was insulted.[264] Free soldiers therefore needed to defend their honour through revenge killings or duels.

From ancient concepts of honour comes the term virtue; the Latin *virtus* comes from *vir* ('man') and in the ancient conception of virtue, strength and courage were the most prized qualities. Unlike later conceptions of virtue, this had the advantage of being visible and that it lent itself to the telling of glorious tales. But of course the opportunity to perform memorable deeds of bravery – and to excel in the eyes of others – was given only to free soldiers, independent warriors and, later, generals; only occasionally does this opportunity fall to heroes from other social classes, such as Eumaeus in the *Odyssey* or the countryman David against the professional warrior Goliath.[265] Even Socrates' courage at the battle of Plataea is reported in an almost accidental manner.

In less organised and less warlike societies, a counterpart to martial courage was generosity – one of the most appreciated qualities of a tribal chieftain. This, like courage, was a visible (and therefore undoubted) 'virtue'. It was also, of course, the preserve of the rich. But social prestige

---

264 Socrates gives an account of the things that one should be ashamed of on the basis of Achilles' conversation with his mother (*Iliad,* 18.70): his mother warns him that he will die after Hector.

265 These opportunities were severely limited by the further development of warfare. The military successes of the Athenians have – probably correctly – been attributed to the *phalanx* organisation of fighters, in which little room for individual initiative was left. As soldiers replaced warriors, discipline outweighed individual bravery.

cannot be based merely on wealth – quite the opposite; the rich man who lacks generosity is a target of opprobrium in many myths and folk tales.[266] It is precisely this generosity – largeness of spirit – that gave legitimacy to 'good' tribal chieftains; although wisdom in judgment and energetic responses to danger were also highly prized.[267]

Already in the heroic times another form of virtue (albeit also an aristocratic one) was also prized – faithfulness. Firstly, the 'virtue' of a wife consists in her unbreakable faithfulness to her husband, as represented by Homer's Penelope. Her action is, of course, also visible, but a wise woman can manage to keep her internal motives hidden for a long time. Also highly prized, though admittedly in Penelope's shadow, is the crucial role played by the loyal swineherd Eumaeus, who assists Odysseus in his return to Ithica.[268] Although faithfulness is still presented in the *Odyssey* in line with aristocratic conceptions and ideals, this is no longer the same notion of excelling in the eyes of others. On the contrary, this kind of virtue is not certain in the eyes of others; it is open to doubt, so that its final arbiter can be none other than the faithful person himself (or herself).[269] In this altered conception of virtue, the focal point gradually moves from external honour and virtue to an internalised understanding of morality as an affair of the individual conscience.

* * *

Another expression of this change is the profound transformation in our understanding of religion. Already in the dynamic urban societies of Late Antiquity, where people from various cultures collided, the previously self-evident, undoubted authority of local religious cults is weakened to the point that they lose their exclusive standing. The experience of different cultures, different rituals, myths and divinities necessarily raised the question: which one is 'right', and why? All that had once been unthink-

---

266 In Czech, and other Slavic languages, the word *bohatý* ('rich') has the same root as the word *bůh* ('God'). Both are derived from the Sanskrit verb *bhajati* – to give, to deal out. The rich man, therefore, resembles God in his generosity. A similar relationship exists between the Latin *Deus* ('God') and *dives, divitiae* – 'wealth'.

267 See, for example, the well-known phenomenon of the potlatch, which we mention elsewhere.

268 In the *Odyssey*, pigs are a symbol of affluence and prosperity; none of the later opprobrium that attaches to these animals is in evidence here.

269 An extreme example of this is to be found in Shakespeare's *Othello*. To take a girl's 'honour' or 'maidenhead' has traditionally meant to take her virginity. The Christian church fought in vain against this strongly 'sexist' idea by attributing the sin of unmarried sex to both parties equally.

ingly, collectively accepted and respected was now open to question. In the culturally mixed, individualised urban environment, the individual unwittingly becomes the judge of traditions to which his predecessors had unconditionally submitted themselves.

Our of this shattering of traditional group religions there grew individualised and universal monotheistic religions, which address themselves to individuals regardless of their social origin; but there also grew a new individual morality with no external support. The individual feels himself bound by the invisible authority of a single God whose will he accepts as his own (as in late Judaism and Christianity); or he comes to see himself as the sole judge of his own decision and action, on the basis of internalised principles and rules. That this must necessarily lead to internal (and almost unresolvable) conflicts was demonstrated by Greek tragedy, for example in the characters of Creon and Antigone.[270]

The demand placed on all citizens, that they be able to 'share in the sense of right and wrong' – the ability to judge their own actions critically – is already regarded in Plato's *Protagoras* as a necessary condition of communal life.[271] The sharp distinction between virtue and 'disgrace' is the chief moral characteristic of Plato's Socrates, and it runs like a thread through all his dialogues (but these dialogues are also 'humanised' by experiences of beauty, friendship and pleasure). When Socrates, standing before the Athenian court, gives a 'summing up' of his moral beliefs, he says that a man should not submit to the pressure of society or the judgments of others, but rather stand by those conclusions which his own reason has led him to. 'To think not of death or of anything other than disgrace' – so long as he does not 'contradict and clash with (him)self.'[272]

The fate of Socrates throws into sharp relief the conflictive character of this fundamental transformation. Plato's Socrates carefully observes Athenian religious customs and defends himself against Dionysodorus: 'I also have an altar and I observe ceremonies like every other Athenian'. In his final moments (according to Plato's *Phaedo*) he reminds Crito that he owes Aesculapius a cockerel; when Crito promises him that he will pay this debt himself, Socrates dies peacefully.[273] Nonetheless, his

---

270 Oedipus is presented as a tragic victim of fate – although he is only 'innocent' in the eyes of the new conception of individual moral responsibility. He did not do anything dishonourable. Creon and Antigone, on the contrary, both experience internal conflicts between their duties to loved ones and their duties to their community. It was entirely self-evident to the Greek audience that Creon must give precedence to the community and Antigone to her dead brother.

271 Plato, *Protagoras*, 322d.

272 Plato, *Defence of Socrates*, 28e; *Gorgias*, 482c.

273 Plato, *Euthydemos*, 302c; *Phaidon*, 118a. See also *Symposium*, 176a.

stance, founded upon rational investigation, is by its nature critical – and therefore conflictive. In the dialogue *Euthyphro* he starts by declaring that Meletus accuses him of 'making new gods and disbelieving in the old ones'. It then emerges, however, that Euthyphro, a 'learned man in questions of divine law and in all things divine and sinful' is taking his own father to court for allowing a slave to die because he (the slave) had killed someone else. Euthyphro is convinced that he must make the charge, but Socrates demonstrates to him that his belief is misguided; it contains within itself a conflict between his (Euthyphro's) duty towards his father and his responsibilities as a citizen to prosecute crime. Euthyphro is unaware of this conflict and is convinced that he is acting in accordance with the will of the gods. Socrates then explains to him that some of the gods may give priority to one of these beliefs but other gods would give priority to the opposite belief. The unspoken conclusion of the dialogue, then, is that a man cannot appeal to the Athenian gods as a guide for action, but must rather seek justice according to his own conscience.

* * *

The moral systems of Late Antiquity, especially Stoicism, appeal to this new conception of conscience and honour as indispensible components of the free person, who is able to bear responsibility for his own actions. The Stoic ideal of complete self-mastery (or *autarky*) demands that we give up our longing for external happiness as this is not in our reach. We should restrict ourselves to that which is in our power, and recognise that those things which are beyond them are, from the viewpoint of honour and virtue, to be classed as *adiaforon* – indistinguishable, and therefore insignificant. 'Do not want what is not, want what is, and you shall be content' says Epictetus. People are therefore classed as either wise or as fools, who chase after the chimeras of health, riches and earthly pleasures, which cannot satisfy the wise, while fearing illness, poverty or unhappiness, none of which can truly hurt the wise. On the contrary, the wise man is not shaken by any of these things as he knows that they are of no lasting importance and that he carries his happiness within himself. This is the Stoic ideal of *ataraxia* ('unshakableness'), which defies all fate and remains firm in its path.

This, however, does not mean that Stoic teaching is fatalistic or deterministic, as many consider. It emphasises the area of responsible human freedom, which lies 'inside' each of us – the only thing in our power –

virtue and virtuous action. 'The soul should be turned away from all that is external and submerged in itself; it believes itself, delights in itself' (Seneca). We cannot control the outside world, and the external circumstances of our own lives; but we certainly should master ourselves and act accordingly. And only if we really live and act according to reason, and in harmony with our nature, can we take pleasure in knowing that we have acted honourably, bravely and wisely – regardless of success or failure.

The strict ideal of Stoicism – of purely individual virtue, as envisioned by Zeno and Chrysippos and as later represented by Cato, Seneca, Cicero and Marcus Aurelius, has always had a major significance for practical philosophy. This is primarily because everything it demands is within the power of every individual and not dependent on any external factors. The ideal Stoic fears nothing 'apart from disgrace' but also has no expectations from life. For this reason there has always been something rather cold and 'inhuman' about Stoic virtue; any kind of hedonism is alien to it. An almost heroic degree of self-control is demanded from the Stoic, along with a full acceptance of responsibility for his own actions, but also for the outside world. The Stoic expects nothing from the outside world, but has a fundamental responsibility to it, which permits no excuses.

But Stoicism is also the first philosophy to clearly defend and demand freedom and autonomy for every individual, even against the community. Until the Stoics, no one had really needed such freedom. Another important factor in this individual autonomy is Stoical universalism; the 'value' of each person lies within the person himself, and in his actions; it has nothing to do with his origins or position within society. In consequence, Stoical individualism is also one of the first philosophies of human equality. Of course this should not be taken to mean that, for example, a Stoic Emperor could abolish slavery or social stratification of the Empire; nonetheless, the generous extension of citizenship to all free residents of the Roman Empire under Caesar Caracalla in the year 212AD was a result not only of practical considerations, but also of Caracalla's Stoic worldview.

The Stoic life of honour, conscience and responsibility is not for everyone, and very few people can live up to it – which is why it has always enjoyed such respect.[274] When early Christianity abandoned the idea that the end of the world was close at hand, and began to establish itself in

---

274 Pascal comments that Stoics 'conclude that you can always do what in reality you can do only sometimes' (*Pensées,* fragment 350).

the world, it took inspiration from the Stoical (or Cynical) morality of self-denial: the taming of individual inclinations, appetites and passions through the exercise of virtue – although this was always motivated by hope and expectation, which were existentially foreign to Stoicism. Elements of Stoicism are therefore to be found throughout the whole history of Christianity, from the letters of Paul, through St Augustine to the preachers of the late Middle Ages, such as Master Eckhart.[275]

Stoical asceticism is what provides the 'Hellenic' element in Christian morality, something which is almost entirely missing from Judaism. Having said that, the idea of the courageous individual, owing nothing to anyone and acting at all times in line with his own freedom and sense of responsibility, was unacceptable to Christianity. When Stoicism experienced a marked reawakening in the context of the Italian renaissance and the attendant humanism, it was rejected, especially by Luther's Reformation. The arguments surrounding 'free will' are, to a large extent, directed against this revived Stoicism. Despite this opposition, however, the Stoic ideal of individual freedom and autonomy was to be a major inspiration for European modernity, from Erasmus through Immanuel Kant all the way to the existentialists.

We must not, however, overlook the extreme form of 'Titanic Stoicism', as presented by the leaders of the French Revolution, for example Maximilian Robespierre, for whom the demands of virtue trumped any human considerations. With such terrifying examples of fanaticism it is easy to point out their most fundamental error: while they may appear as responsible people, in reality they seek to absolve themselves of all responsibility for their actions by ascribing them to an imaginary 'virtue', such as their duty to the revolution, or to their country. It is not I, Robespierre, but rather civic duty, civic *virtue*, that sends thousands to their deaths in the name of the Revolution.

Perfection of the Soul

We have already spoken of the collapse of the ancient *polis* as a place for good human life, and the corresponding transformation of ideas of happiness, in connection with Epicurus. In the chaos of multitudes of beliefs

---

275 The entire argument of Eckhart's *Book of Divine Consolation* is thoroughly Stoical. The specifically Christian characteristics of love and hope make almost no appearance. Stoical argument is also common in the Christian literature of the time. Spaemann's *Basic Moral Concepts* also ends with a surprising defence of Stoical motives.

and voices, there is only one thing left for people to turn to: their own selves. As we have already mentioned, however, this depends on how people imagine 'their own selves'. In addition to the empirical, immanent, complete and self-sufficient 'self', which Epicurus took as his starting point, Socrates discovered different, perhaps more interesting, aspects of this same 'self': the conscience and the soul. He seems to have been inspired in this, partly by Democritus[276] and partly by Pythagoras' discovery of geometry – not as a practical skill, but as a remarkably different world of objects, which do not exist anywhere, but which are unchanging, are amenable to discovery and are equally true for everyone who is able to recognise them.[277]

The 'Socratic turn', which is sometimes spoken of in this context, does not mean merely that the attention of philosophers should turn away from the foundations of the universe towards the internal thought-life of man. If an uneducated slave was able to recall the precise and indubitable geometrical laws, this to Socrates is proof of several further things. Firstly, that there is at least one part of our soul that is capable of conceiving and understanding a different kind of object from the objects that we deal with every day. The capacity to glimpse these eternal, precise and universal 'objects' suggests that, 'if all of nature is harmonious and the mind has known all things' then the mind is, in a certain sense, immortal. But, if left to itself, it will also most likely forget them again; and it can only glimpse them under direction.

Geometrical order is not accessible to the senses, and yet our knowledge of material objects is somehow governed by it. And so there is a great hope – almost a certainty – that something akin to geometrical order could also govern something far more significant: human action. Like Heraclitus or Parmenides before him, Plato cannot accept that human action should be governed merely by experience, or the traditional wisdom of the ancients, which is so unclear and full of contradictions, and which can sometimes lead to outright wickedness.[278] For this reason the most important task, for individuals and the community, is that everyone becomes aware of this and that they start 'cultivating', caring

---

276 'He who commits an injustice is unhappier than he who suffers it.' (Democritus, fragment DK 68 B 45)

277 See the famous episode with the illiterate slave and diagonals in squares, from *Meno* 85b–85b. Socrates here does no more than ask questions, and the slave is able to solve a non-trivial task by himself.

278 See Heraclitus' sarcastic fragments (e.g. DK 22B29, B 112 or B 116), or the above-cited *Euthyphro* of Plato.

for their own minds; or at least take guidance from someone who cares for their own mind well. When Socrates, in the *Apology*, gives an account of his ordinary conversations with fellow Athenians, he says this very clearly:

> My very good friend, you are an Athenian and belong to a city which is the greatest and most famous in the world for its wisdom and strength. Are you not ashamed that you give your attention to acquiring as much money as possible, and similarly with reputation and honour, and give no attention or thought to truth and understanding and the perfection of your soul?[279]

'Soul', in this context, means something like a long-term memory, which gathers together the experiences of life into one whole and leaves, upon itself, the permanent marks of that life. Human actions may be transient, but their marks on the soul remain, giving it its all-important form.[280]

It is not entirely clear what Socrates – or Plato – imagines this cultivation of the soul to look like *in concreto*. What is sure, however, is that it entails a committed search for truth, in human affairs as in geometry; and it requires that we lead our lives according to the truth discovered in this way. This involves developing critical judgment of our own actions and continually asking whether we are not confusing 'good' with 'pleasant' or 'comfortable'. Socrates saw this as the only salvation for the quarrelsome Athenian community; after all, there is no need for quarrelling in geometry if we can all convince ourselves about the truth that it holds.[281] Socrates tried, in all his discussions, to encourage his interlocutors to reach their own insights into the true state of things; his only hesitation in this point was in the question to what extent a teacher can help them in this process. However, his conception of the 'geometric' nature of practical philosophy did not find a large audience; Aristotle, his closest pupil, understood the Socratic fidelity to truth not as fidelity to his master. The truth is to be preferred even if it would contradict our friends.[282] He took no interest in geometry, and stated that ethics could only be 'proportionately' accurate. Later on, Descartes adopted a 'geometric'

---

279 Plato, *Apology*, 29d. This dialogue is also known as the *Defence of Socrates*.
280 Martin Heidegger calls this the 'potentiality-to-be-a-whole' – *Ganz-sein-können* (*Being and Time*, § 48). We have already noted Socrates' concern with not being 'in contradiction' with himself.
281 Thomas Hobbes describes his method in similar terms in *Leviathan*.
282 See the proverbial '*amicus Plato, sed magis amica veritas*', based on *NE* 1096a15.

approach to philosophy, but only in the areas of knowledge and science; and Spinoza's attempts to base his system of ethics on the certainties of geometry were largely unsuccessful.

However, the idea of the caring for the soul – as man's fundamental duty towards himself – took root and has lived on, in various guises, to this day.[283] Its revolutionary importance to the Western tradition rests in its appeal to the individual. As man starts to become more deeply aware of himself as a thinking and acting person, and to reflect upon his actions, a new region of freedom opens up to him. Only in this context does it make sense to speak of things like individual morality, responsibility and conscience.[284] In one of his early dialogues, Plato has Protagoras pronounce the categorical demand of Zeus himself: 'anyone who has no sense of shame and justice must be thought of as a contagion to society and put to death!'[285] A community of free agents can only flourish if all its members are able to judge their own actions, not from the viewpoint of their own interests, but from the viewpoint of justice.

The classic account of morality in Plato's *Gorgias* begins with Socrates verifying the terms of the discussion.[286] He says of himself that he is as happy to be proved wrong as to prove another wrong (458a), a principle to which his interlocutor, Gorgias, also adheres. And so the dialogue can begin, and does, with a famous paradox: Socrates wishes to have nothing to do with any wrongdoing, 'but if I had to choose between doing wrong and having wrong done to me, I'd prefer the latter' (469c). 'Good things are not the same as pleasant things, and bad things aren't the same as unpleasant things either' (479d); suffering wrongdoing is merely unpleasant, while he who commits it comes into conflict with himself. The rational and brave man is the one who is 'in control of (him)self' (491d) and for that reason, we should not be concerned about how long we live. 'A real man ... isn't worried about how long he lives, and isn't attached to life', but, rather, 'considers how best to live' (512e). For this reason it is essential to gain clarity in the question of what is evil, and why do people do evil. 'No one wants to do wrong, and ... every wrong act is done un-

---

283 See the Czech philosopher Jan Patočka, *Péče o duši* (The Care for the Soul), Collected Works II. An even more traditional interpretation of Plato's 'unwritten doctrine' is defended by G. Reale, *Toward a new interpretation of Plato*.

284 It is with reference to Socrates that we considered the difference between social custom and individual morality.

285 Plato, *Protagoras*, 322d.

286 The numbers and letters in the brackets above refer to sections of *Gorgias* which are to be found on the margins of modern editions.

wittingly' (509e) because the person who commits it 'isn't doing what he wants' (468d): he is trying, in committing the act, to attain some good.

But any wrongdoing, even if it is unseen, leaves a permanent scar in the soul of the perpetrator; this is why it is better to suffer wrong than to commit it. And this is why Socrates says 'it is preferable for everyone else in the world to find my beliefs unfounded and wrong rather than for just one person – me – to contradict and clash with myself' (482b). Nonetheless, his morality is not – in the modern usage – subjective, but rather appeals to the overall order of the world: 'co-operation, love, order, discipline bind heaven and earth, gods and men. That's why they call the universe an ordered whole (*cosmos*) ... rather than a disorderly mess' (508a). This is also why wrongdoing must be judged and punished; for the cleansing of the perpetrator – 'a person who pays a fair penalty for his crimes is relieved from the wickedness of his soul' (477a) – but also as a deterrent to others. For courts to be just, however, free from the influence of 'attractive bodies, noble birth (and) wealth', the soul must approach the court unclothed, naked, and without the support of relatives – something which is only possible after death (523).

This account of courts and punishment in *Gorgias* is meant symbolically, something which should be obvious, given Plato's frequent use of images in other dialogues – for example, the 'migration of souls' in *Phaedrus*. This, of course, does not mean that we should take them lightly – quite the opposite; Plato was well aware that the most profound and serious things can only be spoken of in images.[287] It is then up to us, the readers, to try to understand them as best we can, either as direct messages, as an impetus to further thought, or something to simply ignore.

Autonomy and Heteronomy

The originally political concept of autonomy – the independence of a community which is free to make its own laws – is already used in Greek tragedy to describe a heroine who obeys her own 'law', even at the cost of her life.[288] The Stoics also considered themselves autonomous, but then the concept disappears into the background until the 14th century, when it is rediscovered and given unprecedented voice by Dante.

---

287 Democritus declared that 'words are spoken images' (fragment DK 68 B 142).

288 Sophocles, *Antigone*, verse 821.

He is not speaking about autonomy in the modern sense, but rather of full, unconditional 'mastery over oneself'. Towards the end of the second section of the *Divine Comedy*, the narrator must part with his guide, Virgil, who, as a pagan, cannot enter into Heaven. Virgil departs with these words:

> No longer wait for words or signs from me.
> Your will is free, just, and as it should be,
> And not to follow it would be a fault:
> I leave you master of your body and soul.[289]

From the 17th century on, the concept of autonomy reappears, primarily in law. It was introduced into practical philosophy – as the opposite of heteronomy – by Immanuel Kant. In the *Groundwork of the Metaphysics of Morals* Kant says:

> If we look back upon all previous efforts that have ever been made to discover the principle of morality, we need not wonder why all of them had to fail. It was seen that the human being is bound to laws by his duty, but it never occurred to them that he is subject *only to laws given by himself but still universal* and that he is bound only to act in conformity to his own will, which, however, in accordance with nature's end is a will giving universal law.[290]

This formulation juxtaposes both sides of a twofold emphasis: the law to which man must unconditionally submit himself is 'given by himself', but at the same time 'universal', in accordance with 'nature's end'. So while he may, with Dante, have 'mastery over himself', this cannot mean mere licence or caprice, as he would then fall prey to his own inclinations and desires, losing his freedom in the process. He is free only inasmuch as he accepts 'nature's end', and learns to decide, not according to his own 'demands' but rather according to universal law, as expressed by the categorical imperative.[291]

Kant struggled with the human and political implications of this tension, which he tried to transcend in his overall concept of humanity's historical progress. While independence and self-mastery play an important

---

289 Literally 'I give you the royal and the papal crown'. Dante, *The Divine Comedy. Purgatorio*, 27, 139–142.

290 Kant, *Groundwork*, AA IV. 432.

291 See 3.1.

role in his earlier writings,[292] his later work – perhaps influenced by the French Revolution – places great emphasis on the idea of Providence, of nature and its 'end', which man must be governed by. Human nature is wicked and needs government to keep a tight rein on it. Hopes for progress should not rest on what we alone can achieve (through education, for example) but rather on Providence, the way in which nature compels us towards free citizenship.[293] Morality and law must necessarily begin with compulsion[294] and only when people learn to 'honour the authority of the law, as if it were a physical force, will they be able to become their own lawmakers'.[295] Revolutionaries, those 'despotic moralists', must learn from experience that the implementation of new ideas of freedom, at a time when the State is in danger, goes against the wisdom of the State (*Staatsklugheit*) and against nature. Therefore, the introduction of such ideas must be postponed.[296]

And so it emerges that the seemingly simple idea of autonomy is in fact full of paradoxes, a situation which Kant himself was evidently aware of:

> Only the man who is himself enlightened, who is not afraid of shadows, and who commands at the same time a well disciplined and numerous army as guarantor of public peace--only he can say what (the sovereign of) a free state cannot dare to say: "Argue as much as you like, and about what you like, but obey!" Thus we observe here as elsewhere in human affairs, in which almost everything is paradoxical, a surprising and unexpected course of events.[297]

The paradox does not, perhaps, occur so much in the course of 'human affairs' as much as in Kant's relentless struggle to separate 'pure reason' and experience, as if they could each do perfectly well without the other – or were indeed directly opposed to each other.

We tried, in the preceding discussion, to cast light upon at least part of this paradox. We have seen that the way in which children develop

---

292 'Nature has willed that man should, by himself, produce everything that goes beyond the mechanical ordering of his animal existence, and that he should partake of no other happiness or perfection than that which he himself, independently of instinct, has created by his own reason.' (*Ideas for a Universal Commonwealth*, A930)

293 Kant, *On the Common Saying...*, A278.

294 *Toward Perpetual Peace*, B75.

295 Ibid. B79.

296 Ibid. B79.

297 *What is Enlightenment?*, A494.

a sense of basic 'social custom' is similar to the way they learn their native language – by picking up cues from their parents and the surrounding environment. At first they learn about what is and isn't 'the done thing' through simple imitation; only later do they grasp that there are universal rules at work behind these situations. According to Jean Piaget, children learn about rules through playing games – again through imitation to begin with. Around four or five years of age, they become aware of these rules as a given, but they do not understand them and simply accept them as an authority. It is only around the age of nine, according to Piaget, that children make the step from heteronomy to autonomy and internalise these rules, accepting and understanding them.[298] However, they still have to accept them from others, and under a certain societal pressure.

In our account of the difference between social custom and individual morality, we quoted the Bible: 'Thou shalt not follow a multitude to do evil.' Individual morality demands of all of us that we should not be governed by social custom alone, and what is more, that we should stand up against it if need be, as Socrates did. This is a fundamentally important step in the direction of autonomy; but if we are to be able to distinguish evil, we need the help of some general rules which we did not create ourselves – such as the Ten Commandments.

These are purely moral and 'categorical' rules, in the sense that there is no sanction attached to them and there is no reason for obeying them other than 'respect for law', as Kant demands. But if these originally moral rules establish themselves in a society, they then become the basis of law and obedience to them becomes a matter of compulsion. And so, sensitive individuals may feel that they are in fact not acting freely or autonomously – especially if the interpretation of these rules, and the means of enforcing them, are in the hands of a social, political or religious authority which could abuse this power.

Despite all the Utopian attempts to force a change for the better in human affairs, the dilemma of individual freedom on the one hand and peaceful co-existence in society on the other is as troublesome today as it was in Kant's time. One difference is that most societies today offer their citizens some basic rights; but societies are considerably larger and more complex, and citizens often do not share the same basic moral principles. Another important difference is that the concept of reason, as being common to all and binding to all, seems to have become lost – to say nothing

298 Piaget, *The Insights and Illusions of Philosophy*.

of 'nature's end'. The idea of 'natural law' becomes problematic when we consider that nature is probably responsible for the bad parts of human nature as well as the good ones. 'Nature' cannot, therefore, be a reliable moral criterion.

Many of us today consider 'autonomy' to mean being in harmony with ourselves – namely, with our interests and inclinations. This is in direct contradiction to Kant. This false 'autonomy' manifests itself in the notion that my – or our – private interests are sovereign, and if they clash with each other, there is nothing for it but to see who wins. I may overcome my opponent in the most inconsiderate, selfish manner while staying well within the law. Free morality – the voluntary acceptance of important self-restrictions – is becoming lost to society, and needs to be replaced with the external pressure of laws and rules. This has contributed to the conflict-filled nature of contemporary economic and political life. It has also led to the disenchanted realisation that, in a society devoid of free self-restriction, even law is ineffective.

To this extent, MacIntyre's sceptical evaluation of modernity is justified, even if his ideal of a 'return' to an age of shared authority is probably illusory. We will, therefore, in the closing chapters of this book, attempt to provide an alternative basis for autonomous morality: one which is founded, not on the problematic 'force of nature' but on the unconditional responsibility of people and society towards that which it has inherited and from which we all evidently live. This responsibility to a distant, common future corresponds to Kant's idea of autonomy, if anything better than the speculative and timeless 'dictate of reason'. It develops and clarifies the somewhat vague notion of 'nature's end', with the help of lived experience, including the conclusions drawn by biology. But on the other hand Kant, and the demand of autonomy, will provide us with a defence against the 'naturalism' and scientific reductionism which has plagued so much modern thought.

Man is undeniably a part of nature, and he must submit to the limitations of his finite existence. But nonetheless, he differs from all other living creatures in his ability to speak and to reflect, and to know things that are not available to sensory perception.[299] Even the 'will to life', Spinoza's *conatus essendi* and Nietzsche's 'will to power', which in other crea-

---

299 The Pythagorean tradition correctly observed this, although it limited itself to the field of geometry, and probably tried to take too much from it. The almost hysterical attempts of Spinoza and Kant to separate, divide and distinguish, are no doubt an inheritance of this ancient wonder at the possibilities of 'pure reason', which can compel us accept conclusions that we do not want to accept. This is the starting point of the whole of philosophy.

tures is largely instinctive must, in man's case, submit to this reflection, and can be secondary to other interests. Of course, even human freedom is not absolute. This is partly because it most likely arose from the ever greater possibilities of movement and observation of other animals, and partly because man is not born with freedom but must work to achieve it, as part of growing up.[300] It is for this reason that it makes practical sense to speak of freedom and to work to attain it.

There has never been any doubt that young children cannot be autonomous, and that their parents must take responsibility for them. Children are supposed to find their way towards autonomy, through education and upbringing. But what about aged people, or the sick? A person in a coma, or in shock or an advanced state of drunkenness, does not have full command of his or her faculties, and therefore cannot be autonomous. The same can be said for people with learning disabilities or the mentally ill. Even if they are judged by a court to be *sui juris*, they may still need others to make decisions and act on their behalf. These others may not have explicit authorization of the affected person, but nonetheless they are acting in her interests.

This gives rise to a dilemma which every day confronts doctors and firemen, care workers and police officers, family members and many other people: in which circumstances, and to what extent, should such a person be regarded as an autonomous adult? And, on the contrary, when is it necessary for them to act on this person's behalf in his or her own interest? As increasing emphasis is placed on the human rights of patients, and as the risk of legal action in the event of the violation of these rights, the dilemma comes into ever sharper focus. The French philosopher Raymond Ruyer has described this as the 'hunger-striker's paradox'.[301] A prisoner on hunger-strike is a free person who cannot be compelled to do anything. However in the instant that he loses consciousness, the prison doctors must do everything in their powers to keep him alive – but as soon as this is achieved, the prisoner becomes once more an autonomous citizen and the cycle can begin over again.

The situations we have to face in everyday life are not nearly so extreme, but they are more frequent, and more complicated; and legal intervention would most likely make matters even more complicated rather than helping to resolve matters in the interest of the affected party. Indeed, the fear of legal ramifications is such that people are often hesi-

---

300 See Jonas, *Evolution and Freedom*.
301 Ruyer, *Paradoxes de la conscience et limites de l'automatisme*.

tant to help a stranger in trouble, and health professionals sometimes make patients sign disclaimers before agreeing to treat them. And so the original idea of 'informed consent' can degenerate into a mere formality or even caricature, the only effect of which is to terrify the patient and weaken his faith in medical professionals.

Even people 'of sound mind and body' often need the help of others, even though this may represent a compromising of their own autonomy. The abuse of legal autonomy is the basis for the financial abuse of various confidence tricksters, who specifically target the aged and inexperienced with offers of savings or the like. It takes a courageous and free-thinking judge to cut through the pretence of 'free decision' that is the backbone of these conmen's defence.

3.4 The Idea of Good and Ethical Realism

Long before the arrival of such neutral concepts as 'evaluation', people used general terms like good and bad, or evil, in much the same way as we do. That for which we strive is good, that which we do not care for is bad, and that which we fear, or which is abhorrent or to us, is evil. Plato's Socrates attempted to refine this general opinion, and to understand what people really meant by these words. Good – as we have seen – is not the same as pleasant, and evil is not the same as unpleasant. What is it that differentiates them? Socrates (or rather Plato) thought he had found the answer to that question: he called it the Good – or the idea of the good.[302]

Since Nietzsche's famous denunciation of the idea of the good, it has been fashionable to respond to it with a grimace, or at least a shrug of the shoulders. But perhaps we should ask whether we can afford to be so dismissive; Nietzsche himself doubted it and Immanuel Kant, or the Czech thinker Emanuel Rádl – who saw some of the horrific events of the last century at first hand – were convinced that we could not.[303] Before moving onto a critique of Plato's idea of the good, we should first

---

302 Plato's own account is to be found in *Republic*, 505a. See also *Hippias Major*, in which Socrates comes at the concept of good from a discussion of the concept of beauty.

303 See Rádl, *Consolation from Philosophy* (Útěcha z filosofie). Rádl's beautiful metaphor of the 'white swans' provides a gentle warning against the temptation to 'overpower' the idea of the Good by submitting it to definition through other terms. In this point he was perhaps closer to Plato than many declared Platonists. And even Nietzsche, after declaring that 'God is dead' because 'we have killed him', he asks whether we can allow ourselves such a step.

make an effort to understand it. It was – and is – one of the main ideas of the Western philosophical tradition, and it has had a profound effect on the formation of the spiritual world we have inherited. It is almost impossible to imagine Western civilisation – to say nothing of philosophy – without it. When Alfred North Whitehead said of philosophy that it was 'a series of footnotes to Plato', he was referring in particular to Plato's idea of the good.

Where did this idea come from? It seems to be founded on two important phenomena: the ubiquity of evaluation and the experience that people are rarely satisfied for long with any individual 'good' that they have attained.[304] It is as if a person who is striving and labouring for something is, in reality, searching for something else; something which transcends every individual 'good' thing. We have already spoken about the ubiquity of evaluation. However, what is remarkable is that, while the objects of our evaluations are as different from each other as you can imagine, the actual process of evaluation itself is always more or less the same. It is always based on some sort of comparison, it always involves an element of hesitation, and it always concludes with a verdict, which in turn leads to decision or choice. It is as if all human evaluation, all more or less 'rational' choices and decisions, had something in common. Something separates it from unthinking decisions, which seem to have more in common with unconscious reactions, and which the ancients called 'the passions'.

The search for the good must therefore be guided by reason; and yet of course even rational decisions can turn out to be bad, or even tragic. But they are always *my* – or *your* – decisions; it would be better if we had decided otherwise. In other words, even bad decisions – provided they are not so utterly foolish that we are embarrassed to acknowledge them – help to mould our experience and can help us to be on our guard against repeating them.[305] This is extremely important to life in society, and is inded the basis of education: next time, you should do better!

Thoughtless action, on the other hand, whether we regard it as mere reaction or whether we attribute it to inclinations or passions, does not offer any such hope. Whether it turns out well or (more likely) badly, it nonetheless represents momentary weakness and a falling away from our role. People often struggle to explain why they behaved as they did, and sometimes have the feeling that it wasn't even them. In this they resem-

---

304 Robert Spaemann speaks of the 'frustration' that follows the attainment of a goal we have been striving for (*Happiness and Benevolence*).
305 'If you make a mistake and do not correct it, that is called a mistake' – Confucius.

ble Homeric heroes whose minds were 'fogged' by Athena or Apollo, so that they did things they had no recollection of.[306] In such cases there is almost no guarantee that they will not repeat these actions.

Such reckless actions, typical of little children who have not yet learned self-control, represent a serious problem to societal life. They are incompatible with individual freedom and they create a general atmosphere of fear and suspicion. Freedom is only acceptable when everyone can depend on its being kept within certain limits. Even dogs are expected to keep their behaviour (and bodily evacuations) under control. If they did not they would have to be kept in a cage like a tiger.

A certain degree of composure and self-control is, therefore, essential if we are to feel safe in allowing others the same freedom that we would wish for ourselves. This nervousness concerning the imponderable behaviour of others helps to explain why the Western tradition has had such a visceral fear of the 'passions' and why it has placed such emphasis upon mastering them – especially in those areas where it has most fervently sought to expand the realm of individual freedom.[307] This emphasis on 'reason' in evaluation, decision and action is therefore a necessary condition – and an original manifestation – of the Western project of expanding individual freedom.

Even reason – as we have seen – is not, of itself, a sufficient guide; even reason can go astray. Nonetheless, as the highest component of the soul, reason alone is able to glimpse such permanent, clear and precise things as ideas. The experience of disenchantment with that which we had held to be good suggests that our varied evaluations are in fact transcendent. We were not, in reality, searching for beautiful clothes, but for beauty – or *good* – which showed itself to us, fleetingly, in those clothes. This idea has been with us at least since the time of Democritus: 'For all men, good and true are the same; but pleasant differs for different men'.[308] While 'pleasant' belongs to the realm of mere opinion, good is something that is common to all, unchanging and dependable. In contemporary debate, this viewpoint is called 'ethical realism'.

This seemingly insignificant innovation turned out to have serious consequences. As long as people had contented themselves with the common evaluation of 'better' and 'worse' it was clear that the word

---

306 This ancient idea is still with us. It lives on in daily language, in expressions such as 'what's got into you?'

307 'We are all slaves to the law so that we may be free,' *Legum omnes servi sumus ut liberi esse possimus*. Cicero, *Pro Cluentio* 53, (146).

308 Democritus, fragment DK 68 B 69.

'good' meant nothing on its own, but rather in conjunction with other words. The English logician Peter Geach reminds us that the word 'good' – in the phrase 'a good doctor', for example – is not to be understood independently of what it refers to; it does not necessarily follow that a good doctor will also be a good person, or a good athlete.[309] In the common usage, 'good' means 'good for something', 'good for me or for someone else'. 'Worse' almost always means that which I would not choose if something better was available to me. If the better thing was not available, the worse one would probably be 'good enough' – I would be content with it. This is why the adjective 'good' has a comparative and a superlative form: good, better, best.

These are the common, indispensible evaluations that we all make dozens of times every day. But when we combine these with the idea of the good in the strong sense, the good turns into something else. Primarily, it loses its situational context and important attributes (such as 'for something' and 'for someone') and it comes to seem as if everything in the world has fallen under one kind of evaluation. We no longer speak of everyday ends, great or small or of my or our interests; instead we think of good itself, as something which must govern every action. This strong concept of good, without attributes or degrees, is a human concept; however it refers to something which we humans ought to be guided by, and which cannot therefore be in our own hands. Despite this, however, there is the danger that we could wrest this concept and start to judge and evaluate, not as humans, but from the position of supernatural wisdom which in the past was the preserve of the deities. As a consequence we could lose sight of the obvious truth that *my* evaluation could be mistaken and that, in any case, I have to bear the responsibility for it.

And so good gradually became a philosophical and metaphysical concept, detached – at least in the realm of thought – from everything else, and therefore *absolute*. Plato, who played such a significant role in making this epochal step, believed that knowledge of the good is reserved exclusively to the gods; and that the main – if not sole – task of man is to come closer to it, and to somehow share or participate in it (*methexis*). However, by gaining this share, or even thinking we have gained it, we have transgressed the Platonic *chorismos* – the abyss between the human and divine worlds – and we start to use Good like other concepts, namely as an instrument of logic.

---

309 Cited in Ricken, *Allgemeine Ethik*, p. 50. The indication of 'good' in this case applies only to the person's professional role; this is an important distinction, and one to which we shall return later.

Aristotle was the first to observe the paradoxical consequences of the idea of absolute Good; and he applied two significant corrections to it. Firstly, he said that there cannot be only one good, but rather each being has its own good, its designated nature – this is what makes a person a person and a fox a fox.[310] The only difference between these two is that, while the fox's nature guides the fox more or less automatically towards the fox's ends, a person can rebel against this 'guidance'. The search for the good, then, involves the investigation of this nature, which is the end of man and every being. The word 'good' therefore means something different when we say 'a good knife' than when we say 'a good person', and could in fact probably be left out; a bad knife lacks something which is necessary in order for it to really be a knife, and a bad person is not enough of a person. However, because neither knives nor people can have an infinite number of natures, the idea of universal evaluation remains, although it differs according to the character of various beings.

Of course, Aristotle was not only a thinker but also a diligent observer who sought support for his arguments not so much in geometry as in lived experience.[311] As good, for Aristotle, means different things for different beings, so it is necessary in the arts and sciences to distinguish between their characters and objects. The *Nicomachean Ethics* starts with a consideration of method and precision which we have already cited. Aristotle also claims that justice – in the judging of people's actions and the resolution of their disputes – cannot be defined exhaustively by universal laws, but that it is necessary to consider each case individually.[312]

Ethics, for Aristotle, does not therefore resemble geometry and cannot appeal to one axiomatic good; this does not, however, mean that it is founded on thin air. We need only to look around us and notice how reasonable people are guided in their actions and how they evaluate them.[313] Ethics is interested in action in society and among people; the words we use, and our ideas of honour and virtue, suggest that there is at least some general agreement among people about how they should act. That people live in societies is possible only becasue they have all

---

310 'The good, therefore, is not a general term corresponding to a single idea.' (*NE* 1096b25)

311 It is remarkable that this founder of so many sciences seemed to take so little interest in geometry, which was the science *par excellence* of his day. Practical reason does not concern itself with eternal things, but rather with 'particulars'; it therefore demands experience. A young man 'may become a mathematician, but not a philosopher or a physicist.' (*NE* VI.8, 1142a17)

312 See the above discussion of morality, Ch. 2.4.

313 Plato also adopted a similar approach in the *Laws*, where he does not mention the Good.

understood that there is a binding common order of 'political justice', which is divided into 'natural' and 'lawful'. Natural in this context means that which applies to all human societies, so that it most likely did not emerge as a result of human intervention and, unlike the lawful part, is unalterable. The natural law therefore represents a counterpart to Aristotle's teaching on the virtues and in our classification it belongs to the region of morality; this is why it was able to develop into law.[314] Both of these components of Aristotle's ethics were transplanted into the philosophical framework of Christianity, where they were developed by Thomas Aquinas, His doctrine of natural law has been summarised in seven points by American philosopher Mark Murphy:[315]

> 1) The natural law is given by God the Creator, and 2) it necessarily applies to all human beings, 3) who can, through the exercise of reason, come to know it. 4) The good logically precedes the right, so that 5) right action is that which corresponds to the good and 6) is not fundamentally flawed or blemished. 7) Some of these flaws in action can be proscribed by universal rules, such as the Ten Commandments.[316]

The fourth and fifth points connect the natural law with the searching after ends and virtues, whereas the sixth precludes the possibility that a person could attain a good end through bad means. In this form, the idea of natural law determined a considerable amount of modern moral thinking and Christian doctrine. It also played a decisive role in the formation of modern natural law as unconditional corrective against the despotism of lawmakers; our notion of human rights is also based on this.

Most modern theories of morality have attempted to avoid referring to the divine origin of natural law, emphasising instead its accessibility to reason. But if the content of natural law is not positively expressed in divine revelation, it must have as a prerequisite some form of 'real existence'; this is why we speak of 'moral realism' in the contemporary debate. Critics of the ethics of knowable good object primarily to this 'existence'; this is really a formal objection. Others point to the variety of moral ideas in different cultures and finally to the problematic na-

---

314 *Dikaion fysikon* and *nomikon*, (*NE* V.7, 1134b). The first exists 'by nature', whereas the second only exists 'by convention', Ibid. 1094b16. See also the discussion of justice in Plato's *Republic*, IV. 17, 443b et seq.

315 Aquinas, *Summa theologica*, II.I.90 et seq.

316 Murphy, *The Natural Law Tradition in Ethics*. In: Stanford Encyclopedia of Philosophy.

ture of all general moral rules. According to Bernard Williams, debate is made more difficult as many thinkers regard moral theories as 'aggressive weapons' with which to destroy their opponents (through logic). The correct response to that is a reminder of Aristotle's 'proportionate' accuracy; practical philosophy is not logic.

Good and Evil

Around the close of the 4th century BC, at the time of Alexander's expansion into Asia, Eastern ideas made a dramatic entrance into the spiritual world of Late Antiquity. One of the most significant was the idea of dualism. According to this idea, the world is the arena for the endless struggle between good and evil. In the Far East this idea led to the relativisation of all moral questions; but in Persian Zoroastrianism (and its holy book, the Avesta) the opposition of the 'twins' Ahur Mazda and Ahriman, the personification of good and evil, formed the axis of all moral thought. Dualistic conceptions of the world made their way to the Mediterranean in the form of Mithraism, which profoundly influenced late Judaism, early Christianity, Manichaeism and Gnosticism.[317]

The concepts of good and evil also appear in the Bible, but usually alongside such other pairings as 'life and death' or 'light and dark'. According to the apocryphal book of Sirach, 'good things and bad, life and death, poverty and wealth, come from the Lord'.[318] The world and everything in it is the work of the Lord, who 'saw that it was good'; but nonetheless, in the telling of the Creation there appears the serpent as the origin of all evil. In later biblical literature, influenced by Hellenism, there appear other embodiments of evil, for example Satan the informer, accuser and enemy in the book of Job. He is subordinate to the Lord and will eventually be destroyed, but for the time being he is free to wreak his havoc upon the earth. In a similar capacity, and more frequently, the devil or the 'evil one' appears in the New Testament.

Although the New Testament makes frequent use of the words 'Satan' and 'devil', and makes abundant reference to other 'powers' between Heaven and Earth, the mainstream of Christian thought was mostly im-

---

317 It is of course open to question how much we should regard these mostly symbolic religious texts as rational expressions of well-defined beliefs and positions. The texts seem to contradict themselves, at least on a superficial reading.

318 Book of Sirach 11:14. It is clear from the context that this is not 'absolute' or metaphysical good or bad.

mune to the temptation of dualism.[319] The main argument was God's creation, and His unambiguous evaluation of it. But when early Christianity moved into the Greek world, it found another valuable prop in Platonism. In the same way that the Greek and Latin gods were not embodiments of good, the idea of embodied evil was, for Greek and Latin religion, entirely alien and incomprehensible.[320]

The Platonic belief that evil is simply an insufficiency of good, which has no 'being' of its own, took over entirely in later Christianity and was dominant until to the late Middle Ages, thanks especially to the authority of St Augustine. Redemption in Christ means that the reign of evil powers over the world and men is decisively ended; there remains only foolish superstition – and human evil. Only with the individualisation of religious ideas, and the awakening of the need for individual salvation – and perhaps with the separation of philosophy and theology in the late Middle Ages – does the idea of embodied evil start to play an important role again. This idea then returns in full flower in the crises of the incipient modern age. The surprising upsurge of superstition among educated people in the 16th century, and the witch-hunts of that era, are not insignificant in this context.

In their argument against the Platonic humanism, reformers could draw upon their deeper knowledge of the Bible and reject the cheap optimism which made light of the reality of evil in the world and in the hearts of men. The radical, in places almost dualistic ideas of the German reformers in particular, and their belief that human nature was irredeemable, were mostly rejected by their successors. So in Leibniz' or Comenius' conception of the world, evil forces are once again tamed and restricted and represent, if anything, a call to better education – entirely in line with the Platonic view.

For the enlightened, the idea of embodied evil is something that can safely be ridiculed; it makes no appearance in the work of Kant. However the concept of the good – at least from the practical viewpoint – remains indispensable to him, and he handles it with the utmost respect, to the extent of attributing it to only one thing in the world: 'it is impos-

---

319 See Mark 13:25; Acts 7:42; Ephesians 1:21 and others.

320 The Greek and Latin religions did not undergo the same 'moralisation', the fusing together of morality and religion, that characterised biblical Judaism and Christianity. It was precisely this 'shortcoming' that was the target of the 'enlightened' Greek and Roman critique of religion – from Heraclitus (e.g. fragments DK 22 B 5, B 128) through to Plato (*Euthyphro* and others) and Lucretius. The same applies to tribal societies, in which religion simply means collective ritual and ceremony.

sible to think of anything at all in the world ... that could be considered good ... except a good will'.[321] In later philosophy several attempts were made to give an operative description of good. For the utilitarians, as we have seen, it means 'the greatest happiness for the greatest number'; and so the question of what 'good' means becomes a question of what 'the greatest happiness' means. For Hegel, the necessary end of the development of the soul is the full return to itself, the self-actualisation of the Soul. And for a number of contemporary thinkers, good is no more than the absence of suffering.

Friedrich Nietzsche's full-on assault on the concept of good and evil took place against the background of an era of overwhelming religious scepticism. Many regarded – and continue to regard – his work as a flat-out rejection and ridiculing of all accepted values. But nothing was more alien and false to Nietzsche than the hypocrisy and cynicism that he saw all around him. His rejection of the categories of good and evil, while reminding us of the relativity (but *not* relativism!) of evaluation, was also an attempt to take firm hold of something which could give meaning and direction to human action.[322]

This, of course, if a far more difficult aim, and Nietzsche's delicate, romantic soul struggled with the rampant naturalism of his age. His critique of 'good and evil' proved remarkably popular and his insistence that lies and dishonesty are the only real evil, will be important for us as well. His attempts to formulate true 'good', on the other hand, were largely unsuccessful. His theory of 'eternal return', like the celebration of the blind force of the Superman, belong (we may hope) to history.[323] For all that, however, Nietzsche – unlike his many followers – is a worthy addressee of Péguy's aphorism: 'A great philosophy is not a philosophy without reproach; it is philosophy without fear'.[324]

* * *

321 Immanuel Kant, *Groundwork, Section I*. This radical statement is an echo of Jesus' remark: 'Why callest thou me good? There is none good but one, that is, God.' (Mark 10:18).

322 In summing up the exact opposite of his own position, Nietzsche says 'Everything deserves to perish' (*Alles ist Werth, dass es zu Grunde geht*' – from *Thus Spoke Zarathustra*), which he also – not entirely convincingly – imputes to Platonism and Christianity.

323 *Thus Spoke Zarathustra*, 'The Vision and the Enigma'. This famous passage demonstrates, among other things, that the whole concept of evolution was alien to Nietzsche. For him the world is an ever-changing array of eternal elements, which continues to exist only as these elements repeat themselves precisely.

324 Péguy, *Cahiers de la Quinzaine* (1914), from Nietzsche, *Thus Spoke Zarathustra*..

No matter how strenuously philosophers have sought to avoid the general concepts of good and evil since Nietzsche's time, they still have currency in our everyday lives, public and private. In everyday life they are capable of wreaking major havoc, largely thanks to their popularity with political demagogues, who deal mainly in controversial, unconsidererd ideas. For this reason we should not ignore them. We have already sketched a critique of the Platonic idea of the Good; and it is now our task to carry out a more detailed phenomenological analysis and 'deconstruction' of the concept of evil; not so that we may dismiss it with cheap irony, but rather that we may more clearly understand its meaning and significance.

What is Evil?

As we have seen, centuries of meditation over the philosophical concept of good led thinkers to consider also the character and origin of evil. Ancient cultures vacillated between the extremes of either eradicating 'evil' from the good world, attributing it to 'evil demiurges', or else proving that 'evil' had no independent existence and is in fact simply an insufficiency of good. However, exposure to scrutiny quickly reveals the cracks in both concepts; and so thought continues to hover between them.

In the first of the two (dualistic Manichaeism), the world is essentially divided, the battleground of two equal, mutually limiting forces, or deities; while in the second, 'evil' is a mere shadow cast over the whole of the good world. In the first, it seems as if 'evil' receives too much attention, whereas in the second it is trivialised and marginalised. This idea is perhaps typical of historical eras that are successful, optimistic and self-satisfied; which of course only makes their awakening all the harder.[325]

Judaism and Christianity both chose the second of the two, as expressed in the Creation story; later, St Augustine would provide a more definitive formulation of it.[326] So the dualistic, 'Manichaean' conception entered into both religions as a foreign element. It could hardly be otherwise for monotheistic religions, in which the idea of the highest good combines with the idea of the one and only God; but this also had the

---

325 The almost dualistic *Ethics* of Dietrich Bonhoeffer can be seen as an expression of horror at the emergence of Nazism.

326 Genesis 1:31. In the so-called second account, a significant role is played by the 'serpent' (Genesis 3:1), a symbolic hint of the contrary, 'Manichaean' conception; then, like a promise of what is to come, there appears the definitive 'shattering' of evil.

consequence of embroiling Him in the problem of evil. So the unhappy and oppressed may very well reproach God as well as praying to him, much to the displeasure of the prophets: 'Woe unto him that striveth with his maker! Let the potsherd strive with the potsherds of the earth!' (Isaiah 45: 9) 'O house of Israel, cannot I do with you as this potter?' (Jeremiah 18: 6).

This rejection of the question, however, does not sit well with the Christian conception of God's closeness and love towards us, and this creates a theoretical problem – if God loves his children so much, why does he subject them to so much suffering?[327] Why does he allow terrible things to happen to innocent people? There is, naturally, no answer to this question; and every attempt to 'resolve' it inevitably gets tangled up in its own arguments. And is it not strange that humans should try to defend God? This is the paradox of theodicy – philosophical attempts at a defence of the world and its creator.

This problem stems directly from the very nature of monotheistic religions, inasmuch as they cast doubt on human freedom and insist that an almighty God causes, or at least approves, every single event – and is therefore 'responsible' for everything that happens. At least part of this problem lies in the concept of 'evil' itself – or, more precisely, in its seeming obviousness and the emotive force of horrific events (many of them quite recent) which prevent us from submitting the concept itself to closer scrutiny.[328] However, as long as it escapes such scrutiny, there is probably no sense in asking, for example, where all the undifferentiated 'evil' in the world comes from. To avoid these generalised, abstract discussions, which have been going round in circles for centuries, we should pose the question differently: where do we see or experience real, undeniable evil?

There are of course the obvious things: hunger, pain, disease and death. We fight against these as best we can; doctors may give us medicine to ease pain and stave off death. But everyone realises that these are part of being alive; the living differ from the inanimate precisely because they can experience hunger, pain and death itself. The possibility

---

327 This idea is at the origins of Greek scepticism. The classical argument, ascribed to Epicurus, says: If God is unable to prevent evil, then He is impotent; if He is not willing, then He is malevolent; in either case, why call Him God at all?

328 Plato touches upon this in *Gorgias*, when he writes: 'good things aren't the same as pleasant things, and bad things aren't the same as unpleasant things either' (*Gorgias*, 497d). Similarly Heraclitus: 'It would not be better if things happened to people just as they wished.' Fragment DK B 110.

of suffering and the final certainty of death are the inescapable flip side of human freedom. They give life its dramatic gravity and force us to understand and accept them as such. This is of course a highly abstract and impersonal view, whereas each single death is unique, and often tragic. The death of loved ones is always a destructive event, no matter how reconciled to their death they themselves may have been.[329]

Secondly, we must also separate natural death, which could not be postponed, from pain, suffering and death inflicted by another person – murder, warfare and torture. These are 'evil' in a very different sense than death itself. They have something in common with cruelty and terror, with envy and vengefulness, with disdain and humiliation, with destruction and vandalism. We can speak here of evil intent, willed evil and targeted hatred, which can, in some circumstances, turn against itself.

The third type of 'evil' is characterised by being cold and impersonal: selfishness, disregard, avarice, indifference and cowardice belong here. What connects them is not wickedness so much as the fact that they do not take any account of other people; others have no importance here. It is simply the victim's bad luck that he or she must serve as a means to the perpetrator's end – there is nothing personal about it. Nazi concentration camps, as a coldly efficient way of eliminating 'undesirables', probably belong in this category.

The last type of evil could be summed up as fraud, dishonesty, the breaching of promises. While not violent, this evil nonetheless harms its victims, damages human relationships, and undermines trust in society. Unlike the other types of evil, this one only harms those who 'fell for' it, those who relied on the perpetrator keeping faith with them. It is perhaps for this reason that this evil has always struck morally sensitive and honourable people as being particularly repulsive. Cicero spoke of two types of injustice: force and fraud. 'Both are wholly unworthy of man, but fraud is the more contemptible.'[330]

However uncertain and imprecise these divisions may be, they nonetheless show that genuinely moral evil is in fact human evil, evil committed by people. It is of no consequence whether it is violent and bloody or cold and calculating. Its victims may be individuals or entire societies, the natural world or the cultural wealth of nations. Biblical religion, and the concept of 'cultivating the soul' both insist that what makes an act

329 'For a truly religious man nothing is tragic.' Wittgenstein, *Personal Recollections*.
330 Cicero, *De officiis*, 1.41. Kant was a proponent of the extreme view that truthfulness is the 'sacred and unlimited imperative' of reason, so that a lie may be excused in extreme cases but never permitted. See Über *ein vermeintes Recht aus Menschenliebe zu Lügen*, AA VIII. 423–430.

evil is that it harms the perpetrator himself – as expressed by the images of 'courts' or 'scars on the soul'. Philosophy can provide only a very limited answer to the urgent questions of how far this damage to the soul can be repaired through forgiveness and reconciliation.[331] The problems of modern societies, with their 'unexpurgated' pasts (colonial, racist, fascist, communist), attest to the limited power of courts and laws; but civic society has no other instruments at its disposal.

On the contrary, the undifferentiated and unreflected concept of 'evil' is altogether too general and too 'autocentric' – that is, based on *our own viewpoint*. It encompasses everything that we fear, that we dislike, that upsets and offends or impedes us. And yet none of this is necessarily evil; a man with whom I have come into conflict may be bothersome to me in all sorts of ways, but it would be very dangerous for me to consider him 'evil'. We have already discussed this dangerous temptation to regard every impediment as evil and every opponent as an enemy.

3.5 Moral Sense

Practical philosophy – as we have seen – stems from an urgent need to somehow reconcile individual morality and its reflective evaluation of oneself, as dictated by the 'discovery' of one's inner self and conscience, and the necessity of a certain public or social consensus when it comes to outward-pointing evaluation and decision, including the moral ground stones of the law. The mainstream of Western thought turns to reason as a faculty to recognise, to curb our predilections and passions, as well as to build an argument, an ability seen as the only reliable basis of that social harmony which is essential to the functioning of society. It is the good common sense (*le bon sens*), shared by all people and 'of all things among men the most equally distributed', as Descartes notes, half-ironically.[332]

The founders of this school of thought still apply various ways of tempering the reliance on reason and its argumentation. In his Socratic dialogues, Plato is unsure whether virtue can be explained and learned, or whether it is an entirely autonomous and irreducible 'gift' or a bid-

---

331 See Jankélévich, *Forgiveness* and Sokol, *Filosofická antropologie*, Ch. 29.

332 For everyone thinks himself so abundantly provided with it. Descartes, *The discourse on method I*. Similarly Heraclitus: to all people is given the capacity to know themselves and to be rational (*sofronein*, fragment DK 22 B 116); 'reason is common to all' (*froneein*, fragment DK 22 B 113).

ding of the gods. Socrates himself is presented as real person of flesh and blood, who does not only contemplate and present arguments, but also rejoices in beauty and friendship. Aristotle's take on rational justice does after all concede that individual cases cannot be entirely encompassed by general rules, in the end he relies more on good judgment and decency (*epieikeia*), wherein there lies 'more truth'.

But already great Stoics, who by no mere chance happened to be eminent Roman politicians, whose job it was to preside over the fate of millions anonymous individuals, could not imagine anything like it. Their vast and amorphous state did not allow them to strike up casual conversations with the citizens and to take into account 'the individual'. They saw before them two options: either a society of strict rational rules and procedures, or despotism of powerful individuals, which must inevitably end in anarchy. The historical reality itself, the fact that they succeeded in providing their subjects with several centuries of peace, goes to show that it was not a complete fallacy. *Pax Romana* thus became the model for the builders of medieval empires, who sought to graft the Stoics' idea of a good state onto a dramatically different 'substratum' of wild warrior tribes, while also seeking support in Christianity.

The rationalism of medieval theology was also kept in check by the binding content of the biblical revelation, rich in paradoxes and centred on individual fates and stories. The notion of natural law, which is not subject to human judgments, but must on the contrary guide them, also delineated the boundaries of individual evaluations and their mandatory rationalisation. The nominalist theology of the late Middle Ages was already trying to bring the whole of human life under the control of strict logic, thus laying the groundwork for modern rationalism.

With the development of cities and the religious and civic individualism which inevitably came with them, European societies resembled the situation of Late Antiquity and they began to see the medieval authorities as a cumbersome obstacle on the road to further emancipation and expansion. The internal and external dissolution of medieval authorities only strengthened the new change of direction, which sought truth in the individual soul with such vehemence that it thrust Europe into centuries of civil and religious conflict. It is no wonder that thinkers such as Erasmus of Rotterdam, Jean Bodin, Hugo Grotius, René Descartes, and especially Thomas Hobbes abandoned medieval authorities and sought refuge in reason, if possible untouched by the complicated speculations of preceding philosophies. Their 'reason' is no longer a mere tool designed to make sense of the wondrous order of the world, as it was for

Socrates and Aristotle; it is an *authority*, whose main purpose is to help set up a new and binding order of society.

Already in the 17th century, thinkers who did not want to accept that moral life was secondary to the rational knowledge of social necessity were voicing their opposition to the extreme rationalism which led to more or less enlightened theories of absolute power (Hobbes, Spinoza, Leibniz). Descartes saw the springs of action in desire and other passions, both good and bad. It is then the task of reason to select the best ones and to ensure that the will obeys the reason.[333] Others regard moral evaluation as a separate, autonomous area, perhaps even more crucial than the area of rational knowledge, judgment, and argumentation.

One of the first advocates of the autonomy of moral evaluation was the French scientist and philosopher Blaise Pascal. In a collection of aphorisms, which were planned as a defence of Christianity and which have come down to us as unfinished fragments, Pascal explicitly defends the role of 'the heart' in the life of an individual as well as the whole society: 'The heart has its reasons of which reason knows nothing'. Elsewhere, he quotes de Roannez: 'Reasons come to me afterwards, but at first a thing pleases or shocks me without my knowing the reason, and yet it shocks me for that reason which I only discover afterwards' (fragment 276).[334]He himself counterbalances the 'geometrical spirit' of axioms with the 'spirit of fineness' which responds to the quiet calling of mercy and love.

That, however, is not to say that we should blindly trust our judgment: 'Men never commit evil so fully and joyfully as when they do it according to their conscience' (895). 'Man is but a reed, the feeblest thing in nature; but he is a thinking reed. A vapour, a drop of water suffices to kill him. But, if the universe were to crush him, man would still be more noble than that which killed him, because he knows that he dies and the advantage which the universe has over him; the universe knows nothing of this' (347). Man can never find happiness of his own accord for 'we think either of the misfortunes we have or those that threaten us' (139). 'Happiness is neither without us nor within us. It is in God, both without us and within us' (465). Based on that then, moral thinking cannot be just purely individualistic: 'In each action we must look beyond the action at our past, present, and future state, and at others whom it affects, and see the relations of all those things. And then we shall be very cautious.' (505).

---

333 Descartes, *Passions of the Soul (Les passions de l'âme)*, particularly art. 69 and 144 ff.
334 The fragment numbers refer to the French Brunschvicg edition.

Pascal was not alone in objecting to the Rationalists reducing moral judgment to mere knowledge of the rules and their observation. Unlike Pascal's pessimistic view, the British tradition of 'moral sense' draws on a much more optimistic view of humanity. The Earl of Shaftesbury (1671 – 1713) rejects and rebuts Hobbes' theory of selfishness as the sole human motive. He attempts to describe the process of evaluation and action, and rejects the simplistic distinction between selfish and unselfish. Man always acts out of some interest, which however does not always have to be egoistic. 'Never was love or gratitude or bounty practised, but with increasing joy, which made the practiser still more in love with the fair act.'[335] Moral sense, then, has a great deal in common with a sense for aesthetics and harmony, which Shaftesbury also regards as a part of human nature.

Shaftesbury's essayistic portrayal of measured, gentlemanly dignity became highly influential, earning enthusiastic approval from Leibniz, Voltaire, and Diderot, and, later on, from the philosophers of the German Enlightenment (especially Mendelssohn and Herder). In Britain, it provided inspiration most of all to the Irish theologian and philosopher Francis Hutcheson (1694 – 1746), one of the instigators of the Scottish Enlightenment. Hutcheson considered man to be equipped by nature with a number of 'senses', defining these as 'Determination of our minds to receive Ideas, independently on our Will, and to have Perceptions of Pleasure and Pain.'[336] Among these 'senses', Hutcheson gives primacy to awareness of oneself, the 'sense of community', or *sensus communis*, so that we rejoice in the happiness of others and feel sorry for their misfortunes, moral sense which enables us to distinguish between virtue and vice, aesthetic sense, a sense of honour, of praise and blame, of ridiculousness, and so on.

Like Shaftesbury, Hutcheson seems to reject Hobbes and Locke's conviction that humans act primarily from selfish motives; he also rejects the emphasis which the German Reformation placed on radically curbing human nature. On the contrary, he views it as a valid principle for evaluating human actions. Hutcheson regards the moral sense with which we are all endowed as stemming from our instinct for self-preservation, enabling us to evaluate good and bad actions nearly as quickly and effectively as taking decisions to prevent us from physical harm. Moral sense even manifests itself as a 'perception of pleasure and pain' and even self-

---

335 Ashley-Cooper, Earl of Shaftesbury, 'The Moralists'. In *Characteristicks of Men, Manners, Opinions, Times*, 2 (1711). Oxford 1999, p. 30.

336 F. Hutcheson, *Essay on Nature and Conduct of the Passions*, 1 (1728).

ish behaviour does not merit complete condemnation, as it is beneficial to the preservation of society.

The collocation 'moral sense' may, however, easily lead to misunderstanding, making the entire process of moral evaluation appear almost spontaneous and automatic. Hutcheson maintains, on the contrary, that it is always preceded by a stage of deliberation and evaluation, only after which the individual can spontaneously feel agreement or disagreement, acceptance or rejection. While this final feeling is always the same, automatic, and unerring, mistakes may however be made during the preceding deliberation stage; it is therefore desirable to develop the skills of judgment and thought through education, and to reinforce them through repetition.[337]This aspect of Hutcheson's theory was developed in detail by one of his most influential followers, David Hume, whose ideas were then in turn advanced by Adam Smith.

Again like Shaftesbury, Hutcheson is rather sceptical on the subject of the speculations of 'moral philosophers', creating an impression that he would prefer a spontaneous and instantaneous 'judgment' based on emotions. However, he also views as necessary the follow-up test of the correctness of a decision in the form of evaluating the consequences of the particular action. This theme was later developed by the Utilitarians, in particular by Bentham. Hutcheson actually uses the well-known phrase about 'the greatest happiness for the greatest numbers'. He makes a connection between moral sense and perception of pleasure and pain, which brings him close to moral naturalism – the belief in the organic nature of moral judgments – and leads to the rejection of Plato's distinction between the good and the pleasant. This was vehemently criticised by the British Utilitarian philosopher Henry Sedgwick (1834–1900), who maintained that man's ultimate goal should be personal self-improvement. He regarded the term 'good' as absolutely fundamental, beyond any logical analysis and impossible to equate with any notion of pleasure of utility.

* * *

I shall include one highly original take on ethics in the context of moral sense – although it considerably deviates from it. It is the view of ethics as 'unlimited responsibility for the other', as proposed by Emmanuel Lévinas (1906–1995) in his book *Otherwise than Being*. The notion of the

---

337 Reworked echoes of Socrates' conviction that man cannot knowingly commit evil.

pre-eminence of ethics, which as 'the first philosophy' precedes any ontology, like the concept of the 'encounter with a face', frequently recurs in Lévinas' writing. But it is only in this book that he gives a systematic (if not entirely accessible) explanation of it in phenomenological terms.

Already in his previous book, *Totality and Infinity*, Lévinas had challenged the unquestioning habit of modern thought to give primacy to knowledge and freedom, which – as we have seen – also mean power. Through cognition, man takes hold of the object of cognition, destroys its otherness, thus spreading his mastery not just over the world, but over people, too. This unchecked licence can however only become freedom once it encounters the face of the other and hears its categorical order 'Thou shalt not kill'. The face does not pose as a force or an obstacle; on the contrary, it is defenceless and 'naked', thus offering me a chance to take the first step towards real freedom: to feel shame.[338]

Lévinas' seemingly paradoxical claim that 'ethics precedes ontology' is based on what we have here described as 'omnipresent judgment': the concept of man as an acting and evaluating being.[339] For we first and most often do not encounter the world as a dispassionate objectivity, given to us at our leisure, prey to our curiosity, probing, and conquest ('ontology'), but as a place to live, and as the source of everything that we need in life. The first counterpart of a young child is after all not the world of objects but the world of other people's faces, beginning with his mother's face. In the first stage of his life, the child learns to stand on his own two feet, and as an adolescent begins to conquer the world; but his wilfulness must inevitably be curtailed – not by obstacles which it would begin to overcome and subdue, but by the 'commandments' of a defenceless face.[340] Only when we have 'heard' it and realised the

---

338 Lévinas describes this opposite of the aggressive 'imperialism of the Same' as a 'metaphysical' or 'ethical' relationship.

339 'The ontological level is preceded by the ethical level' (*Totality and Infinity*, III.B.2). 'Morality is not a branch of philosophy, but first philosophy' (Ibid.). Likewise Patočka: 'Ethics is not founded on metaphysics, at the most, metaphysics as a form of questioning can stand on a moral foundation.' *Evropa a doba poevropská* (*Europe and the post-European Era*), in Patočka, *Sebrané spisy* (*Collected works*) 2, p. 132.

340 Lévinas' paradoxical concept of the face of the other always being placed 'above me' (as in *Totality and infinity* IV.) caused much misunderstanding: are we not all equal? But that is the viewpoint of a third person who observes an encounter without taking part in it. On the contrary – as we have seen in our discourse on politeness – even in everyday social situations we address each other with expressions which at least feign this asymmetry of encounter, addressing the other as 'sir' or 'madam'. We can disregard this simple phenomenon as purely formulaic, but we can also choose to see a deeper meaning in it. Equality is then based in both parties feeling and expressing respect toward the other.

unjustifiability of our perceived freedom, we may possibly be able to take a step back from our immediate aims and situation in life and perhaps devote some time to learning, that is, 'ontology'. [341]

In *Otherwise than Being*, Lévinas opens with an analysis of human perceptiveness;[342] he shows that just as speech (*le dire*) as a way of addressing, 'purely for the other', precedes the pronouncement of a judgment (*le dit*), sensual perception does not begin with a recognition of 'something as something', but rather with concern, as a sensitivity for something which is pleasing or hurtful, as significance and closeness.[343] This is why perception is a privilege of physical beings. If we examine perceptiveness purely on the example of visual perception, it might appear that it is an impartial cognitive faculty; but if we consider the perception of temperature, taste, or smell, they are not a case of recognising something as something, there is no impartiality, and no 'crystallised idea' or essence at all, as it has been frequently suggested in the philosophical tradition. After all, psychologists also distinguish between 'affective' and 'representative contents' and Husserl's intention, aiming at its subject may be fulfilled, or on the other hand disappointed. To 'feast your eyes' or 'devour with your eyes' are not mere metaphors.

Before a subject can be *thematised* it has to evoke a certain 'non-indifference' – significance, closeness and 'vulnerability' – otherwise the subject could hardly become a subject. First, there is desire, and only then consciousness of something. After all, life too, rejoices in itself even before any reflection is undertaken, before it begins to denote itself as 'I'. 'Significance which awakens affectivity, activity, sensitivity, hunger, and thirst, desire or admiration, is not dependent on thematisation.'[344] Only subsequently can it be neutralised into a peaceful attention to the subject, which possesses particular qualities. 'Space and nature first cannot exist in their geometrical and physical inertia and only have man – and his desires and passions – bestow upon them a cultural layer, which would provide them with significance and expression.'[345]

---

341 'The freedom that can be ashamed of itself is the foundation of truth' (*Totality and Infinity*, I.C.1).

342 The French *sensibilité* has a wide range of meanings and can denote both sensual perception as well as emotional sensitivity.

343 Lévinas, *Otherwise than Being*, III.1. The term vulnerability denotes here both the enjoyment of pleasure as well as pain and suffering. – A discerning man will only dismiss banal and uninteresting things by 'recognising them as something', i.e. file them away among the well known, but something which 'captures our interest' cannot be simply dismissed in this manner.

344 Ibid. III.3.

345 Ibid. III.6.a.

In connection to the world, there is not just an intention aiming towards the subject, but also a reverse movement, which Lévinas refers to as 'obsession by the other, maternity':

> As if I had received a command from without – a wounding command – which I do not internalise by any notion or concept of the authority commanding me. I do not ask by what right, I do not even ask what is it I have done that I am suddenly a debtor.[346]

Based on these – truly daring – phenomenological analyses, Lévinas constructs his concept of unilateral, unconditional, and unlimited responsibility, within which I become 'a hostage of the other'. He is well aware that he is approaching the realm of religion here; nevertheless he is certain that he is not misrepresenting phenomena.

Sentiment and Reason

Theories of moral sense – like Lévinas' concept of closeness, sensitivity, and vulnerability – are right to stress, that human actions and decisions cannot be understood merely by surveying the moral commandments which regulate them. Custom and morality only provide auxiliary rules when choosing ways and methods, a map of sorts, or warning markers at the junctions, they cannot however be that which instigates action and spurs it on. On the contrary, human actions are motivated and driven by 'positive' goals, from life's basic needs to Aristotle's 'search of the best', and Spinoza's 'desire'. Whether they are on the basic level of instincts and needs or whether they search for ways to impress others and to make their mark in history, or perhaps gleaning the 'infinite and unexplored land of goodness',[347] all are characterised by there being something at stake.[348]

These theories quite rightly reject attempts to found practical philosophy merely on rational arguments and syllogisms. Good actions do not have to be – and, indeed, often are not – a result of thorough and

---

346 Ibid. III.6.a.

347 Lévinas, *Totality and Infinity*, III.C.5.

348 Heidegger's well-known description of existence as 'a being which is concerned in its being about that being' (*Being and Time*, § 41), perhaps excessively individualises human existence: in reality, the concern cannot be solely for the individual's being, but also for that of their family, children, and much more beside.

meticulous deliberation, the correctness of which an acting person could logically prove. A classic example of action which all societies have valued and value still is the ability to see the need of others and to interpret it as a call to action. A generous and kind person will often not reflect and deliberate, but simply 'see' the need of others and cannot merely look on – just as the theories of moral sentiment suppose. The human capacity for compassion can of course sometimes be abused, and there are certainly instances of false compassion which is only displayed but not acted upon; or it may be acted upon, but at the expense of its object's freedom. But this certainly does not mean that we would fare better without such sentiments.

The term 'good' in its full moral sense is not a characteristic like any other, it cannot be included in any higher category, and therefore it cannot be defined by other terms. Evaluation is a more general and fundamental activity than the impartial and disinterested cognition which the sciences strive for. But all scientists live their own individual and 'unscientific' life, in which they make judgments and choices every day; and after all, their particular science does not stand completely apart from them, as it can be of service, perhaps in enabling them to make better predictions and decisions.

As well as these indisputable qualities of various theories of moral sense there are also attached grave weaknesses and shortcomings. Just as the 'heroic' moralities of the Stoical or Kantian kind overemphasise 'activism', laying almost unachievable absolute demands, the message of 'moral sense' perhaps errs on the side of optimism. If it is somehow inherent to human nature to be so mindful of the good of others, if we are so equipped with sensitivity and abilities which self-activate upon encountering the Face, we can too easily give in to what Lévinas refers to as 'rejoicing' (*jouissance*), 'egotistical joy' of pure being without want or need.[349] As Cicero puts it: 'The philosopher who claims that the highest good has no connection with virtue, and measures it by his own interests rather than by what is honourable, cannot cultivate friendship, justice

---

349 Lévinas maintains that the first and most fundamental setting of a human life is not Heidegger's 'care' but simple enjoyment, pleasure, or 'bathing in the element', from which we are only disrupted by hunger, cold, or another need. Only then do we begin to worry, scramble for things, possibly work. A condition for this happening is a separate dwelling, a home where we can store up, gather our possessions, where we can also invite another into. See the brilliant outline in *Totality and Infinity*, II.A.2. Hospitality also features strongly in late Heidegger, see e.g. *The Thing,* in *Poetically Man Dwells.*

or generosity so long as he remains consistent in his views and is not prevailed upon by his own better nature.'[350]

On the one hand, then, there is the calm ideal Stoic hero, who regards all his motions almost with suspicion, mercilessly subjecting them to the supreme judgment of reason, prepared to give up his life at any time in the name of Titanic honour and an almost neurotically vigilant 'virtue'. This ideal is, however, hampered by a much too lenient judgment of our own nature, which regards reason as a mere tool for small improvements of our otherwise satisfactory welfare and comfort, as demonstrated for example by Adam Smith. Bernard Mandeville maintains that a properly arranged society lays no further claims on man other than to be thoroughly dedicated in following his 'selfish interests' and comfort, and to banish all idle fancies, which would only 'spoil his peaceful sleep and healthy digestion', as Nietzsche remarks disparagingly.[351]

If Kant and the Stoics relied solely upon reason and the 'goodwill' determined by it, the theory of moral sentiment would appear to have sent reason packing, perhaps into the realm of learning or science, wanting to completely bypass it in practical thought. The fly in the ointment of the theory of moral sentiment seems to be that it is blind to rational concern about others who are not close at hand, in a way as it is encapsulated by the notion of justice for example – Mandeville, entirely cynically, counts on this. In contrast, Cicero regards justice as the ground stone of any well arranged society, calling it the 'mistress and queen of all virtues'.[352] Aristotle remarks that 'justice is another's good' and emphasises regard for the distant and unfamiliar.[353] Lévinas places great importance on justice and it is repeatedly mentioned in the form of 'regard for the third'. He however endeavours to base it on the meeting with the Other in the singular, with Buber's 'You'. 'We call justice this face to face approach, in conversation,[354] it calls on us to cross the line of justice and 'enter the realm of goodness which extends infinite and unexplored, necessitating all of the resources of a singular presence.'[355] It would suggest that justice were only a secondary and auxiliary tool only leading on to the very

---

350 Cicero, *De officiis* 1.5 – Cf. Also Lévinas: 'The original form of relationships between people, the personal relationship, blossoms in the strictness of justice, which judges me, and not in love, which defends me' (*Totality and Infinity*, Summary, 11).

351 Mandeville, *The Fable of the Bees*.

352 Cicero, *De officiis*, IIIc28.

353 *NE*, 1134b5.

354 *Totality and Infinity*, I.B.4. It is 'just' to let the other speak, to let them have their turn.

355 Ibid., III.C.5.

subject of ethics, i.e. the absolute and unlimited responsibility for the Other, which turns me into their 'hostage'.

Only when contrasted with the theories of moral sentiments does the true significance of Kant's morality of abstract equality come into sharp relief.[356] It is impossible to build justice, and by extension good society, only on human sentiment, on closeness and compassion for the others. Justice represents an independent and rational 'perspective of the third', at which point critical reason can come to the fore and to uproot my own life from this warming but often problematic 'closeness'.[357] For that is not only love and friendship which stem from this, but equally envy and hatred; and it therefore cannot serve as a reliable criterion. Nietzsche knew what he was talking about when he opposed 'love of one's neighbour' and its psychological risks with 'love of those far away' (*die Fernstenliebe*), although he limited himself to an aphoristic appeal and projected the 'far away' into the concept of a future *Übermensch*.[358]

The problem of 'reason and sentiment' is highly topical in present-day practical philosophy. The measure of equilibrium which Kant still tried to maintain between them (for example with his emphasis on 'beauty' and the 'starry sky') is nowadays endangered from the opposite direction. Many regard the Stoic ideal of unshakeable firmness and calm rational virtue as remote, alien, even repulsive. We tend to find the voice of compassion – an undoubtedly important part of our mental makeup – much closer and more naturally convincing. We should, however, certainly not forget how unreliable sentiment can be in itself.[359] 'Our dark emotions do not merit reckless trust (…) We cannot rely on emotion as such. To use emotions by way of justification is naive and avoiding the objectivity of what we can learn or think.'[360]

Unreflected compassion can, moreover, be abused for blackmail and mass mobilisations. Little else has the power nowadays to move the masses like images of children or animals suffering. Legal injustice, on the other hand, is often regarded as an argument against the law as such. Many people are actually convinced that all the great miseries of the world can be put down to the impersonally rational order of mod-

---

356 See Kant, *Groundwork*, Concluding Remark.

357 In Judaism and Christianity, this is above all the view of God, whose finite and unconditional validity is encapsulated in the notion of judgment.

358 Nietzsche, *Thus Spoke Zarathustra*, I.16.

359 The ability to feel is also regarded by W. Marx as a 'criterion of responsible actions'. Quoted after Greisch, *Ethics and Lifeworlds*, p. 49 ff.

360 Jaspers, *The Question of German Guilt* (*Die Schuldfrage*).

ern societies, so that they fail to see the opposite, 'emotional' aspect of bloody revolutions, chauvinist and terrorist movements, or totalitarian regimes.[361] It is as if they have forgotten what the Nazis and Communists alike used to mobilise whole societies and stir up hatred towards the plutocrats, Jews, or imperialists.

The trouble is, of course, not rooted in the ability to feel compassion and to help, without which humans – and human society – would not be human. The trouble begins when rational control and criticism are by-passed. It then becomes possible to turn the manipulated 'emotion' into hatred towards perceived perpetrators and to provoke the masses into knee-jerk actions. The manipulated nationalism in Bosnia provides a recent example of nationalist sentiment being turned into blind hatred. By the time the affected societies realised that the manipulators had succeeded in exclude rational criticism of their projects and to relegate reason to the role of mere tool for their implementation, it was already too late.

---

[361] Nobody saw the dangerous, threatening nature of emotions, particularly compassion, as clearly as Nietzsche (see for example the *Genealogy of Morals*), who rightly suspected that compassion would be 'his doom' (*Verhängnis*). The problematic consequences of the morality of compassion can also be traced in the work of the Australian Utilitarian philosopher Peter Singer.

4. The Ethics of Heritage

Man's happiness does not come from freedom,
but in the acceptance of a task.[362]

People have always lived in the company of others and life in society, by its very nature, can be conflictive – individual interests and aims often clash, and are often at odds with one another. As we become more and more dependent on others, we must coordinate our actions with them, modifying these actions in various ways. Practical cohesion and, ultimately, the success of human societies depend increasingly on the extent to which acting individuals can rely on each other – and, conversely, to what extent they are afraid of each other. In order to feel free, individuals should be able to conform, and restrict themselves voluntarily, even if no punishment threatens them. It is the task of practical philosophy, then, to search for such conditions and prerequisites which would make free co-existence a long-term possibility; to discover what is detrimental to this co-existence and what makes it flourish, and what universally valid arguments can be employed to convince everyone that this is so.[363]

The brief overview of moral and ethical theories which we have sketched out in the preceding chapters suggests just how much effort people have poured into the search for some solid, unshakeable and universally accepted basis of morality. As we have already learned, some schools of thought in practical philosophy seek to achieve universal validity and plausibility for their postulates by restricting themselves to purely rational knowledge and arguments; they share Descartes' belief

---

362 Gide, *Journal*, 8th February 1932.

363 That is why Socrates – unlike Kant – poses his main question in the plural: 'How should we live?'

that 'good sense is, of all things among men, the most equally distributed', and upon which we are all most likely to agree.[364]

But reason, which is the instrument of deliberation, is therefore also the instrument of doubt and uncertainty. Indisputable conclusions can only be reached in axiomatic systems, such as logic or mathematics – and even here, only on the strength of the axioms.[365] However, the world within which a person lives and acts is not an axiomatic system. Even Kant, while stressing the autonomy of moral decision-making, presupposes that our shared reason will compel every one of us to accept the categorical imperative based on the postulate of freedom and equality. This is a very elaborate position, with considerable persuasive power in discussion, but nevertheless much too abstract for action. As a motive of decision, it can hardly be expected to withstand the onslaught of other, stronger motives.

The other main branch of practical philosophy is based on motives, particularly the strongest one of those, the desire for happiness. But happiness is a feeling rather than a concept, and as Pascal noted, even those who hang themselves do so out of desire for happiness.[366] Aristotle defines happiness through virtue, while the Utilitarians try to quantify it. They cannot, however, agree as to what should be measured and over what period of time; besides, measurable quantities have little to do with the feeling of happiness. And if the consequentialist emphasis on the outcome of our actions was taken to mean that the end justifies the means, then we would be a very long distance away from ethics.

In the present academic discussions, deontological and consequentialist systems are often understood as being in opposition to each other. The former makes exacting claims on us, without being quite able to explain convincingly why we should conform. The emphasis on *a priori* decision and its rules belongs in the realm of morality (as we defined it above), and as they seek to strictly separate moral decisions from any consideration of personal profit, they tend to dismiss the other side of human deliberation, namely the motives of desire, seeking purpose and achieving one's aims. The consequentialists, on the other hand, tend to emphasise the *a posteriori* view of actions, their anticipated consequences as well as their retrospective evaluation. While this is a very important check, it will only come into play as part of retrospective evaluation. Thus

---

364 Descartes, *Discourse on Method*, I.1.

365 That is why Spinoza, for example, attempted to build his ethics *more geometrico*, 'in a geometric fashion'.

366 Pascal, *Pensées*, fragment 425.

the only criterion we have to guide us in the decision-making process is an estimate of a future state of affairs, which is by definition uncertain, while we are denied the pivotal support of shared morality and rules. This unfortunate, and (in my view) academic dichotomy – the artificial separation of things which naturally belong together – does make for endless discussion but also makes life complicated for those who have to make decisions and want their actions to be good.

As we have already mentioned (Chapter 2.6.), both these positions have in common a certain disregard for time and temporality, including the finite nature of human life. They overlook the fact that actions happen in time, and that the way they appear to us in the decision-making stage is quite different to the way they appear after they have been completed. Kant himself tried to exclude time, as an empirical category, when discoursing ethics, not least so that the evaluation and decision would not depend on any future course of events and could not be subject to change. The consequentialists, on the other hand, disregard the significant difference between the view forward into the future and the retrospective view of evaluation after the fact.

Only when this temporal distinction is made does the connection between decision, action and responsibility become obvious, as it successfully spans this artificial dichotomy. Even though *a priori* rules may make decision making easier, the whole moral issue will only fully emerge over the whole period of time. What binds the various phases together is the phenomenon of a lasting, diachronic pledge and responsibility, as manifested in 'accountability', the willingness and ability to be accountable for the consequences of one's actions – with the (*a priori*) knowledge that each action may have such consequences. Unlike the abstract Kantian duty, which simply says 'obey!' without offering any further definition of its contents,[367] the pledge of responsibility is usually specific, often pertaining to a particular person: even to the extent that it may become the subject of a court case, and is one of the basic characteristics of law.[368]

4.1 Ancestors and Descendants

The following chapter will be an attempt to delve a little deeper into the ethics of obligation and responsibility, on a rather broader basis than is

---

367 Kant, *Was ist Aufkl*ärung, A 494, in Werkausgabe, XI.
368 Pospíšil, *Anthropology of Law*, p. 8; Knapp, *Teorie práva* (*Theory of law*), p. 46.

customary. Our first step will be to look into how obligations are created, and we will seek to disprove one serious error in contemporary thought. The next step will be to consider the phenomenon of gift-giving as a one-sided act, which creates a certain obligation to reciprocate; we will see, however, that this obligation is purely of a moral, unenforceable character. The next step will then be to demonstrate how an obligation in the form of heritage can be devoid of the restriction of reciprocity, and can cross beyond the boundaries of the present.

We will use the example of 'tribal religion', the religion of home, hearth and grave (as it is likely to be traced in all settled cultures) to show how the phenomenon of patrimony and the responsibility for it has successfully connected the care for the past and the future and how it has contributed to forming a generally human, albeit highly particular, morality. This specific 'pagan' religion is long extinct in Europe; and elsewhere, it struggles to resist the advancement of the urban, individualistic way of life. We cannot really go back to it and, in truth, we would not want to either. But nevertheless we believe that even in our modern-day societies, we draw on an ever-richer 'inheritance'; not only in the biological sense but also culturally and socially – and it is to our detriment that we tend to overlook this important factor.

* * *

When David Hume vehemently rejected that from any state of affairs there might arise a moral obligation, an 'ought', he seems to have overlooked that there are situations, even quite everyday situations, where a person's factual actions do create something of an obligation, whether it be his own or that of another. In a contribution to the polemics regarding the so-called 'naturalistic fallacy', the American philosopher John Searle mentions the phenomenon of the promise, a speech act by means of which a person creates an obligation which he would otherwise not have.[369] Another, slightly different, example is the giving of gifts – an action by which one gives something up for the benefit of another, who in return feels obliged for this act. Both these phenomena seem to play an important role in the constitution and maintenance of human societies

---

369 As we have seen earlier, this term as used by G. E. Moore meant the attempt to define good through other terms, something quite different from Hume's problem with factual actions creating obligations. Mixing up the two confuses the debate. Alasdair MacIntyre objects to Hume's original idea on the ground that with objects which are 'defined by their function', such conclusion is obvious – a watch that doesn't go is bad (MacIntyre, *After Virtue*).

well from the ancient times.[370] Let us then begin with the promise and the contract.

A remarkable theory on the almost biological origin of promise, pledge and contract has been developed by the French ethnographer Georges Davy, a pupil of Durkheim's, in his book *La foi jurée*.[371] He postulates that the possibility of relying on the help of others when in need stems from the blood relationship into which we were born, and which creates a strict kinship obligation. Attempts to extend this to other, unrelated persons start with the various 'blood brotherhood' ceremonies, which are known to us from many different cultures. A shared meal, too, during which people of unrelated origin come to share something identical, is often understood as forging an almost physical form of alliance, thus allowing us to choose our 'relatives'. Further steps lead through marriage and the associated exchange of gifts, with a couple's children presented as the unifying element. These are, however, merely a promise at the time of the wedding; so a marriage can gradually develop into a pledge and, eventually, a contract. The significant difference here lies in the fact that each familial brotherhood creates a 'total', unconditional duty to give help in everything, including matters of life and death; while the pledge and the contract usually have a defined subject and duration.

The pledge and the contract, in ancient societies construed as a twofold mutual promise, are binding, but only to those who have made the pledge and only within the scope and conditions specified by it. The contractual parties have, freely and with full autonomy, based on the principle of contractual freedom, taken upon themselves certain obligations, thus guaranteeing each other corresponding rights. In this sense, the contract forms the cornerstone of private law to this day, and unless it is in contradiction of binding norms, its contents are legally enforceable.[372] The contractual parties have stated their rights and obligations in the contract, so the eventual ruling will only state if these have been breached or not.

---

370 For example all theories of social contract are based on the validity of a promise and a pledge. It is not a valid argument, therefore, that they themselves inevitably presuppose some sort of legal system.

371 Davy, *La foi jurée*.

372 See V. Knapp, *Teorie práva*. In Roman law, an obligation can be created by a contract, but also through damage caused or a delict. The only difference here is that the latter may be punished by a fine as well as compensation. Modern law makes a clear distinction between civic obligation and criminal responsibility, where the convicted offender is liable to the state, not to the aggrieved party.

Today, the general view of an obligation has, influenced by the legal interpretation, been narrowed down to that which a person has pledged to do themselves, of their own free will – and possibly to that which is binding based on the currently valid norms. Practical philosophy, however, cannot be satisfied with this notion. The aforementioned Georges Davy's exposition of the origin of the pledge begins with the 'familial' pledge, one we were simply born into – and in a similar way we are nowadays born into societies, states, and their laws. Not even the fiction of a social contract can change anything about this and it would be ridiculous to present some such thing to a soon-to-be adult to sign. That is why, as late as Kant and Hegel, the state is not considered a contractual establishment but a categorical necessity, into which every person may be coerced.[373] Before we attempt to explain this, however, we should note the general phenomenon of the gift as a unilateral act, which nevertheless creates a certain moral obligation in the recipient.

The social importance of the gift has been highlighted by the Polish anthropologist Bronislaw Malinowski in his book *The Argonauts of the Western Pacific*. A group of small islands off the eastern coast of New Guinea is culturally held together as a community by the ritual circulation of symbolic gifts. While the circulating bangles and necklaces do not have any practical value, and nobody can claim permanent possession of them, they nonetheless perpetuate the network of obligations between the inhabitants of these remote islands. Malinowski's discovery was then generalised by the French ethnologist Marcel Mauss in his renowned book *The Gift*. Mauss stipulates that free men in many archaic societies are bound by three rules:

1. to participate in gift giving,
2. to accept gifts, and
3. to reciprocate within an appropriate time.

Mauss argues that this social institution is, in various forms, manifested in all known archaic societies; and its traces can also be found in fairy tales and fables, in popular culture as well as in ancient literature.[374] Claude Lévi-Strauss considered the exogamic exchange of brides between villages as the oldest form of this 'exchange', and he also mentions the significance of an invitation to a feast, while the sociologist

---

373 Kant, *Metaphysics of Morals*, AA VI., p. 306; Hegel, *Philosophy of Right*, § 75.

374 According to Heidegger and Derrida, hospitality is an important form of gift – something which anthropologists can also confirm.

Pierre Bourdieu based his theory of social capital on Mauss' work.[375] Within our context, the cyclical system of gift giving is significant in that it promotes a positive obligation as an anthropological constant, which complements and gradually even replaces the unconditional familial relationships, while requiring reciprocal action.

The promise and the contract require some sort of 'fulfilling' and after all, that is a trait of the nature of the gift, too, usually to be completed during the participants' lifetime. They may be characterised with the old principle of *do ut des*, 'I give that you might give'. Some radical critics therefore reject any moral significance of gifts. Jacques Derrida says that the true gift would have to be completely unselfish, but also invisible, so that it would not bring the giver any benefit whatsoever.[376] That, however is too radical a demand, and actually a misguided one. A gift is characterised by its voluntary nature, and if it really does benefit the recipient, any symbolic benefit to the giver makes no difference to this.[377] A bribe, on the other hand, is quite a different matter. It poses as a gift but its aim is to profit the giver; we will return to this topic later. In our modern society, voluntary gifts are still of huge importance, not just for people in dire need, but for the maintenance of good relationships as such. The notion of reciprocity cannot be completely separated from the promise, contract, or the gift, thus somewhat limiting their social reach.

There is yet another remarkable phenomenon, one that rules out any chance of reciprocity: heritage. It is impossible for the heir to reply in kind to a deceased giver;[378] any possible expressions of gratitude will be purely symbolic. If the recipient wishes to comply with the giver's wishes, he cannot return the favour to the giver but must turn his attention to the inheritance itself – how he manages it and looks after it. The nature

---

375 See Bourdieu on the theory of action. Slight weaknesses in Mauss' account – especially his idea of the magical power (*'hau'*) which somehow adheres to the gift and prompts reciprocation – have been criticised by Malinowski and others (without actually refuting his proposition).

376 Derrida, *Donner le temps*.

377 The New Testament also makes a demand on the giver of hidden, anonymous gifts: 'But when you give to the needy, do not let your left hand know what your right hand is doing, so that your giving may be in secret. Then your Father, who sees what is done in secret, will reward you.' (Mathew, 6:3–4). Here, however, the distinction needs to be made between a believer relying on the unimaginable future reward and the everyday building up of social capital in the here and now. Besides, the idea of absolute selflessness seems to be an illusion anyway – if nothing else, 'feeling good about oneself' can never be ruled out. Cf. Parry, *The Gift and the Indian Gift*.

378 The current legal term is the 'testator'.

of the relationship is thus not 'I give that you might give', but on the contrary, 'I give, for I have been given'.

The phenomenon of patrimony has played an enormously important part in the past development of human societies, but one which has almost disappeared in modern times – and hardly anybody would regret it. Our farming ancestors were also bound and restricted by material patrimony. However, the entire concept of inheritance seems to have disappeared along with this system. As we mostly no longer live off inherited wealth, we tend to stop noticing the temporal connection of our present existence with the past, and especially with the future, which goes beyond us. As we have become emancipated from them both, regarding them as a burden and encumbrance, we have boxed ourselves in the narrow space of our individual 'now', which we may have improved and refined wonderfully but we have also succeeded in ridding it of its natural context and meaning. This process has now gone so far that, although we still live off various forms of 'inheritance' (material, cultural or social), we have ceased to view these as our inheritance. If we wanted to give currency to this very basic human phenomenon, and to understand it, we would need to turn to a fairly remote past. Not because we seek (or are even able) to return to those ancient institutions, but because they may serve as a reminder of something that the modern age has forgotten about.

We will demonstrate the importance of the phenomenon of heritage, as illustrated by the symbolic system in which our ancestors lived for millennia: the kin 'religion' of settled agricultural societies, somewhat inaccurately labelled in religious studies as ancestor-worship, or 'Manism'.[379] The directness and hardness of this 'religion' may appal contemporary readers; we are making a journey into a very distant past. The French historian Fustel de Coulanges provided an intriguing (and still widely accepted) account of this 'domestic religion' in the first part of his remarkable book *The Ancient City*. His exposition is largely based on an extensive study of ancient Greek and Roman literature, but we now know that similar arrangements were widespread among almost all known agricultural societies, or indeed all settled societies in general. Significant traits of domestic religion may for example still to this day

---

379 The reason for putting the word 'religion' into inverted commas here is that this symbolic system does not correspond to the usual definitions of religion – there are no deities, scriptures, preachers, or shrines. No religious treatises have come down to us; most likely none were ever written. What is of interest to us, however, is not the status of such religions *as religions*, but rather their social and existential aspects.

be found in rural China and its traces are present in folklore and folk culture around the world.[380]

The transformation to settled husbandry, the 'Neolithic Revolution' as Gordon Childe called it,[381] brought a whole range of far-reaching changes to human life. Although it did not take place overnight, as the world 'revolution' might suggest, but rather happened over thousands of years, it had a profound effect on man and his environment. In the temperate zones, the gathering of whatever food was chanced upon, which necessitated being constantly on the move, was replaced by settlement, which enabled intensive food production, an exponential population increase, and in turn an ever greater 'investment' into land and dwellings. Survival became less dependent on changeable natural conditions, but it did require an incomparably greater effort, and constant hard work. Unlike hunting, which required the co-operation of the whole group, a (more numerous) farming family could achieve almost complete self-sufficiency.

Grain – at a cursory glance a problematic foodstuff[382] – keeps well if stored properly, but its yearly cycle with only one harvest does require rational long-term planning. A person who, come spring, has no grain left sowing, is likely to starve to death the following year. But a person who manages his resources well may set something by, create a surplus and generate wealth, which then makes it possible to introduce barter and the division of labour to the society. Later it gave rise to crafts, commerce, and cities. The strict division of land was of utmost importance to all ancient societies; it helped to restrict conflict, and moreover the shared interest in safeguarding provisions from predators and thieves enforced a lasting, if limited, co-operation.[383] A family farmstead may be self-sufficient, but each and every person must work hard and every pair of hands counts; therein lies the reason for the de-

---

380 For ancient Greece, see Gernet, *Anthropologie de la Grece antique* and Nilsson, *Greek Folk Religion*. For China, see Fung Yu-Lan, Selected *philosophical writings*, or Yan, *The flow of Gifts. Reciprocity in a Chinese Village*. For South-East Asia see Rappaport, *Pigs for the Ancestors*. A good overview for more recent times is Friesen (ed.), *Ancestors in Post-Contact Religion*.

381 Childe, *What Happened in History*.

382 This is partly because grain requires fairly complex processing, but mainly because uncultivated grasses offered only a small yield and ripened gradually, so that harvesting the grain was extremely laborious. On the origins of grain agriculture, see Gellner, *Plough, Sword and Book* and a rich ethnographic literature.

383 In the *Laws*, Plato tries to ensure that the number of family farmsteads in the ideal Magnesia never changes. He describes boundary stones as 'boundaries separating friendship and enmity' (*Laws*, 834a2).

mographic increase in agricultural societies. And once all the land has been divided and claimed, then each man is destined to his fate from the day he was born: he who has not inherited a farmstead will have to eke out a living as a slave or a menial worker in the family farmstead, or elsewhere.

Just as with husbandry and livelihood, the religious life of the early farmer centres around the household. The farmstead or simply house (*oikos* in Greek and *familia* in Latin) is first and foremost an economic unit. At its head is the 'father' or 'master',[384] who oversees the whole farmstead. The household comprises hereditary land, buildings, livestock, the master's wider family, including all his un-provided-for siblings, and often other dependents, household slaves.[385] All of them live off that which has been passed down to them by their ancestors – and these ancestors are the subject of their reverence. It seems likely that the burial of the dead in the most ancient agricultural societies happened in two stages, as was until very recent times the case with some South American, African, or Pacific tribes. The dead body is first carried out into the open countryside or tied up in a tree, and when there is nothing left but bare bones, it is laid underneath the floor inside the house, later outside underneath the doorstep, and finally in the communal burial ground.[386] Thus the living literally live together with their dead, and must take due care of them.[387]

A constant fire in the domestic hearth marks the presence of the ancestors and the perpetual nature of the dwelling, which in fact belongs to them; the current master is only a temporary steward, whose main duty it is to ensure that there is someone who he can pass it down to, to ensure that the line of family's sons continues unbroken.[388] Otherwise all the deceased would be deprived of the service which keeps them alive in their shadowy existence in the underworld, and the master himself could not expect to receive it after he died. In return, the fire and the ancestors offer much-needed protection form intruders to the house, as well as to

---

384 *Despotés* and *despoina* in Greek, *dominus* in Latin, later came to be used as rulers' titles.

385 Linguistic connections show that underage children also ranked among these: the Greek *pais* and Latin *puer* can mean both. The Russian word for 'youth', *otročestvo*, stems from the root *otrok*, which in Czech means 'slave'. Machek, *Etymologický slovník* (*Etymological dictionary*), p. 426.

386 Fustel de Coulanges, *The Ancient City*, Book I.

387 The ancient Indian *Law of Manu* (Book 3) prescribes in detail when and how food should be brought to the graves of the dead.

388 'So I, as lawgiver, make this ruling – that both yourself and this property are not your own, but belong to the whole of your race, both past and future.' (Plato, *Laws*, 923a.)

the family fields. The fields are defined by boundaries and boundary stones, which are under the auspices of special deities. Once a year, the master must walk round them all and offer to them a sacrifice of flour and honey. Boundaries and boundary stones are thus literally 'untouchable'; damaging a boundary stone carried the death penalty, and by wilfully entering another's property, the intruder risks the vengeance of the domestic deities, that is the family's ancestors.[389]

The strict separation of individual farmsteads did however clash with the firm rule of exogamy: the bride must come from somewhere else.[390] How to arrange matters, then, so that the ancestors accept her, rather than killing her as an intruder? This made the Neolithic wedding a fairly complicated transition ritual, some elements of which have to this day survived in the form of customs and superstitions. First of all, the bride's father had to release her from all ties with the household's deities (afterwards, she must never return home again) and the groom's friends were to at least pretend an abduction of her. Even in ancient times, when nobody would otherwise travel in such manner, the bride was carried away from her house in a covered carriage.[391] When she was brought to her new home, the groom would carry her over the threshold and first present her to the hearth. Then they would offer a sacrifice to the deceased ancestors, by which act the bride was accepted into the groom's household.[392] After the bride and groom shared a round cake made of white flour, they were united in an irrevocable bond.[393]

It is most likely that this whole remarkably intricate and rigorous system was (with minor variations) a general practice in settled agricultural societies, and in some places, it has survived down to modern times.[394] Our notions of privacy, as something guaranteed by the constitution and laws, into which not even public law enforcement can encroach, stem precisely from this agricultural tradition, as do our concepts of 'untouch-

---

389 Fustel de Coulanges, *The Ancient City*, II.6.

390 'Each man lays down the law to his wives and children, and disregards his neighbours,' says Homer of Cyclopes, those who do not live in a community (*Odyssey*, 9, 112).

391 The modern-day version of decorated wedding cars is not quite so conspicuous in our motorised society.

392 This is the where the habit of the bride taking the groom's surname originates.

393 The ancient form of Roman wedding was for a long time still called *confarreatio*, 'united with white flour'.

394 Precisely this model was observed in a Muslim village in the mountains of Northern Turkey as late as the 1980s. The 'abductors' of the bride were armed, the bride was completely covered from head to toe and the groom would not get to speak to her until after the wedding night, see Schiffauer, *Die Bauern von Subay* (*The Farmers of Subay*). Also Nilsson, *The Greek Folk Religion*.

able' property.[395] The strict separation of family property had a long-term stabilising effect on agricultural societies, it restricted the opportunities for conflict, and supported intensive farming and long-term investment. In places where this system has not taken hold, such as in central Russia,[396] agriculture was found to be lagging behind and the notion of private property has not been firmly established even to this day.

The care for deceased ancestors and the on-going cohabitation with them are the most marked aspects of the domestic cult and it led Herbert Spencer to coin the term Manism, i.e. 'ancestor – worship' to describe this symbolic system. However, its other aspect, the one facing towards the future, the strict obligation to ensure the continuation of the family line, would appear to be far more important.[397] The dependence on inherited property for his livelihood broadened the farmer's time horizon by including both his deceased ancestors, and above all his progeny, in his day-to-day considerations. The Indian manuscript *Laws of Manu* makes it every man's duty to marry and to father at least one son. Chinese Confucianism contains a similar idea: 'A marriage ought to unite two families and to ensure for the past worship in the shrine of the ancestors, and for the future, the continuation of the family line.' 'There are three things unbecoming in a son. The worst one of them is not to father a child.'[398] The Persian *Avesta* holds that 'the three most virtuous things are to procreate, to work the land, and to plant a tree.'[399] Plato explains that the human race shares in immortality by 'leaving behind it children's children', he urged all men between the ages of 30 and 35 to marry and have children, or else have to pay an annual fine 'lest he imag-

---

395 'What is more sacred ... than each citizen's home? It houses his altars, his hearths, his household gods, this where sacrifices and religious ceremonies take place. This is the asylum of every one, so holy, that it is impious to drag any one away from it. (Cicero, *De domo sua*, 109) – When boundaries were being ploughed up to create large fields during Communist collectivisation in Czechoslovakia, many farmers saw it as the final abolition of domestic religion.

396 The collective possession of land in some Slavic cultures was seen by the Romantics as a sign of the unselfishness of the Slavic nature; in fact it is merely a sign of less intensive farming – typically cattle-grazing – which does not require investment but rather a form of usage regulation to allow the pastures to regenerate. The highly intensive forms of agriculture on the other hand, such as orchards and vineyards, were never communally owned.

397 Even in ancient times the Persian *Avesta* strongly opposed ancestor worship, while laying great emphasis on tilling the land and procreation. There might be a similar meaning to Heraclitus' rather dark fragment suggesting that 'Corpses are more suited to be thrown out than dung.' (DK 22 B96).

398 Li-chi, *The Book of Rites*, quoted after Fung Yu-lan, *Selected Philosophical Writings*. See also Fustel de Coulanges, *The Ancient City*.

399 Avesta, in *Vendidad*, 4,47. The commentary adds that 'a childless person who has not left an equivalent on earth will be barred by the angels from entering paradise' (Sad Dar 18, Ibid.).

ine that single life bring him gain and ease'. Such a levy really was paid in ancient Rome and even Immanuel Kant, himself an attentive reader of Plato, argues that bachelors – of whom he was one – should pay a tax for being unmarried.[400]

Monotheistic religions have considerably moderated this strict law. The Bible merely gives the commandment to 'honour thy father and thy mother', and demands a certain level of attention to burial and graves.[401] In the Old Testament too, though, children are a 'blessing'. Woe to them who have none; who will take care of them in their old age? Nevertheless, the 'iron law' of family property was still current among farmers in Europe as late as the 19th century, and the literature of the time offers up a wealth of tragic stories of doomed lovers and the tyranny of property. This lead Bergson to suggest that the task of familial or 'closed' religion is to 'balance out a possible insufficient clinging to life in beings endowed by the power of reflection.' He saw religion as 'nature's defence mechanism against everything in intellectual activities which might cause an individual to feel despondent and a society to disintegrate'.[402] We should probably take with a pinch of salt Rousseau's observations of man as the first creature to be 'released' from nature and to be 'born free'. Even if we accept the metaphor of personified 'nature', we must concede that it held the reins of human freedom in a firm grip for some considerable time, and has only released that grip very gradually.

The greatest limitation of domestic religion was the strict separation of individual homesteads, which was the source of considerable difficulties – as we have seen with wedding arrangements and, later, during the foundation of the Greek city-states. The Greek city-state also incorporated a number of elements of home religion and set itself up as a sort of large homestead; it worshipped its founding fathers as its ancestors; the Athenian *boule* housed a perpetual flame; and when Socrates stood trial, he stated in his defence that he too has his hearth and shrines and therefore is a proper Athenian.

These narrow limits were broken in a much more radical way by Judaic monotheism and its idea of the one and only God, His Creation and His promise. This perhaps stemmed from the broader and less exclusive solidarity of shepherds. It gradually united them into tribes and would eventually bind the whole of Israel by the unifying authority of the Scrip-

---

400 Plato, *Laws*, 721, Ibid. 774. Kant, *Metaphysics of Morals*, AA VI.

401 Here 'honour' means to care for them in their old age. The inclusion of the mother alongside the father is significant; this was not the case in all tribal religions.

402 Bergson, *Two Sources of Morality and Religion* II., p. 159.

ture and Abraham's promise of a great future.[403] In many parts of the Old Testament we encounter the notion that the Lord's blessing and His rule ought to pertain to all peoples, as they are all related from the dawn of Creation and the Lord's Promise extends to them all and they can all turn to it. On the other hand, laying so much emphasis on blood relation and exclusive rules about purity caused Israel to stand apart from the neighbouring societies and later, in Halachic Judaism – again under the pressure of hostile neighbours – this emphasis was strengthened further, as it became a practical condition for the continuation of the message of Judaism.

In some parts of the New Testament, a distinction is still made between the Israelites and pagans but then the view prevailed, most likely championed by Paul of Tarsus, that the exclusionary commandments lost their validity and that everyone who converts to the belief in Christ is a Christian. This universalism has its most radical expression in the following quote: 'There is neither Jew nor Gentile, neither slave nor free, nor is there male and female, for you are all one in Christ Jesus.'[404] This is what enabled Christianity to spread throughout the whole of the ancient world, and although it went through various periods of 'nationalisation' in the course of its history, it never gave up the principle of universality and belief as a matter of personal conscience. In contrast, the recent revitalisation of Islam is largely connected to national and political movements.

It seems that religious morality and ethics are, even today, the most important practical factor supporting good cohabitation within society. Only a morality based on religion can issue commands naturally and only goals based on religion can be accepted as indisputable and unconditional.[405] This, on the other hand, makes them vulnerable to abuse, as demonstrated by various monarchs, misusing religion in order to strengthen their power. The Enlightenment's critique of religious morality as heteronomous was in its day justified, but the argument is somewhat weakened in a free society, where religion is no longer imposed on the individual. It is however also true that most people are born into a religious world and they accept it as natural, often before

---

403 'I will make you into a great nation, and I will bless you; I will make your name great, and you will be a blessing' (Genesis 12:2). According to Genesis 46:3 and Deuteronomy 26:5, this was supposed to happen in Egypt and according to Genesis 18:18, his blessing was supposed to extend to all the nations on Earth.

404 Galatians 3:28.

405 Cf. Burkert, *Creation of the Sacred*. Hans Jonas actually proposes that without religion, the requirement of moral self-restriction cannot be justified at all (*The Imperative of Responsibility*). Practical philosophy, however, attempts to find a way around this condition.

they are able to make decisions for themselves. If they do part from it in adulthood, they may then come to regard it as 'heteronomous'. This is perhaps why in affluent European societies it is only the trace of religious life that we see. Nonetheless, even these have a significant practical importance.

The real issue with religious morality and ethics is actually not heteronomy, for even voluntary and conscious acceptance of religion means an unconditional acceptance of authority, which man fully complies with. For truly religious people, this bond is extremely strong and exclusive – just as religion brings people closer, it inevitably excludes others from their community. Religion is thus a very powerful tool of societal integration – all too powerful, some believe. The French sociologist Émile Durkheim was convinced that through ritualistic religion, human societies maintain their cohesion; this religion helps them to create and identify themselves, and make themselves self-aware.[406] That is why religion could be so easily hijacked to further political power, as many politicians still attempt to do even nowadays, and not only in Muslim countries.[407]

What is crucial in our context, however, is that religious morality and ethics are by definition exclusive and therefore also partial and particular within modern societies; they are only binding for the believers of that particular observance. This is no problem in homogenous societies, where belonging to the society naturally also means belonging to a certain religion, and people do not necessarily take notice of it. But in a situation where 'our kind' come across strangers, a strong and discordant distinction comes into play, which misled people, with some ease, to queer moral conclusions. 'You may charge a foreigner interest, but you may not charge your brother interest, that the Lord your God may bless you.'[408] For Pascal, this 'relative' morality was unacceptable: 'Why

---

406 Durkheim, *The Elementary Forms of Religious Life* (1913). The book is mainly based on descriptions of Australian Aboriginal cultures.

407 Marcel Gauchet also believes that the awareness of a pledge or debt is 'a basic form and simultaneously a general reason of religious belief'; however, he bases his thinking exclusively on its misuse for the purposes of power. (Gauchet, *La condition politique*) In reality, though, the problem of the relationship between religion and politics is not limited to the possibility of misuse. Democratic theory presupposes that voters monitor politicians' behaviour and potentially 'punish' them the next time round. If, however, the voters' connection to 'their' party is too strong – for example based on religious or nationalist basis – this control mechanism ceases to be effective.

408 Deuteronomy 23:20. – Previous, possibly older parallel sources (Exodus 22:24, Leviticus 25:36) say almost the same, not mentioning foreigners though: perhaps that question was not

do you kill me?' 'What? Do you not live on the other side of the water? If you lived on this side, my friend, I would be an assassin, and it would be unjust to slay you in this manner. But since you live on the other side, I am a hero, and it is just.' 'A strange justice, that is bounded by a river!'[409]

There has been a significant shift since then, and our contemporary situation is different. The thinkers of Late Antiquity concerned themselves with the themes of universal humanity and universal morality, and monotheistic religions largely shed their original tribal and closed nature. Bergson distinguishes between closed and open religions, and the majority of religious communities are aware of this nowadays. But no matter how open they may be, they do practically represent a minority and, as well as providing inspiration, they can enrich their environment by their willingness to accept everybody. But to do this, they must retain their somewhat separate identity – otherwise they would dissipate. Their function therefore lies elsewhere – Jesus spoke of 'the leaven in the bread' – rather than in providing a basis of binding, but less specific, universal morality and ethics; for that reason, they are not a topic for this book. Practical philosophy must not rely on religion too heavily, and although it is never likely to achieve a similar impact, it must search for other foundations, which may be weaker but also more general and fully universal.

4.2 Life as Inheritance

The kinship arrangement of agricultural societies, including their religion, seems entirely foreign to us nowadays, and some of its aspects may repel us. We may acknowledge its significance in forging the demographic and cultural success of humanity; but we ourselves would never accept such conditions. There are three reasons for this. Firstly, traditional agriculture, without energy, industry, and commerce will, in the best possible circumstances, sustain no more than about thirty people per square kilometre. Secondly, as it binds people firmly to inherited property and land, it severely restricts their options. And finally, it also creates an insurmountable divide between those who have inherited land and those who have not: the landless. This is why early 19th century social

yet posed in their time. The Qur'an actually distinguishes three categories of believers ('people of the Book'), i.e. Muslims, Jews and Christians, and non-believers.

409 Pascal, *Pensees*, Fragment 291, 294.

movements viewed it as totally unjust and sought to abolish inheritance altogether.[410]

What is of interest to us, however, is something more general: the notion of man not as the 'master and owner' of the world, but rather as the heir of a fortune which he has taken upon himself and which he in due course should pass on to those who come after him. As we nowadays mostly do not inherit our livelihood and we use our own means to make a living, it is easy to overlook the fact that we, too, live from an 'inheritance', on several different levels in fact – life in itself first of all. Various tribal societies viewed life as a 'heritage', as the English anthropologist A. M. Hocart reported: 'We are to teach (our children) the meaning of life, so that they hand it down from one generation to the other', he was told by a Winnebago tribesman, and he came to the conclusion that even the objective of their rituals is to ensure life, 'a prayer for children so that the tribe may increase and be strong; and also that the people may have long life, enjoy plenty, be happy and at peace.'[411] There are countless examples in all great literature, whether religious, philosophical or fictional, of the joy parents feel at the birth of a child, especially if they have been waiting a long time for it.[412]

The specific meaning of physiological 'inherited life' has been unexpectedly opened back up to question by biology, in particular by genetics; each of us has been given life by our parents and each was given a certain basic 'equipment' of abilities, talents, and limitations.[413] Nobody would dispute that these days, but we must mention two important reservations. First of all, it cannot be treated as just a matter of children and livelihood, as was the case with domestic religion, but rather a much wider 'heritage', not just in the biological, but also the cultural and so-

---

410 For example the early forms of socialism, especially Saint-Simonianism. They sought to solve the question of what to do with a deceased person's property either by abolishing ownership as such, or simply not posing such questions at all.

411 Hocart, 'The Purpose of Ritual', in *The Life-giving Myth and Other Essays*, p. 49. Similarly Ovid: 'that I'm even alive is a gift from the gods' (*Tristium*, I.1.20): he may have only discovered that during his Black Sea exile. Cf. Burkert, *Creation of the Sacred*.

412 The child as a promise and hope crops up in numerous places in the Bible, and even the Romantic Nietzsche does not fail to see innocence, 'a first motion, a sacred Yes' in the child (*Thus Spake Zarathustra* I.1, 'The Three Metamorphoses'). On the phenomena of eros, fertility and fatherhood as basic forms of transcendence, see Lévinas, *Totality and Infinity* IV.C.

413 It is characteristic of certain general pessimism of modern times that 'heredity' is usually mentioned only as of an unavoidable threat and the damage of 'depravity', a modern form of fate. The notion of irredeemable hereditary defects is what biological racism and eugenics are founded on.

cial sense.[414] Today we count language and culture, institutions and law, science, technology, and politics among the necessary equipment of life; and these too must attend to their own 'reproduction'. They too must find people to take them over, analyse them, cleanse them, deepen and develop them, and then pass them on. Secondly, many ancient texts, both religious and philosophical, speak of 'the debt of life' in this context and demand that it be repaid.[415] In the *Laws*, Plato emphasises the worship of gods, 'the Olympians, the gods who keep the State, the gods of the Underworld, as well as ancestral deities', as, he puts it, 'for to these duty enjoins that the debtor should pay back the first and greatest of debts, the most primary of all dues, and that he should acknowledge that all that he owns and has belongs to those who begot and reared him. ... thus making returns for the loans of care and pain spent on the children by those who suffered on their behalf in bygone years, and recompensing the old in their old age, when they need help most'.[416]

This, however, is only one aspect of man's obligation, one turned towards the past. But how could one 'repay' life itself, received from one's parents?[417] To whom – and how – should we pay this 'debt' for our language, culture, and institutions into which we were born and which we were 'given' for free? The 'debt' metaphor is somewhat misleading in this case, in that it would make life appear as a loan which we are given and which we are somehow supposed to pay back to someone else. For this reason it is more precise to speak of an inheritance, which one is also gifted in a unilateral act but with which there is no question of 'repayment', as there is no one to repay it to. This is not to say that that inheri-

---

414 'Those who do not have children should not feel diminished. Biological sonhood is only the first model of sonhood, which can also be understood very well as a relation between people even without biological relations.' (Lévinas, *Ethics and Infinity*)

415 For the Hindu texts, see Malamoud, 'La paiment des rituels dans l'Inde vedique', in Aglietta – Orlean, *La monnaie souveraine*.

416 Plato, *Laws*, 717.

417 Ancient burial rituals show a pronounced ambivalence in the relationship of the living to the dead. On the one hand, there is the fear of their return among the living, as evident from crouched burials or cremation of the dead bodies; the term 'revenant' is proof of the fear people felt of such 'returns'. There is ample evidence in folk literature, too. On the other hand, there are those not very coherent notions of 'the underworld' and of the dead living on in their grave thanks to the care provided by their ancestors, as described in detail in the *Laws of Manu*, and subconsciously suggested by a grave being referred to as a 'resting place'. The living bringing food to their dead ancestors' graves can be viewed as a symbolic 'compensaiton' for the life they have been given. A more thorough thinking through of this relationship led the Persian *Avesta* to a strict ban on burials – a ban which was, however, very difficult to enforce in practice.

tance does not contain any sort of obligation, for that is exactly what we have been discussing here. This obligation, however, lies in that the heir does not regard this inherited 'wealth' as merely something for his own consumption but rather as something that he himself should look after and one day bequeath to someone else. He should, then, not see himself as the sovereign 'master and owner', but as a temporary steward, who will do best by his duty if he takes on the inheritance which has been entrusted to him, and then sifts through it, furthers it, and finally passes it on.[418]

Every one of us is on this planet because our parents did not regard themselves as 'owners' of life just for themselves but – just as the unbroken line of their ancestors did – as guardians and intermediaries of life. The seemingly unremarkable reality of life being passed on shows how precarious, and dependant on the unbroken line of progeny, it really is. A biological line which does not continue simply comes to an end.[419] But then each such apparent 'line' constitutes a series of interruptions, for new life is most certainly not just a continuation of previous lives. It is not the parents' *oeuvre* or a project and strictly speaking not even an *a priori* given option. Speaking of 'inheritance' is metaphorical, too, for there is no 'heir' yet. The passing on of life is thus a sort of singularity, difficult to talk about as the words are not quite there and each attempt to formulate it leaves us tangled up in paradoxes.[420]

Perhaps only once a new life has been created can we talk, however cautiously to begin with, of 'heritage', as there is no outward ownership in question but this life itself and the things without which it could not be sustained. There are many factors in our lives, which we have also 'inherited', or adopted – from our parents, teachers and others. First among these factors is socialisation, being introduced to our close society: learning to look after ourselves, learning established patterns of behaviour, and of course, our mother tongue, which then becomes the principal medium of further 'cultural wealth', required by one and all at ever greater measure in a modern society.

---

418 The basic fact of responsibility for the entrusted 'wealth' resembles Jesus' parable of the talents (Mathew 25:14–30; Luke 19:12–25). It has traditionally been understood in the way there is not just life itself which matters but also all the endowments which we are equipped with; therefore the Greek talanton (originally cca 25 kg of silver) could become a metaphor for 'talent', an individual skill or ability. The gravity of this responsibility is illustrated in religious terms by the image of 'judgment'. 'Whomsoever much is given, of him shall be much required: and to whom men have committed much, of him they will ask the more.' (Luke 12:48).

419 That is – as we will see – quite different as opposed to passing down culture, which can be taken up almost at any time.

420 Cf. Lévinas, *Totality and Infinity*, Section IV, 'Beyond the Face'.

Human life must take place in society, and its prerequisites are not just those things which we are given individually. We may picture ourselves living as South American Indians do, living in a jungle and sleeping underneath a shelter made of leaves.[421] But we are fortunate to have been born as Europeans, and we have 'inherited' a tried and tested environment with fields and gardens, roads and streets with public transport, flats with bathrooms and tenements with lifts. After dark, we are not afraid to walk in our well-lit streets unarmed. When we are unwell, we call on a doctor, or we can even get a doctor to come and see us in the comfort of our own home. And when occasionally some of these things temporarily fail (when there is a power cut or no hot water) we regard it almost as a violation of our human rights.

All of this would have been the stuff of dreams for our ancestors, and it still is for our less fortunate contemporaries. Although our ancestors (like the vast majority of the people on this planet even today) had to make do without such conveniences, their cultures show clear signs of how much they valued (and value) all that they live on. Feasts and festivals, sacrifices and dances expressing their joy at having survived thus far, offering their thanks to a river or a forest, at the same time trying to make them amenable so as not to withhold their gifts in the future. The huge variety of forms of celebrations and festivals, this fundamental human expression of the joy of living and concern for the future is the subject of comparative religious studies, and we will not discuss it further here. We should nevertheless take note of one obvious paradox: the poorer, more dangerous and precarious the life of our ancestors was, the more they were able to come to the view that they are living off what they had inherited and been entrusted with.

It is not difficult to imagine the reasons for this. While our ancestors had the fragility of their own existence constantly in plain sight and encountered death on a daily basis, modern man has – at least in the wealthier parts of the world – managed to bring many things under his own control. Society has been organised in such a way that we can live wealthier, more comfortable, and safer lives. Hygiene and medicine can prolong life and defer death for so long, that it may make seem like an unfortunate accident, one which should perhaps been prevented. Naturally, we have to pay for a lot of these conveniences – whether directly or through taxation – and we may therefore consider them rightfully ours,

---

421 For a non-idealised view on native societies, I would recommend Biocca, *Yanoama*, or Clastres, *Chronicle of the Guayaki Indians*.

without owing anybody anything for them. It is quite easy to overlook that even though we do, in one way or another, pay for a specific medical procedure, the very institution of medicine, with its sum of knowledge and experience, has been passed down to us for free. The same goes for all of culture, science, law, and institutions in general; we only pay those who maintain and practise them. Homer, Shakespeare, and Mozart are 'free'; we only pay those who translate, print or perform them. Pasteur, Röntgen, and Einstein never patented anything, and as a result we do not have to pay for any of their discoveries or findings.[422]

It is even easier to overlook more obvious and basic things, which legal, economic, or even linguistic categories cannot express. My life as such – as we already know – is not something that I could have inherited in the usual sense of the word. Only our parents could accept us as a 'gift', if we were so fortunate as to have such parents. Without their participation, we would not have been here at all, but only an ignorant person can fail to see the striking disparity between this 'participation' and its result. All the great minds and Nobel Prize winners put together would not be able to 'make a child', let alone your poor ordinary parents, who have no idea what such a child should consist of and how exactly is it all supposed to 'work'. And yet, two perfectly unaware, ordinary people can have a healthy baby; and while they have to provide love and care, the job of living and growing is up to the children themselves..[423]

This equally wonderful and ordinary experience of the beginning of a new life served Hans Jonas as a basis for his 'ethics of responsibility'.[424] Jonas conveyed precisely its unique 'non-reciprocal' and unconditional nature. From the very fact of conception and birth, an unconditional obligation arises for the parents to take care of the human being who is ac-

---

422 The possibilities of the internet have also freshly opened the issue of copyright, which, while enabling successful artists to make a living without depending on rich benefactors, also introduced market rules, so that more challenging art and literature still depend on subsidies.

423 The parents' relationship is however put to the test if they have a disabled child. Typical modern care of the disabled is probably a not completely reflected and very 'natural' reaction to the Utilitarian view that such life is 'not worth it'. The majority of parents, too, devote an almost heroic level of care to their disabled children, although they are well aware of the very limited success it can confer. They seem to have a deep understanding of what is the real point in the passing on of life, and they are confirming the non-reciprocal nature of their relationship. In contrast, the recently publicised case of a disabled person who brought a legal action against doctors for the wrong ante-natal diagnosis, on the basis of which his parents went through with the pregnancy, confirms a rather brutal misunderstanding of the same. Also surprising is the logical absurdity of such a case: as part of the perceived damage, I am able to take legal action, the purpose of which is a further continuation of this 'damage'.

424 Jonas, *The Imperative of Responsibility*.

tually not quite here yet, or to be precise, is just beginning. This care is of such utmost importance to the society itself that its neglect is punishable by law. In the early stages of a child's life this care, for obvious, and not only physiological, reasons mainly the 'obligation' of the mother, who carried the baby for nine months, gave birth to it and nursed it. However demanding it may be, this most natural of all human relationships is also far more than a mere obligation.

The care that parents are expected to provide for their children (and the length of time that they need to look after them) is far greater in humans than in any other animal, and it has undoubtedly increased throughout history. That is why human cultures have tried to spread the care for offspring onto both parents and tie them together in a permanent bond. Older societies tried at all costs to prevent the grave danger of the mother being left alone to care for her children, and much cultural and social emphasis was put on the role of the father.[425]

The ancient notion that the man 'sows' the child into the woman and that the woman merely carries it (from which comes the scientific name *sperm* – 'seed'); the patriarchal arrangement of family and property; the one-sided concentration of decision-making into the hands of the father; all of this cultural effort has been expended throughout history to prevent men from shirking their share of the unconditional obligation to care for their offspring. The shocking abuse of these 'male' privileges (all the more noticeable in the present day, in the absence of any unconditional corresponding duties or responsibilities) most certainly deserves the negative label of 'sexism'.[426] For the sake of future generations though, it would be an unforgivable step back, and a serious betrayal of our biological and cultural heritage, if we accepted that the duty of childcare should fall solely to the mother – as is the case with so many animals.

---

425 It is hardly possible to decide nowadays, whether the obvious preference for the 'male gender' in various languages is a cause or a consequence of this general 'strategy'. Its influence, however, cannot be overestimated. A newborn child did not enter an ancient society by being born but by paternal 'initiation' or acceptance, as in ancient Rome. When this acceptance was replaced by circumcision and baptism, so that the child was 'accepted' by God, it meant a significant weakening of the authority of the *pater familias*.

426 Even 19th century liberalism – with the honorary exception of Jeremy Bentham and John Stuart Mill – still concerned itself with the freedoms of an individual man; women only succeeded in getting the right to vote, for example, after the franchise had already been extended to all classes of men. It is, however, also true that at the time, the right to vote was largely demanded by eccentric upper-class ladies, whereas women from poorer backgrounds were scarcely interested.

The cohesion of the parenting couple in humans is further strengthened by an unusually highly developed sexuality, which is not strictly connected to procreation. In agricultural societies, there was no alternative to the family as a unit of organisation, for a solitary person would quite simply not have been able to eke out a living.[427] If a threat arose to this life-preserving cohesion, ancient societies would counter it with drastic measures: strict punishments for marital infidelity (especially for women, it has to be said), legal discrimination against children born out of wedlock,[428] and the rules of property inheritance. Everything was set up to strengthen the family and to protect it against any influences which would undermine it.

All this has changed dramatically over the past hundred years, and it is changing still. The family unit is no longer an existential necessity, children are no longer a welcome helping hand around the family farmstead, nor are they the only reliable provision for our old age. On the contrary, they have come to represent an undeniable career complication; working women everywhere expend a great deal of energy and effort looking for ways to balance out the two aspects of their lives. The Draconian measures taken against unmarried men, which we mentioned earlier, have left a certain social stigma; and even nowadays, it is (for example) hard to imagine the president of the United States not being married.[429] Divorce, which just a hundred years ago was an eccentricity, and the preserve of the wealthy, has become a common occurrence and has lost much of the stigma of impropriety. The care, upbringing and education of children is getting ever more demanding and expensive, so that many people in wealthy societies choose their career over having children. Sexuality has been largely separated from its original function; it has been removed from the realm of intimacy and become a commercial article; it is only slowly dawning on us that it has lost a part of its attraction.[430]

---

427 This has been an age-old problem of widows and orphans in agricultural societies, well into the 19th century.

428 In these parts up to mid 19th century. In contrast, adopted children were considered legally equal to one's own.

429 As confirmed by the somewhat scornful terms 'spinster' and perhaps also 'bachelor'. In contrast, the ancient phenomenon of mandatory celibacy helped emphasise the exceptional nature of certain religious functions. In the Middle Ages, the mandatory celibacy of Christian priests still functioned as sort of sign – among others an expression of the courage to forgo the natural social security, represented in agricultural societies only by children.

430 Thus women dressing in an ostentatiously provocative manner cause a heart-felt outcry among European Muslims, who react with the exact opposite; while commercial and media outlets

These dramatic changes have naturally led to a weakening of the family and have inevitably been reflected in the demographics of wealthy societies. Closely connected though these phenomena are, it is useful to consider them separately. The crisis of the family, in the sense of its being in serious danger, has been discussed for at least half a century and – as we have seen – with good reason. Almost all the forms of outward social support of the family have indisputably been weakened, and the elementary mutual dependence between spouses has all but disappeared. The increasing number of divorces and alternative family arrangements has its cultural and social causes, too; so it is not really appropriate to adopt a moralising approach to it. On the contrary, the fact that the majority still opts for it is a testimony to the lasting inner strength of the family institution. And if a functioning family survives at least into its children's adulthood, that is a praiseworthy accomplishment these days. However, as is also obvious in most wealthy countries, the numbers of such families are rather dwindling.

Another fact is that there seems to be no substitute for the 'complete' family setting for ensuring a good upbringing for a child.[431] Only a very primitive naturalistic approach might make it seem that the male's role is limited to the sexual act, as certain interesting but cynical ethological theories would also have us believe. The notions of male and female 'sexual strategies', for example, are rather plausible and they may explain the origins of man's social development and some fundamental institutions. But somewhat speculative interpretations, popularisation, and the reductive generalisation of these theories have helped spread the impression that no such development had actually taken place and that man is in reality still no more than a 'naked ape'. Indirectly, they give currency to a state of affairs which human societies have striven to change for millennia. The obvious fact of different roles, and the 'sexual strategies' connected to these, has led the creation of institutions which would suppress natural human tendencies in the name of the successful continuation of life and society.[432] So nowadays, when some scientists preach generalised ethological findings as something akin to the law of

---

offer increasingly more extreme forms of sexuality – perhaps because the 'common' kind does not have a sufficient 'pull' any more.

431 See. e.g. Ivo Možný, *Rodina a společnost* (*Family and Society*).

432 It suffices to mention such anthropological constants as the ban on incest, the rules of exogamy, the cultural imperatives of dressing and body decoration, as well as the intricate institutions of courtship and wedding. It was through these that man distinguished and differentiated himself so early on from related animals and based all his further development on culture – with all the benefits and risks it carries.

nature and the general public views it as refutation of traditional moral-ity, it is in contrast to the principle of preliminary caution, to which we adhere so closely in matters of far lesser importance.

In reality, it is not just the obvious role of the father[433] in the up-bringing of children approaching adulthood which is at stake here, but the whole act of transmitting culture, something no society can afford to do without. The father no longer needs to be the breadwinner, but he should certainly be there to lend support, to offer a third voice in the resolution of conflicts, to lead his offspring out from the intimacy of the nest and into broader society. He should be there to offer his children first objective criticism, for them to get used to negative criticism, and to take responsibility for their own actions. When children are denied these aspects of socialisation, it fosters lifelong infantilism, about which teachers, employers and others continually complain.[434]

This careless naturalism, which so casually likens human children to the young of, say, gibbons, and considers their behaviour almost as the norm, thus concealing, or even casting into doubt, something more as well. While young people in archaic societies could make their living by using skills they learned unconsciously, just by watching their parents, modern human societies require them to acquire much more varied and complex skills – which their parents do not practise at home. So woe betide young people without education and qualifica-tions. Whereas language, a handful of rituals and storytelling were suf-ficient to perpetuate cultural reproduction in archaic societies, modern societies are based on an immeasurable wealth of experience, knowl-edge, and wisdom, of which the young generation must somehow par-take. They are growing up in an incredibly intricate net of scarcely noticeable but important institutions and organisations, which they will one day take over and develop themselves. In traditional societies, power was concentrated in the hands of a small elite, and the prosper-ity of the whole depended largely on the quality of this elite class. In contrast, in a democratic society, we all have our share in decision-mak-ing. And whereas the archaic man's world ended on the horizon he could survey and nature could have seemed an inexhaustible source,

---

433 Or, to be more precise, a man: in some traditional societies, the upbringing of children falls to the mother's brother.

434 As early as the beginning of the 1960s, the German psychologist Alexander Mitscherlich warned that in contemporary society, the role of the father is vanishing and that there is gen-eration growing up who have discovered that 'there is no need to grow up'. Mitscherlich, *Auf dem Wege zur vaterlosen Gessellschaft*.

we nowadays live in one world, which is growing ever smaller and coming ever more into our power.

Perhaps the crisis of the family in wealthy countries, and the resulting demographic stagnation, could be regarded as an overall change of human reproductive strategy. It would not be completely implausible. Just as man differs from other animals by having relatively few offspring and investing an incomparable amount of effort into their upbringing, it could be argued that we are gradually departing from the expansive strategy of conquering and colonising the Earth, and supplanting it with striving for a better and more human life in accordance with our ideals. Such a change cannot happen over the course of just a few years, and it is doubtful whether everyone will take it on board – or rather if everybody will be able to afford it. Even in wealthy countries, its consequences are likely to be unforeseeable; it should however suffice to list those, which are already evident.

The aging of the population must necessarily result in restrictions of public social services, at least in increasing the retirement age. The shrinking of the working-age population, and the corresponding pressure on immigration, will lead to a further erosion of national 'identities' and greater cultural diversification in these societies. Global competition among producers as well as job seekers will steadily increase the pressure on performance and skills, and will most likely lead to a considerable reassessment of the notion of what it means to be 'qualified', with flexibility and adaptability playing an increasing part. We should start factoring these changes in right from the present moment.

Let us return to Hans Jonas and his unconditional responsibility of the mother towards her child, which however – as we have just seen – we must significantly expand. Jonas is right in rejecting that the mother's obligation towards her child could be reciprocal, based on mutual benefit, and he insists that it is of a different nature, as care for something which is not yet 'there', or is only just beginning. This then forms the basis of his 'categorical imperative': 'Act in such a way so that your actions were in harmony with sustaining truly human life on Earth.'[435] Much as I agree with Jonas' basic intention in this matter, the way he deduces and argues it has at least two weak points. Firstly, the logical leap from the mother's child to the future of all mankind seems rather abrupt and unconvincing. Secondly, Jonas' imperative is perhaps exceedingly 'cat-

---

435 Jonas, *The Imperative of Responsibility*. The wording resembles that of Brentano's and Moore's – see above.

egorical', as he does not even attempt to expand on its universal obligation and explain it.[436]

The foregoing should make it clear that even the truly exceptional relationship between mother and child is not altogether unique, as it might seem, if it is taken out of broader context. Parents are not – as Jonas also suggests in his book – the 'immediate originators' of a new life, rather they pass on their own existence as their own parents once did.[437] They act, therefore, as its stewards, whose task it is to take the best possible care of the life entrusted to them. From an individual's viewpoint, it might be difficult to justify why a being which does not yet exist should be given any priority over those who are already here. Seen in the context of the continuation of life, however, it is not surprising at all: had all our ancestors not acted in this way, we would not be here now.[438]

4.3 Heir and Steward

The legal institution of patrimony is certainly of much less importance nowadays than was the case in agricultural societies – and who would wish to return to those times? Most of us do not live off inherited property and we are glad not to have to tend to the family plot; we make a living with our own abilities and skills. But that is why we can so easily overlook the more substantial part of our 'inheritance', starting with life as such, the countless hours and days of parental care, and the years of upbringing and education, during which we acquired these skills, gradually becoming what we are. First and foremost then, there are 'investments' put into us by other people – our parents, teachers, and others, who we – at least in older age – occasionally remember.[439] In all ancient cul-

---

436 Jonas weakened his argument by linking this responsibility (with hardly any logical steps) to the responsibility of (for example) a politician. But, unlike a politician, a parent cannot simply 'step down'.

437 According to Pavel Barša, 'the moral source of a social bond lies in ... the ethics of immanence, i.e. to put it in the Christian idiom – love which gratefully accepts and passes on the gift of life.' (*Imanence a sociální pouto*, p. 110)

438 The priority of reproduction over an individual's own life is otherwise common in nature, in some species, an individual dies after reproducing.

439 The Czech theologian Josef Zvěřina, who spent many years in Nazi and Communist prisons, once told me how shocked he was to realise that every one of the criminals he encountered daily – from murderers to informants and interrogators – had a mother who would lose sleep worrying about them at night if they had a fever.

tures, these 'investments' formed the basis of a strict and strictly enforced obligation to take care of them in their old age. During the 20th century (at least in wealthy countries) this duty started to be taken over by the pension system and the welfare state.

While this development eased the relationship between parents and children, it also removed an element which made this relationship seem straightforwardly reciprocal: we are providing care for you, so that you will one day take care of us.[440] In agricultural societies in particular, where children were also needed as labour, the other, less noticeable element was almost lost: that which goes beyond any utilitarian interest of parents in their children, and which belongs to the mysterious reproduction of the whole of life. The incredible and highly 'improbable' complexity of life being passed on only began to be discovered less than a century ago; nowadays, it is probably the most vibrant area of science.[441]

Less attention is paid to the equally complex act of transmission, or tradition of human culture in its broadest sense – all that man is not born with but which he could not live without. Just as physiological life has been passed on for billions of years, and human life for millions (without any of the participants being aware of the process, let alone understanding it),[442] this specifically human aspect of our 'heritage' is also passed on, almost involuntarily, in a wondrous harmony of parental and educational care on the one hand, and the receptiveness of children on the other. Although both are necessary for the success of the transmission, the latter is key to this success. The parents' role may be less 'automatic' than in biological transmission, but here too, it only has a supportive role. Parents and teachers can offer children countless opportunities, but it is up to each individual child to what extent he or she takes these up and acquires what is on offer. There is no point trying to 'fast-track' the process. Parents' attempts to teach the child can only have an auxiliary role.

For that matter, views on education have been oscillating between various extremes for thousands of years – from the 'Nurnberg funnel'

---

440 This is probably also the meaning of the fourth Commandment, which gives an explicit reason: 'Honour your father and your mother, that your days may be long upon the land which the Lord your God is giving you.' (*Exodus* 20:12)

441 Among other things, because it promises economically interesting results, or 'outcomes'.

442 According to ethnographic reports, people in many archaic societies were not even aware of any connection between a sexual intercourse and the conception of a new life – yet, they did not die out.

on the one hand, where ready-made knowledge is 'poured' into children's minds, and in contrast, Socrates' idea of the 'midwife role', helping children to arrive at their own conclusions.[443] As in many other cases, we should probably forgo the appealing notion that such a complex process could be causally explained by a single 'cause'.

For all the obvious similarities and parallels between the passing on of biological and cultural heritage, there is a difference between them, which is of growing significance. Biological inheritance is – as we have seen – fortunately transmitted over our heads, and even the most scientifically minded couple are not likely to have their minds focused on ribonucleic acid in the decisive moments of 'making a baby'. Their body and mind will be in the 'natural world' where all-important human matters occur. Procreation does not rely on their conscious participation after all, its success is dependent on complex – *sit venia verbo* – physiological mechanisms.

All this changes with birth; the conscious, committed, and informed participation of the adults is then increasingly more crucial during the following years of the child's development. While the child is naturally equipped[444] to learn to stand up, walk, exercise basic hygiene, bond with its mother, explore its surroundings and make the groundbreaking discovery of human speech, the adults' input all this while gradually increases. And when the child enters the realm of speech and starts to 'learn' in the specific sense of the word, this comes more and more from the adults. The child has to take it on itself, i.e. it must become interested and then hold this interest and attention, which would be very difficult without the active and committed participation of adults.

That which is being passed on must now continue without any natural support. It must perpetually maintain its precarious way of being, which characterises the whole realm of human culture.[445] If we allow

---

443 In current terminology, this approach is sometimes described as 'pedocentric' education, e.g. in Montessori schools. On the paradoxes of educators' attitudes and the 'education aporias' of Eugen Fink, see Palouš, *Paradoxy výchovy* (*Paradoxes of Education*).

444 Noam Chomsky proposes the existence of a special 'language acquisition device'(LAD) in the human brain, which enables us to acquire and produce language. This 'device' is how Chomsky accounts for the remarkable structural correspondences and parallels between very different languages, as well as certain aspects of how children 'learn' their mother tongue.

445 In contemporary, highly organised societies, it might seem that, for example, the language or information content of a particular science is securely preserved in books, libraries or databases. But a book only contains information if there is somebody who reads it and comprehends what is being read. 'Information' in an unfamiliar language or alphabet is not real information at all. The problem of 'comprehension' occurs even at the technical level, for example with formatting changes in digital media.

ourselves to use such personification, not dissimilar to the sociobiological notion of the 'selfish gene', then each part and section of any culture must seek human carriers who will transmit it without loss, who will understand it and learn to operate it, who might possibly purify it, develop it, translate it into the younger generation's idiom if necessary, so that they may perform their role in the chain of cultural reproduction and evolution. Whatever does not pass this recurring test of each generation will simply disappear.[446]

As Richerson and Boyd have shown, the mechanisms – or rather processes – of this reproduction are more numerous and varied than those of biological reproduction. Cultural and social transfer is simultaneously more precarious and constantly under threat, but also much more flexible. It allows for much quicker adaptation to a change of situation, devising, spreading and accepting new elements, as well as conscious and reflected selection among these. Clearly the genetic dogma which rules out any passing on of acquired properties or skills does not apply here, not even in the timeframe of one life or generation.[447] As soon as circumstances allow, cultural transmission – or to be more precise culture *as* transmission – becomes communicative, and therefore cumulative. Nobody is limited to acquiring only the costly and risky personal experience; they can take on the experiences of others, both present and past, thus gaining an interest in sharing the cultural wealth among the broadest community possible.[448]

This factor was probably first utilised in the sciences, which, from the Middle Ages and most certainly from the 18th century onward, began to create stable transfer networks, universities, scientific societies, and various discussion platforms – libraries, archives, museums, journals – as a kind of *aide-mémoire* to ensure that what has been gained is not lost. Descartes' notion of universal method played a decisive part, enabling scientists to take over other people's findings, and to build on them. That made way for a more specific division of activities and the truly collective

---

446 As Nietzsche demonstrated, forgetting is equally necessary to us as learning. This perhaps applies to whole cultures, too.

447 On more differentiated approach to this dogma in contemporary molecular biology, see, Kirschner & Gerhart, *The Plausibility of Life*. The authors emphasise the dynamic nature of molecular transcription, where genome parts move about, block, activate, or condition each other. These processes can be influenced by the cell's inner environment, and possibly the outer environment, too.

448 That is the significance of the exceptional human capacity for mimicry, in which even very young children highly outperform for example young chimpanzees. J. P. Richerson & R. Boyd, *Not by Genes Alone*, p. 100f.

and cumulative nature of modern sciences.[449] By the 19th century, the volume of accumulated knowledge was such that science had to split up into individual branches, each with their own subject and method. Present-day science continues to diversify further into more or less disjunctive communities centered around various scientific journals.[450] We will discuss this 'divided inheritance' later.

* * *

When towards the end of the 1930s Edmund Husserl noticed this situation, he believed that the world of modern science is the opposite of the world into which we are born and in which we die (*Lebenswelt*). He juxtaposed the world of our shared human experience, as expressed by language, against the logically structured, but instrumental and parcelled out world of various sciences, lacking the common foundation of understanding. In his view, the gulf created by the mutual lack of understanding between these two worlds is the root of the existing crisis. He believed phenomenology would provide such an indisputable foundation of exact and definite analysis of experience, something individual sciences could refer to. This challenge was taken up by Jan Patočka, who attempted to describe this natural world in phenomenological terms.[451] It would seem to me that this important act has not lost any of

---

449 Descartes was aware of this and frequently mentioned it his letters. In a letter to Vilebressieu (of summer 1631), he recommends a publication of clear theses, so that others be able to improve upon them, and writing to Meysonnier (on 29th January, 1640), he writes of the necessary cooperation of 'thousands searching for the truth'. Descartes, *Oeuvres*. Similarly two centuries earlier Nikolas of Cusa in his 'Dialogue on Weight-Scale'.

450 Bibliometric methods of calculating mutual quotations and impact factor even make it possible to compare these circles and to somehow arrange them in a hierarchical fashion, which strongly motivates competition among scientists. The 'objective', i.e. mechanised, and therefore 'blind' character of these indicators, as based on an idealised market model, is nonetheless a welcome tool when it comes to awarding science grants by governments and other agencies: how much they truly express the real value of various scientific projects remains a question. The concept of evaluation without evaluators is both tempting and problematic.

451 J. Patočka, *Přirozený svět jako filosofický problém* (*The natural world as a philosophical problem*). Both Husserl and Patočka view the natural world as entirely intellectual, centred on language and comprehension/understanding, so that it might seem that its opposite is the world of science. But the 'basis of the world we live in' are other activities apart from thinking and cognitive processes. We must eat and sleep, feel hunger and pain, enjoy ourselves and suffer, rejoice and cry – in short, live. We only perceive the surrounding world of things and people from a certain perspective. Our 'life world' is then characterised by ever-present evaluation, rather than a vague 'naturalness'. Although Patočka regards the natural world as unquestioningly historical, the notion of 'natural world' nowadays unavoidably invites naturalistic misunder-

its significance, and while Husserl's original idea of phenomenological method has survived, the idea of unifying sciences by a common philosophical foundation was abandoned.

A lot has changed however, in the hundred years since it was first proposed, and it seems to me that for the purposes of practical philosophy, the dividing line should be drawn elsewhere. Sciences, characterised as a systematic effort to gain knowledge, continue to develop; but more and more often, they present only 'practical' results, thus becoming a part of a wider phenomenon of technology, business, and mass organisation of human lives in general. What we as humans have to deal with, on a day to day basis, is not tension and conflict between the natural and scientific view of the world,[452] but between private lives, which inevitably play out in the natural world of birth and death, meaning and speech, and beauty, love, and hate, too – and on the other hand the 'world' of organisations and the roles which we all play within these.

Public life in our sense of the word was for the first time distinctly separated from the privacy of the home, which is fully engaged in worries about livelihood and children, among free and equal men in the cities of antiquity in the sphere of competition, rivalry and striving to stand out. In contrast to never-changing domestic worries, where everything recurs in cycles of days and years, from birth to death, it emerged as an area of free action, an opportunity to 'do memorable deeds with everyone bearing witness'. It is no wonder then, that in the minds of the participants, it completely pushed into the shadows the slavish life of *banausos*,[453] the labouring classes, and private citizens, and also women and children, who are only of service by catering for life's ordinary needs, and ensuring its perpetuation.

When this public, or political, form of life flourished again in medieval towns, which often looked to Athens for inspiration, the situation

---

standing. In *Život, svět, hodnoty a dějiny*, J. Moural defines 'life world' as 'the action environment of interested agents', he further characterises it by the dichotomy of familiar/strange, as well as by the cognitive limitations or perspective.

452 The most conspicuous conflicts arise on the very fringes of common life interests, and when we say 'the sun is setting', we can reconcile ourselves with the fact that 'in reality', it is not the case. A harder to comprehend conflict between the common notion of an impermeable substance – e.g. glass – and a physics description employing the theory of atoms and void, can perhaps be shrugged at. It can perhaps help account for the difference compared to Husserl's times that nowadays, we have largely given up on the ambition to understand and explain everything. After all, there are specialists to concern themselves with all that.

453 The Greek *banausos* (from *baunos*, furnace), used to denote those who busy themselves around the hearth and cooking, concerning themselves solely with private affairs of their livelihood.

was somewhat altered. Unlike the nobles, whose task it is to fight, the free burghers mostly work for themselves, although not necessarily in the fields. From this then, stems their pride; and their success and wealth are a proof of their own abilities. They however mostly work in domestic trades and household businesses, so that their working and domestic lives merge to a certain extent. Only with the arrival of industry do they become strictly separated, while the functions of the two spheres become reversed. A person entering a workplace relinquishes his or her autonomy, takes on a role and works in accordance with someone else's wishes, entering this social sphere of dependence in order to earn funds for his or her private and free life. And it is 'at home', in the previously scorned private sphere, where we live our lives in accordance with Kant's 'purposes', while we obtain the means to lead this life by performing various roles within society, in the world of organisations and institutions.

Sociology defines an institution as a 'universally practised, or socially recognised and within the given culture passed on mode of behaviour', while organisation is 'the manner in which we coordinate our activities'.[454] According to J. Jandourek, the purpose of an organisation is to reduce the complexity of its environment. An organisation is characterised by a certain number of members, by boundaries between its own structure and the environment, internal distribution of roles, and a hierarchical system of authority. It is aimed at a certain purpose and it is arranged rationally, it is relatively independent of its individual members, whose activities are strongly formalised.[455] But as both these words are used copiously in ordinary speech, often as near synonyms, it is difficult to observe this distinction. Niklas Luhmann, whose theories we are partly building on here, only speaks of institutions, when meaning both. We will use the word 'institution' in the sense of general and superior structures and patterns of behaviour, while 'organisation' will denote particular specific realisations of such structures; we cannot, however entirely prevent the two terms overlapping.

The role of institutions has been brilliantly described by the German sociologist Niklas Luhmann, employing the theory of the Chilean biologist Humberto Maturana. Spontaneous formation of beneficial and viable structures – in the biological sphere as well as the cultural – is extremely unlikely. They can only take hold if they somehow become stabilised and ensure their own maintenance and reproduction. Matura-

454 Petrusek, *Velký sociologický slovník I. (Great sociological encyclopaedia)*, p. 435; Keller, *Úvod do sociologie (Introduction to sociology)*, p. 71.

455 Jandourek, *Sociologický slovník (Dictionary of sociology)*, p. 177.

na sees the fundamental characteristic of all living things precisely in the maintenance and development of a certain inner structure, something he calls autopoiesis.[456] Maturana observes that autopoiesis is not a feature or aspect of an organism, rather the organism is autopoiesis itself.

In the social sphere, the creation of institutions is an equivalent. They play a crucial part in every human society, even more so in modern societies. We all come into contact with them, and we all participate in them, too. Institutions and organisations are created by separating from their environment, 'functionally closing' themselves. Nevertheless, they only function in various exchanges with this environment; in this, they resemble living cells. Every organisation is then by its nature a partial affair – whether it is defined by a closed circle of members as a club or society, or by its subject matter, focusing on a particular area of social life, for example, various scientific, economic, or legal organisations. Luhmann furthermore observed that all institutions live their own life and evolve 'from within'.[457]

Luhmann considered this concept of the autopoietic system a characteristic feature of every institution and he studied it across a range of subsystems of modern societies. Institutions, like living organisms, separate themselves from their environment, but they communicate with it in various ways; otherwise they would cease to be a part of the society, and therefore cease to exist altogether. Institutions 'themselves' choose the area of their activity, as well as the legitimate channels of communication with their environment. Thus legal institutions for example, separate themselves by specialising in decision making as to what is justified by law and what is not, while they pay no attention to all non-legal matters. To function, though, they need funding which they do not generate themselves; that has to come from outside. Legal institutions clearly demonstrate how important the restriction of economic communication to legitimate channels is: a judge can receive payment only from the court, i.e. the state; any other remuneration represents corruption and must be prevented for the sake of the maintaining of the organisation's integrity.

---

456 From the Greek *autos*, 'self' and *poiein*, 'to make'. An autopoietic system is a permanent structure which maintains itself through the perpetual flow of matter. The author came up with the concept when searching for an answer to a student's question: 'What exactly happened 3.8 billion years ago, so that we can now say that is when living systems first appeared?' (H. Maturana, *Autopoiesis, Structural Coupling and Cognition*. http://www.isss.org/maturana.htm).

457 A caricatured version of 'functional closure' and 'growth from within' has been well described by C. N. Parkinson in his famous book *Parkinson's Law*.

Luhmann was convinced that, as a sociologist, his remit was merely to study ('observe') the functioning of institutions, and their mutual relationships, or 'communications', disregarding the fact that they consist of, and are maintained by, people. He was right to stress that for an institution to function, the people must be, at least to a certain degree, exchangeable and replaceable, that they are a part of the organisation not as unique persons, but as carriers of certain roles, performers of specific activities, which the organisation, according to its regulations, distributes and entrusts to them.[458] Outside their working hours, people live an ordinary civic life of free time, which is common to all and where their work qualifications are scarcely reflected. In their assumed or delegated institutional roles people do not act (only) for themselves, they do not dispose of their own possessions and resources, but they perform clearly defined activities within the framework of the remit entrusted or delegated to them. If they act 'in the name' of the organisation, the responsibility they bear for these actions tends to be specified and limited by a set of rules. Any 'short-circuit' which would occur between their institutional role and their private life would threaten the working of the organisation, and must be punished.

This undoubtedly simplified picture of social reality enabled Luhmann to succinctly characterise the peculiar nature of institutions, but at the same time it also led him to a scarcely justifiable conviction that institutions and their rules have in modern societies come to replace morality and render it defunct. He believes that in the 'de-moralised' society, morality 'lost its job' and has been made redundant, thus losing its legitimacy.[459] Such a statement could perhaps be defended as a critical description of modern reality, but Luhmann himself frequently crosses that line and attempts to justify the *'de-moralised'* state, even using moral arguments such as violence and lack of tolerance in the name of moral principles and rules. A clear and convincing critique of this aspect of Luhmann's thinking was presented by P. Floss,[460] who lists the main arguments against it: besides an evident renewal of interest in

---

458 According to Maturana, 'The elements that compose a system are not its components by themselves, they are its components only as they participate in its composition, and only while they do so.' (*Autopoiesis, Structural Coupling and Cognition*, 1.2).

459 The most urgent role of ethics is to 'warn against morality' (Luhmann, *Paradigm Lost*, p. 198). In contrast, Durkheim considered the absence of morality in economic life, which is run only by human greed, a major issue and the cause of the crisis of European societies in the 1930s (Durkheim, *Physik der Sitten und des Rechts*).

460 Floss, *Ztracené paradigma?* (A lost paradigm?) https://phil.muni.cz/fil/etika/texty/studie/floss1.html.

morals, even in areas which might seem able to do without them, such as banking, as well as a plethora of various 'ethical codices', and most importantly the peril of such an extremely functionalistic view of the meaning of institutions. The apparatus of the totalitarian state – its propaganda and its extermination camps, would in this framework be considered perfectly functioning 'autopoietic' organisations, the running of which was made possible by its employees being able to separate their orderly civic lives from the completely 'de-moralised' functioning within these institutions.[461] We will return to this extremely important issue later.

Despite all the dire warnings of history – recent history in particular – it is simply impossible to imagine modern life without these thousands of organisations. The widespread Utopian despising and loathing of organisations as such is not only futile, but dangerous; it invites us to tar them all with the same brush, making it easier to make peace with those which are really bad. The necessity to distinguish between organisations and to be able to evaluate institutions is all the more pressing in modern society, as any road to a better future most likely leads through them. They can be the very tool which brings together and augments the actions of individual people, who, in modern mass societies, cannot achieve anything on their own.[462]

Instead of the naive, generalised mistrust or rejection of organisations, it is necessary to pay close attention to them, and to be careful to separate the living and acting individuals from their roles within organisations. If an official, employee, or a politician forgets Cicero's requirement to 'use common possessions for the common interest, private property for their own', he or she will be guilty of corruption. This distinction, essential in a modern society, has in all post-communist societies been weakened and obscured by past experience. Not because communist propaganda emphasised collective and supposedly collective interests, but because state socialism suppressed free social and public life, offering instead a substitute diet of various activities in the workplace, especially in labour collectives.[463]

---

461 Can we console ourselves by saying that they did not survive for very long anyway? This fact certainly deserves attention but the harm they managed to do during the brief period of their existence goes well beyond human imagination.

462 Paul Ricoeur therefore is very clear in reminding us that a fulfilling, successful life is 'good life with the others and for them, in just institutions' (*Oneself as Another*, p. 200 ff).

463 Under the communist regime, when stealing from businesses and organisations was mentioned, people often argued that they are merely relocating their property 'to another workplace' – that is to say, their home. Some even considered it an act of resistance.

Equally dangerous, at the other end of the spectrum, is the use of an-thropomorphic language to describe all those things that organisations 'want' and 'do'. This kind of talk can serve as a useful excuse for our own failings, especially failing to act, or as a front for following our private interests. In reality it is always a specific group of people who decide what an organisation 'does' – and then it is usually the job of others to carry this out. Although legal regulations naturally restrict the responsibility of an employee, the increasing power (and danger) of organisations require that their employees evaluate their actions within their roles on moral cri-teria as well as merely organisational criteria. They are often the only ones who have the opportunity to perform such an evaluation; nobody else has the necessary knowledge. Just as organisations live their inner, more or less separate 'lives', there must, from the very nature of things, be a set of independent rules regulating their functions. Organisations feel nei-ther pleasure, nor pain,[464] they do not know how it feels to be free, their sense of 'honour' is different, and as they are set up for a specific purpose, they cannot be guided by the golden rule or the categorical imperative. That is why we will pay them closer attention from a moral viewpoint.

In the meantime, we should make the distinction between the inevi-tably whole and undivided world of personal and private life on the one hand, where we live as people with a name but without 'attributes'. We have been born into it not out of our own will or effort, and we will leave it when we die, but we want to live it as Kant's 'end-in-itself', as unique human beings. Here, we act on our own behalf, more or less freely, we use what is ours, and we usually bear quite palpable responsibility for our actions.[465] It is only in recent times that human life has been accord-ed such high value that a man, having suffered bankruptcy, can pick him-self up, dust himself down, and carry on; both real and literary figures in the past often found the only solution in suicide.[466] And on the other

---

464 This is why contemporary penal law finds it so difficult to find ways of penalising organisa-tions. A private business can be easily penalised, which is much harder to achieve with a gov-ernment institution.

465 A Roman farmer who fell into debt could not separate himself from his farm and had to be sold as part of it. In republican Rome, the law said that a debtor who failed to pay his debts could be quartered by his creditors (*The Law of the Twelve Tables*, Table III); When Shakespeare used this motif in *The Merchant of Venice*, his audience probably did not find it all that far-fetched. In England, debtors' prisons for those who failed to pay their debts were still in use in the 19th century.

466 This significant difference between the owner and the person who is 'only working for wages' is illustrated by the biblical parable of the good shepherd, a prototype of the distinction between life and roles (John 10:12n).

hand, there is the different milieu of always partial and specialised organisations, which we all have to deal with, and where a great many of us also work. We enter employment more or less voluntarily, of our free will, and we also have the freedom to end such employment. We accept the mostly hierarchical setup of these organisations, we carry out activities as prescribed and instructed, and the resources we deploy do not belong to us, but are only temporarily entrusted to us. Corresponding to all this is the restricted responsibility, the 'limited liability' for the results of our work, which is coupled with a requirement of 'loyalty' towards the 'firm' and adherence to its rules and regulations.

This other area of employment, into which we enter in the role of temporary stewards, is meant to serve as a means to achieving the first one, in which we live our own, inherited life as an 'end'. For that purpose, we will distinguish between these terms as 'heir' and 'steward'.

Private Heir

With our birth, we 'enter the world'. To begin with, this world is very limited; and psychologists say that initially, we regard it as part of our own being. One of the first tasks awaiting a young child is to learn to distinguish between itself and its environment, or 'the world'. As this world of ours gradually differentiates and expands, we learn to deal with it in various ways, eventually to search within it our own place and a path to adulthood and our role in life. Most of us adults manage all this with relative success, probably because we have been well equipped for it, and also because the adults around us guided us, corrected our mistakes, and praised our successes. Once we learned to distinguish between ourselves and 'the world', we then learned to distinguish between what is ours and what is someone else's; we started to create our own 'niche', into which we could eventually bring our own children.

The care for what is ours, which in wealthy modern societies comprises of an ever growing number of necessary, useful, or simply desirable objects, which we want to obtain and for which we need to earn money, can be so engrossing that we can cease to see beyond it. The natural concern of everything living for its own life and its perpetuation, which we have already discussed and which is much augmented in humans owing to our capacity for reflection, memory, and conscious planning for the future, can completely engross us too. But thanks to the power of reflection, we are also able to take a step back not just from the world but also from our own life and actions – something which all moral behaviour rests upon after all. And from this distance, we may also – albeit rarely – also come to see that our options are considerably more numerous and varied. This is why moral thought has, since ancient times, tried to turn our attention to other people, both close and distant, and to human societies as such.

There is much truth and currency in the age-old wisdom that our own life is merely a sort of preliminary horizon of human possibilities, and that those who become completely preoccupied with it have actually missed out on the best possibilities available to them.[467] It is perhaps even more valid in the more comfortable setting of wealthy societies. Nevertheless, one must not, even as a private heir, be content with the problematic distinction between selfishness and altruism, to which the moral dilemma is often reduced. Primarily because – as we have seen – it is not strictly possible to separate them; even in the most 'altruistic' act there can be found a kernel of satisfaction, which would put it in the opposite category. Secondly, the scope of options is perhaps outlined too narrowly here. It is not just other people who are our opposite and that which entices us to step out of the closed privacy of an individual life, it is also the world, in which we can all share our lives with others.

Classical thought on egoism and altruism does take note of other people around, who we cannot do without, to whom we are very likely much indebted, and who possibly also need us, but it fails to see the trivial fact that together with life, we have also 'inherited' and took over an already 'ready-made' world. This world is not, at first, the planet of which we learn at school, but as a natural opposite to our consciousness and a necessary 'natural' condition of life as such. Of course the relationship towards it which a farmer or a hunter have who, day in day out, find their sustenance directly in it, differs from that of ours, who look for our food on the supermarket shelves. Because they have seen it being born, growing and ripening, they are more intuitive as to its various, more and less obvious links, they are able to observe the effects of sunshine and rain, winter and summer, and they then channel their wonder and horror of this mystery into common celebrations and sacrifices. From what we know of their contents, we can deduce that man became aware of the mystery of the life-giving world long before he began to uncover the depths of his own consciousness, or of life and its perpetuation.

---

467 As shown for example by the evolution of the Greek word *idiótés* (from *idios*, one's own), which originally meant 'a private man', and later became a form of invective and a psychological diagnosis. We have already discussed the similar case of the word *banausos*.

The mysterious world, or 'nature', as we rather recently started to call it, was only 'rediscovered' by modern man when it became clear that it was not to be taken for granted, nor was it so inexhaustible, as it previously may have appeared. So we actually discovered it indirectly, via a diversion, because it is endangered, and we are all endangered with it. The initially mediated and instrumental character of environmental care corresponds to that, having been instigated by reports of dwindling resources, something that must be dealt with by global organisations anyway. We will return to this point when we discuss remote and in-stitutionally mediated responsibilities. This purpose-driven interest has nevertheless awoken something else and more humanly profound – an almost religious interest in nature here and now, in our own close sur-roundings. This perhaps stems from the Romanticism of the 19th century painters and tourists, including their aesthetics and the somewhat exhi-bitionist nature of their protest.

This interest could perhaps be content with satiating its 'own needs' – such as keeping pets – and perhaps end in mere voyeurism of the typ-ically remote causes which excite media attention, such as the seals in Greenland or the tropical rainforests in Brazil. Where it did escape these trappings, it has emerged as a truly widespread movement, whose sig-nificance we perhaps cannot yet fully appreciate. For it uncovered the completely forgotten relationship to inheritance as to something irre-placeable which has been passed on to us and which sustains us.[468] In its truer forms, it immediately understood that it is a 'personal' inheritance, which belongs to each and every one of us, whether we live surrounded by romantic landscapes or in a high-rise in an industrialised area. In this profoundly 'grounded' form, it began to rediscover the relational world of our ancestors, a connectedness to a place, land, and country-side, which have been entrusted to us as to independently thinking and acting stewards.

Nor is our notion of privacy and human autonomy a 'natural' given, as many have imagined and many still do.[469] It is a result of a complex cultural development, thousands of years of emancipation struggles. There is a whole tradition of practical philosophy devoted to the po-sition, aims, and obligations of an independently acting human being.

---

468 This is discussed quite clearly for example by the French lawyer F. Ost in his *La nature hors la loi*, and does not remain restricted to nature only.

469 For example all those championing the concept of the 'state of nature' and 'social contract', from Hobbes, Rousseau and Kant to John Rawls, or on the other hand the advocates of 'nat-ural law' in the extreme sense.

Philosophy itself only begins where individual people succeed in shedding the collective identity of a tribe, a 'dynasty' or a 'large household', as Jan Patočka calls the ancient empires. These too, could perhaps be termed organisations, albeit of a very specific, 'total' kind: people are born into them unable to choose between them and they will only leave them upon their death.[470] As they were born into them, they 'belong' to them not just for the contractual working hours, but with their whole lives, which they must be willing to risk for them. Nobody 'founded' these 'organisations' either, their origins lie 'in the dim and distant past', 'in the mist of time'.

The rules of their inner working, too, supported by collective festivities, rituals, and myths, could not be placed under scrutiny, let alone criticism, as there would not be anybody who could 'step back' to gain the necessary perspective: they were simply an inseparable part of an ever constant 'natural world', in the same way as the daily and yearly cycles of nature are. From the evolutionary point of view, they carry clear traces of their nearly 'biological' origin, much of which has been preserved to the present day. We have already mentioned the authoritarian character of social custom and the bequeathed language, and to this day, it is a constitutional duty of each citizen to defend his or her country, although they do not actually perform it. Another obvious remnant from the ancient 'total' human organisation is xenophobia, a subconscious nostalgia after simple arrangements inside the 'big households', where all look, act, and talk in a similar way. After all, even the totalitarian regimes of recent times, with their 'scientific' pseudo-myths, emphasising 'the unity of the party and the people', excluding the fabricated 'enemies', can be construed as manipulative 'revival' of the ancient past – but of course they are sham, and eventually untenable.[471]

The first significant step by which human cultures weakened this 'total' naturalness of the tribe, was the introduction of settled agriculture and division of land: with this way of life, a single farmstead or 'house' as the ancients called it, or a wider family, could become an independent living and self-reproducing unit. Within these, nevertheless, 'total' claims were still made to the indisputable fatherly or paternalistic authority, as we have spoken about them. Outwardly though, and between individual

---

470 Exile, or banishment was often understood as a death penalty in these societies. Cf. Wesel, *Frühformen des Rechts*.

471 A subconscious yearning for 'the good old times' may possibly explain the success of totalitarian ideologies among confused and startled masses during the hardship following both world wars.

units, relationships of an entirely different character could develop. The dependent members of the homestead were as a matter of course not allowed to act as independent beings, and they were, until recent times, regarded as 'under the control of another' (*alieni juris*); while the heads of these homesteads had to recognise each other as equals, only willing to submit to the authority of a judge in cases of conflict.

The necessary foundation of this 'segmentation' of agricultural societies lay in the strict division of property, i.e. land – and ancient literary sources show the significance of boundaries and borders was well recognised.[472] Only when land ownership became fully stabilised, could the *paterfamilias* enter into voluntary and equal relationships and by doing so, they weakened the 'total' rule of the former tribal 'kings'. In times of peace, when united cooperation did not represent a bare necessity, a new type of relationship could develop, one faintly resembling the social contract, which could effectively compete with authoritarian domination. So it was that the division of land, which in those times did not have the status of unlimited private property in today's terms,[473] and its 'untouchability' was a condition for a later creation of cities and 'democracy' in its ancient conception. This crucial impact of the division of land and the iron rules of inheritance also explains why property and ownership play such a significant role in the moral thinking of 'segmented', and later individualistic societies (at least in times of peace).[474]

We have already sketched out the situation of the heir: while he is the sole 'ruler' of the family property, he must take good care of it, under the constant scrutiny of his ancestors, present in the domestic hearth. In the early ancient times, there was absolutely no question of selling

---

472 A boundary stone, according to Plato, marks a boundary 'between friendship and hostility', preventing the last (Plato, *Laws*, VIII, 843a; cf also *Laws*, 878b).

473 Interesting legal institute of usucaption comes from the Roman law: uncultivated land, for example, can be taken over by somebody else. Thus, its 'ownership' was legitimised only through its use of providing a livelihood for a family; if they do not till it, they may lose it. Cf. *The Institutes of Gaius*, II.51 and 55.

474 For Aristotle, it is a given that free equals wealthy, independent of anyone else for livelihood. The importance of wealth and the struggle to secure it was taken to the extreme by David Hume who regarded even the concept of justice as stemming from the effort to protect property, and he frequently mentions 'justice and property' with one breath. Kant's *Metaphysics of Morals* (1797) and even Hegel's *Philosophy of Right* (1830) still begins with private law, which is founded on ownership. It was not until the 20th century – probably influenced by the experience of the war years and under growing pressure from the impecunious classes – the human life and safety come to the fore again. Even then, Robert Nozick based his concept of freedom on the thesis that 'every one is the owner of their body'; a curious expression which would have surely delighted Karl Marx as a perfect example of alienation.

it or otherwise parting with it. Not before the Roman *Law of the Twelve Tables* were fathers allowed to choose their heirs by means of a testament. Property was – as we already know – family property; in a sense it also belonged to the deceased ancestors. Just as the current family lives off it, the dead in turn live form their services. Patrimony was not allowed to be distributed; it was, however, burdened with this 'servitude', which at the same time provided it with meaning and legitimacy. Within his family stead, the heir had an obligation to his ancestors, which, in turn, created obligations towards his progeny.[475]

Outwardly, however, between 'equal' free heirs in ancient Greek cities, there appeared a scope, for independent actions amongst equals. That gave rise to the *agora* as a 'public space', where the 'discovery of the soul' may be manifested and separated from common custom, as individual morality and ethics in the sense of individual search for the best life. But the obvious predominance of concern for public matters as gleaned from writers of antiquity, may well be an optical illusion; the 'domestic' people, the *banausoi*, did not write anything, and therefore we know very little about them. These societies survived the fall of the Greek city-states and the Roman Empire, as the homestead – where life is handed on – carried on. In Late Antiquity, clearly under the influence of Christianity, the less 'visible' members of the household, especially women, begin to emerge to the fore.

The notion, or rather the promise, of individual eternal life, for which Christianity took over and re-labelled the concept of the eternal soul, signified among other things an enormous increase in the significance of the individual – each and every one without exception. We are all God's creatures, accepting our souls, as it were, directly from God's hands, not as a part of the heritage passed on from our parents, and therefore answerable only to God for how we treat them. Plato's 'cultivation of the soul' has thus acquired a new meaning: its purpose is not just the immanent beauty and goodness of the soul as such, nor its rational participation in eternal ideas, but the almost inconceivable promise of individual 'eternal life'. Each individual person is thus exempt from many a philosopher's wholesale scorn of 'ephemeral things' and owing to their soul becomes an adept of the best thing one could wish for – futile as it might be to try to imagine it. And precisely because there is more at stake in life than life itself, the need for freedom arises, which from the

---

475 If he does not have his own son, he can fulfil this duty by adoption. The modern concept of 'mandatory heir' – one who cannot be omitted from the will – can be traced back to these rules.

Middle Ages onwards becomes individual, independent even of religious authorities.[476]

Until recently, the concept of the eternal soul coexisted and competed with the concept of inherited life and property, according to which the practical running of earthly life had been arranged.[477] During the High Middle Ages, however, it found a rich breeding ground in towns, with their individualistic way of life, spread amongst all social classes, and became by far the most dominant idea. But it was not until city life gained general predominance over rural life, in the 19th century, that it began to completely oust the notion of life wedged between ancestry and progeny. But hand in hand with the concept of inherited life, the concept of the eternal soul began to dwindle too, and it was gradually replaced by the (originally theological and later legal) concept of a *person*. Although the humanists and philosophers of the Enlightenment bestowed upon various superlatives upon it, human life nonetheless lost some of its transcendental character, both earthly and heavenly.

One of the most important attributes of a person in the legal sense is undoubtedly ownership, through which a person acquires an 'external sphere of freedom'.[478] In an attempt to achieve maximum legal simplification of social life, the understanding of possession has strengthened, becoming nearly absolute, in the Modern Age, so that we nowadays understand it as an 'exclusive, complete, and unrestricted power over a thing'. This very simple, methodically simplified idea of society as a 'mathematical set' of strictly separated private citizens who exchange products and possessions, resonates with both classical economic theory and the majority of modern concepts of practical philosophy. Hume, Smith, and Kant all consider the situation of an individual, free, and independent person who has unrestricted powers over his possessions. He is his own master and he himself decides what he will give to someone else, what he will accept from another, and what he will exchange for something else. Kant's morality, therefore, only judges whether the postulate of equality has been observed during these transactions, and if the individual acted in such a way as everyone should. If we were to limit ourselves only to the 'heads' of families (as the aforementioned thinkers

---

476 'There is no sin except against the conscience.' (Abelard).

477 The evident tension between the dualist notion of the immortal soul and the hope of resurrection in monotheistic religions, which has for thousands of years defied all attempts at rational explanation, is just another form of the paradox of any mortal, who nevertheless lives with the hope of 'death being destroyed' (1 Corinthians 15:26).

478 Hegel, *Philosophy of Right*, § 43.

did), that would reflect the setup of agricultural societies, and in fact the situation of a typical burgher as late as the early 19th century, if they were practising a trade or running a business.

4.4 Institutions and Action in Roles

The ideally simplified concept of society as a group of separate farmsteads and their free owners, who may exchange goods among themselves, has long ceased to fit social reality. It only applied to that part of society which, from Neolithic times up until early 20th century, lived in a 'segmentary' agricultural setup of self-sufficient 'houses', firmly tied to the hereditary estate. We have seen what it achieved and the legacy it left for the future development; it could however, no longer satisfy the growing possibilities and demands. Already with the establishment of first cities, a new element appeared, based on the relationships between individual homesteads, the introduction of the division of labour and exchange of its products. While it was only limited to small-scale craft and trade production, to individual barter and trade, it could be construed as a certain supplement or service, an enrichment of the agricultural life which offers it a broader range of possibilities.[479]

Already in ancient times, but certainly no later than with the rise of large empires, there appear vast and intricate projects, for which this dispersed economic system is simply no longer adequate. Temples, bridges, aqueducts, shipbuilding and manufacture of goods require ever more complex cooperation and organisation, which goes hand in hand with increased demands on the organisation of communal and public life. The 'horizontal' distribution of labour is then joined by the 'vertical' stratification of society and hierarchically arranged political power.

The decline of patriarchal agricultural societies can be regarded as a loss of self-sufficiency of individual estates; on the other hand, it heralds gradual emancipation of the dependent members of the household,

---

479 That is how Plato, too, regards the human society in his later works, proposing an ideal set-up in the *Laws*, designed to maintain this situation and prevent any further changes. His Utopian Magnesia must be self-sufficient, it must not have a coast, markets are to be held only three times a month and the citizens are not to engage in trade, that is restricted to the foreigners who come in for that purpose. Plato, as well as all the Utopists who came after him – all the way to Bernard Bolzano (*On the Best State*), or Friedrich Engels – have such a sceptical stance on trade and exchange because they rightly suspect that it will be exchange which will eventually bring this set-up down. The myth of the Golden Age connects its demise with shipbuilding and sea-faring (Ovid, *Metamorphoses* I.94nn).

who have thus far been completely excluded from public life. The heads of families require tradesmen and experts, who may not be their social equals but who are not totally interchangeable and replaceable slaves any more – they must possess a particular skill. The old landlord (or *despotés* in Greek, *paterfamilias* in Latin) thus loses his unlimited power over his subjects, and he must engage in negotiating with some of them at least.

This corresponds to a twofold parallel process, which Hegel encapsulated in the famous 'master and slave' dialectic.[480] On the one hand, the increasing complexity of life, its demands and needs, entwines even those who are 'free' into an ever thicker web of various dependencies, while the originally rightless menial labourers, or slaves, come to demand certain rights and freedoms. The emancipation of dependent persons was already underway in ancient times, and the majority of city dwellers in Late Antiquity were people who were perhaps not free in the full sense of the word, but certainly were not bound to any kin authority – the Roman *plebs*, and also those without property, *proles*[481], and eventually the proletariat. Those among them who got rich gradually wrested some political rights for themselves, while the rest had to look for a dependent livelihood. In the cities, though, these were no longer slaves,[482] although they were not free in the ancient sense of the word; they were dependent on others for their livelihood. Even in the Early Middle Ages, the landless tenant farmers, *coloni*, were allowed to start a family, and the relationship of unlimited 'service' was gradually transformed into one of contractually defined 'servitude', and eventually employment.

From the end of the 18th century onwards, this change was dramatically accelerated by the industrialisation of Western societies, and it is to Karl Marx's credit that he was among the first to notice it. While the vast majority of us nowadays make an 'independent' living, we do not

---

480 The passage from *Phenomenology of the Spirit* was probably inspired by a fragment of Heraclitus', 'War ... turns some into slaves and sets others free' (DK 22 B 53), Hegel develops it in another direction though: a slave becomes emancipated by acquiring skills, which at the same time makes the master dependent on him.

481 In Latin, *proles* means 'offspring', or 'descendants', originally unindividualised and dependent 'domestics' in any homestead – from children and the master's relatives, to slaves. A *proletarius* is then technically someone who does not have to pay taxes, serve in the army, and his only service to the state is having offspring.

482 There is no precise modern equivalent for the Greek *dúlos* or Latin *servus*. They, too, included dependent relatives, children, domestic servants, and later slaves at large estates. That is how Aristotle can on the one hand describe a slave as a 'living tool', and on the other maintain that a relationship between the master and a slave can be one of friendship (*Politics* I.6, 1255b).

live on what we have ourselves grown, nor do we exchange products: we enter into employment. We do not sell any commodities but rather we sell a portion of our life in the form of working hours, so that we can live the rest of the time as free citizens.[483] That is a profound intervention into human freedom, because an employee does not act in his or her own capacity, but fulfils tasks given out by someone else, being continuously managed and his or her performance monitored. It makes hardly any difference that we have freely chosen our employer – after all, often we have little choice in the matter.

Marx attempted to describe this new situation using the terms of 'alienation' (taken-over from Hegel) and 'exploitation'. As his starting point was Rousseau's concept of the 'natural state', where man live by the work of his own hands, he believed that the exploiter takes, or 'alienates', products from the worker, thus perpetrating violence and plain injustice. What Marx failed to recognise was that this change occurred right at the moment when production began to require many different workers and employees, from planning and funding, to the production itself, and eventually distribution and sales, so that no one person can claim any more that the product is 'theirs'.[484] The alleged 'alienation' then, is not caused by private ownership but by the increasingly complex division of tasks, which, while it may have degraded independent farmers and craftsmen to the position of dependent employees, nonetheless brought about the whole success of modern societies. For sure, a car or a computer cannot be produced by a craftsman alone, and while a single shoemaker cannot compete with the mass-producing shoe factory, it was the latter which made it possible for us all to wear shoes.

The very same process continues on to this day, and since the workers' movement of the 19th century gradually achieved a fairly extensive protection of employees, even the 'better off' would now regard 'dependent' employment in a different light than a couple of centuries ago. Many formerly independent professions – business people, doctors, lawyers, and others – are en masse turning into employees these days. The loss of a certain part of individual freedom is well compensated by considerable relief from worries and 'business risk', which is transferred

---

483 Kant seems to have realised that an employer uses his employees as a means, which is why he carefully states in the second formulation of categorical imperative that others should not be used 'merely as a means to some other end'.

484 Besides, agricultural farm hands were keen to offer themselves for employment in order to shake off the limitations and risks connected to independent farming, the burden of which they had to bear as well. A similar process is happening in modern-day China.

to the employer. The most acute problem of current wealthy societies is perhaps not so much exploitation, as it was in the 19th century Europe,[485] but unemployment, or (to put it provocatively) a lack of 'exploiters'.

Given the growing complexity of modern societies, and the practical interdependence of their members, this is perhaps unavoidable, and there are other aspects to take into account too. The tasks which are laid before business people, doctors, or architects nowadays can no longer be accomplished by a single person. They need other experts – 'specialists', as they are rather tellingly called nowadays. The activities we are able to perform are increasingly more specialised, and we would hardly be able to take them to the local marketplace and barter them for a loaf of bread. Correspondingly, hundreds, or perhaps thousands of people have been involved in the production of the things which we buy, products which have 'changed ownership' several times before they even get to us. But what kind of 'owner' is this? The companies which organise the production, trade, financing, or transport usually do not belong to a single person, but to trusts, banks or anonymous shareholders. Of course a trust or a bank does not decide what should be produced and using what materials, how to transport it where, but only which expert to hire into the management of the company in question, who they employ to make such decisions. This creates a special stratum of 'top managers', who often come from unrelated areas; they are not experts in production but in management.

Karl Marx also correctly noted that this process, which nobody thought up and which nobody directs, leads to an unprecedented accumulation of people and resources, which in real terms means accumulation of power. This give rise to global – and at the same time anonymous – players, whom the liberal economic theory still supposes to be driven by solely economic, or financial objectives, i.e. their own profit. In contrast to the carefully scrutinised political power, which is publicly held to account, the supposedly 'private' economic sector produces ever more gigantic 'powers' – and their inner working is nobody's business but their own. Only the stock markets keep a close eye at how well they are doing – in financial terms, naturally.

But as economic operations cumulate and optimise, these powers naturally gain influence over the sphere of public life and politics. They

---

485 Whereas in the other parts of the world we can even today realize, what the worker's movement was fighting against.

can be misused by politicians, just as easily as they can themselves try to use politics for their own, non-transparent aims. Marx's (or rather Hegel's) concept of alienation is certainly more pertinent here than in the relationship of a worker to 'his' products. The classic theory of the strict separation of the 'private' sphere of business from the 'public' sphere of politics has become disputable nowadays, and it appears more like a consoling relic of the old times, rather than a workable social theory.

But it was this theory that, in the wealthier parts of the world, helped to create living conditions that our ancestors could not even dream of. We may not always be satisfied with the range of options and possibilities open to us, or the level of security, comfort, and public services; but we would not wish to part with them. After the collapse of revolutionary theories and totalitarian regimes, which had promised so much, there is nothing better on offer than the time-honoured endeavour to keep the 'private' power of money in check by the public power of law. That is to say, try as we might to prevent attempts at hijacking the political power by the hidden, rather than 'private' power of money. One of the ways to ensure this could be through a better understanding of institutions and organisations, in particular the human relationships which surround them.

Citizen and Employee

We may spend half of our time as citizens in some form of privacy, where we may contemplate with Kant if all should obey his maxim, but as soon as we emerge from this private space, we meet people who are in a different situation. They do not act on their own behalf, but as employees of offices, organisations and businesses which are exempt from such considerations. And the same goes for us, when we step out of the privacy of our consumer life and step into the other half of our life, where we, as employees – shop assistants, drivers, office workers, or teachers – also act for and on behalf of someone else, and we only bear a limited responsibility for our actions in this capacity. If Smith or Kant would have to understand our situation, they would have to observe other environments, such as in the offices, or in the army. There they would, even in their day, find people like themselves, who were, however, obliged to comply with other people's orders, being answerable to those people, and often carrying out actions whose objectives and implications may not be clear to them, and for which they most likely cannot bear any normal human responsibility.[486] A police officer clearing a public area is acting on orders, just as a soldier, who may shoot somebody while on duty; he may well feel remorse, but we would not regard him as a murderer. The German philosopher Otfried Höffe uses the terms personal and institutional morality to describe this distinction, and its importance for practical philosophy. So how do the two differ?

The position of an acting citizen is characterised – as we have seen – by three essential features:

1. His decisions and actions are based on his own deliberation, he follows his own objectives and interests, his freedom may only be limited by law.
2. The property and resources he disposes of are his own, acquired rightfully and in accordance with good custom – whether these be possessions, skills, connections, or information.
3. As a citizen and a person, he is also able to check himself and he bears a clear personal responsibility for the consequences of his actions, both in the moral and legal sense.

An employee, on the other hand, is a dependent person, although nowadays not normally in the situation of a slave or a servant. Although he makes a living by acting in someone else's interest, he is not hired merely as an Aristotelian 'living tool', he is selected on the basis of their skills and competence, and it is expected that he will act as a more or less independently discerning human being, only following the employer's 'script and direction'. That makes an employee's position akin to that of a theatre actor, and that is why it is often referred to as acting in role.[487] The three above mentioned features look considerably different for a person in a role – whether hired, appointed, or providing only a specialist service:

1. He should act according to directions or orders provided by others, to follow objectives which they have set out for him, and to be mindful of their profit.

---

486 This is why the French revolutionary constitution, as late as 1795, denied the right to vote to servants, employees, and other dependent persons, among others.
487 In his renowned book *The Presentation of Self in Everyday Life*, Erving Goffman analyses everyday situations of work life from a 'theatrical perspective', on the basis of a metaphor of a theatre performance with a stage, set, an auditorium and dressing rooms. Although he repeatedly stresses that a 'role' is an integral part of human life, he occasionally tends to regard it only as pretence and sham.

2. While doing so, he works with property, information, and authority which do not belong to him and which have merely been entrusted to him for a particular purpose.[488]

3. He bears only a limited legal responsibility for his actions in that role, directly proportional to the extent of freedom of action.

This is, of course, a highly idealised description, but it does correspond to Kant's distinction between autonomy and heteronomy, as previously discussed. The extent of heteronomy is naturally great in a soldier, who simply obeys orders, as well as in a manual worker or a clerk, who carry out strictly defined activities, whose purpose they themselves may not comprehend. This is tied in with a low level of responsibility. Responsibility grows with the less narrowly defined relationships, for example management personnel, and it is directly proportional to the volume of the assets and authority entrusted to them.

It is therefore clear that the classic concept of freedom and its indivisible other side, i.e. responsibility, which practical philosophy traditionally draws upon, only applies to a limited extent, or not at all in the case of the actions of a dependent person acting in a role. By taking on a role, we considerably limit the freedom of our decisions, as well as the responsibility for their consequences, while pledging to carry out the particular role conscientiously and to use only the assets entrusted to us for the specified purpose. These are certainly much more complex and less palpable demands than the uncomplicated situation of two people haggling in a market place, each of them pursuing their own private interest.

* * *

We should however distinguish between the allocated and limited actions of, say, an administrative worker from another variant, namely actions in public matters, which are delegated by the public to their elected representatives. They differ in that the area of decision-making of members of parliament or council representatives is much broader, it cannot be clearly demarked, and also an MP does not make decisions on his or her own, but as a vote in a majority. Unlike a prime minister or a town mayor, this represents a typical example of collective decision-making, where apportioning the responsibility is extremely

488 In consequence, nor the fruits of his actions shall be his or her.

problematic.[489] A typical modern feature is also an even more hidden decision-making by various committees and experts, who do wield a significant influence on the outcome, but most certainly bear no responsibility for it.

Nowadays, we regard participation in public life at national, regional, and local levels as part of civic life, as a space for free actions, the Aristotelian *praxis*, which is an end in itself. This is also the principal reason why it is desirable for everyone to take part in political decision-making – albeit in a mediated form through elections and representative democracy.[490] But to execute the decisions it has made, political power must then employ bureaucratic organisations, which we regard as a means for achieving certain aims, namely the Aristotelian *poiésis*. Economic organisations, but to a certain extent also medical, cultural and educational ones, operate in the same way. As we wish to review and evaluate them based on their output and results, whether economic or other, their inner organisation should be guided by the requirement of the highest functionality and effectiveness. Similarly to the army, police, or a hospital, where the main goal is not the human self-realisation of the employees, but the effective performance of tasks, organisations typically have a hierarchic structure of authoritative subordination and superiority.[491]

Interestingly, both of these probably evolved from the most basic groupings of equals, whether driven by a specific (economic) purpose or more lasting and universal ones. This voluntary association for mutual or general benefit naturally comprises both aspects: the internal aspect of the fulfilment and satisfaction found in communal life and the external aspect of attaining objectives. On the one hand, there is a friendly circle, a club as an 'end in itself' of sorts, on the other there is a special-purpose association with clearly defined objectives. But it is exactly because these

---

489 This may be intentional with a firing squad, diffusing the individual responsibility of the members and allowing them to avoid feeling like executioners. Something similar also occurs in elections, where, however, political parties do bear a portion of responsibility, unlike in a referendum, where no individual or group can be assigned responsibility.

490 The concept of direct democracy is appealing in its simplicity. It does however have two important restrictions: firstly, it presupposes that the voters understand what they are making a decision on, and secondly, that no individual responsibility can be attached to the result.

491 Attempts to introduce democratic principles into the factories of Communist Yugoslavia (where elections to company management roles were offered in lieu of real political elections) were generally a failure. In contrast, the strategy of open management, whereby employees are continuously updated on important events and decisions, is nowadays still frequently recommended.

two aspects are not separated here, that voluntary associations and clubs offer fertile ground for the creation of more clearly-defined organisations, as well as a foothold for civic society. It has given rise to gradually broader civic organisations, from the bottom up, focused on areas of public life and politics, such as political parties; and also to organisations with clearly defined, and predominantly private aims.

Only when such groupings outgrow the narrow confines of friends and acquaintances do they need to be formalised, to create efficient hierarchies, and hire employees. The very fact that the majority of our contemporaries earn their living in employment illustrates how advanced this process is in modern societies. Modern public institutions and organisations bear hardly any traces of their roots in the sphere of friendly gatherings, which have been pushed ever further into the margins, an archaic remainder of another era.[492] But only this natural and friendly environment teaches people an understanding of the institutions of politics, community, and state as an expression of the shared interest and care for the whole, while all other perspectives may make them seem merely instruments of partisan or individual interest and domination.[493]

The growing number of organisations, and their seeming ubiquity, are proof of their growing importance in modern societies. Businesses, offices, associations, and other organisations nowadays effectively divide the whole sphere of public and social life, just as government does at the 'top' level with its subdivision into individual ministries. No alternatives seem readily available.

We encounter organisations with every step we take, in two quite different roles: as voluntary or involuntary users (and sometimes victims), and also as their representatives and stewards. In the former role, we approach them from the outside, as 'parties', we come into contact with their 'communication channels' – the registry, the communicating window, the visitors' waiting room, web pages and so on. Our contact with them is occasional and happens almost 'casually', without us gaining any deeper understanding of their working, or their purpose and the reason for their existence; after all, within this framework of division of social actions, they do not need concern us at all.[494] This naturally puts us at

---

492 In the Czech context, this is well illustrated by voluntary fire brigades, which in the 19th century played an important part in the organisation of Czech society, and nowadays still fulfil a vital public role.

493 According to Aristotle, 'between friends, there is even no need for justice' (*NE* 1155a26).

494 The special case of 'total organisations', such as prisons, mental asylums, hospitals, or boarding schools, where the 'inmates' are completely in their care, sometimes even for life, has been

a disadvantage when dealing with the employees of these organisations, that of 'information asymmetry': we are 'laymen', we are not familiar with the rules and regulations and so on.[495]

Often, we seek contact with organisations ourselves, as we happen to need something from them, but contact with state institutions can be enforced upon us. In such cases, we cannot chose who we deal with: clerks, judges, police officers and others are allocated to us – or perhaps *we* are allocated to *them*. Unlike 'private' organisations, or those run for profit, which gain their livelihood directly from their customers, and therefore have a specific interest in them, public organisations typically have no direct profit from us as 'parties', and therefore no personal interest in us – and, often, they let us know it. On the other hand, however, generalised gripes about 'impersonal' bureaucracy are not entirely justified: if the officials' interest in us became 'personal' (i.e. with a particular treatment or objective in mind) that would be far, far worse.[496]

In contrast to the more or less given framework of private life – family, home, childcare – which has been so long established that we consider it 'natural',[497] the origins of social institutions and organisations in the modern sense of the word are unambiguously cultural. They have a (more or less) clearly defined purpose and a history, so they are to a much greater degree in human hands. It follows, therefore, that the very terms *institution* and *organisation* do not refer to just any kind of arrangement, but only those which are able to reproduce themselves, managing to stay 'alive' across the lifespan of their individual 'carriers'. As Max Weber puts it, an estate only becomes an institution when its founders manage to secure its continuation – i.e. by obtaining its hereditary status. Thus on the one hand, people undoubtedly create organisations – possibly even without realising it – but on the other, institutions and organisations also give a 'harsh schooling' to their 'carriers' by promoting in them certain characteristics and suppressing others. In the end, only those which have managed to secure their perpetuation (found the right human carriers) will survive.

---

discussed by the just cited sociologist Erving Goffman in his book *Asylums: Essays in the Social Situation of Mental Patients and Other Inmates.*

495 That is why we hire legal representation in our dealings with the judiciary; in other areas, there are various agents, consultancy firms and the like.

496 Older generations in Central Europe could have experienced such 'personal' interest from the secret police.

497 This 'natural' aspect of social life has recently been brought to the fore by ethologists, see de Waal, *Good Natured.*

Acting in a Role

As we have seen, an organisation is a certain functional arrangement, whose carriers can only be specific (if replaceable) people: manual or office workers, policemen, judges, teachers, and so on. These people, or employees in general, are what the organisation is made of, therefore their attitude towards it is quite different. They typically work for a single organisation, which they have more or less freely chosen for a time and which requires them to perform certain activities, for which they are paid and for the performance of which they are entrusted with a portion of the organisation's 'information superiority', authority and resources. Employees are to use these within the remit of their assignment and in accordance with various rules and regulations, but with some degree of freedom. They act in accordance with their designated task (the 'script') and with their superiors (the 'directors'), as well with each other, but all the while as discerning human beings and not automata. We can, therefore, speak of them 'acting in a role'. The ability to communicate and a measure of self-control, rationality, sanity, and loyalty are implicitly required of every employee.[498]

* * *

Unlike private citizens, employees are involved in 'vertical' and asymmetric, non-reciprocal relationships with superiors and subordinates, as outlined by the structure of the organisation. Superiors delegate tasks to their subordinates, they evaluate and reward them, they apportion a degree of authority to them, and as the authority and resources in question are entrusted to them, these relationships too, are at risk of corruption (of which more later). This basic schema of issuing and carrying out orders in an idealised form turns the organisation into an immense power structure, as dangerous as it is efficient.[499] Fortunately, this ideal is seldom a reality, and the efficiency of an organisation is usually limited by various human factors, including common

---

498 In contemporary societies, lacking these qualities is possibly the biggest handicap, characterising many homeless people. An extensive survey of the 'clients' of one of Prague's charity organisations has recently shown that the only measurable parameter which significantly correlates with homelessness is a lack of formal education. See L. Prudký, *Kudy ke dnu* (*The way to the ground*).

499 One of the oldest applications of this scheme, the disciplined Greek *phalanx*, brought about a revolution in warfare.

sense.[500] Even orders are mostly given verbally, so each utterance almost automatically requires a response, opening an opportunity for discussion (with the exception of the military where 'Yes sir!' is the only answer expected or tolerated).[501]

In every organisation, everyday dealings between employees, superiors and subordinates are guided not only by rules and regulations, but also by established custom within the organisation, a strong sense of hierarchy (for example in the army, in banks, or in hospitals, but typically looser in environments such as factories or laboratories, where there is no contact with the customer). A part of this custom in some places is specific attire, or a uniform. Other issues, such as how much time can an employee spend on non work-related matters during working hours, how much scope for discussion with one's superior there is, or how to ask for a raise are all outlined by this established custom.

Apart from strongly asymmetric relationships of superiority and subordination, employees usually also inhabit 'horizontal' human relationships, not institutionally organised, with colleagues and co-workers; or competitive relationships with their rivals. Friendly, familiar collegial relationships, even if they are not always sincere, are characteristic of a workplace in post-communist societies, where these restricted communities for a long time substituted the lack of public space and the extremely regulated opportunities for gathering.[502]

Among the 'moral', i.e. individual requirements which organisations impose on their employees, reliability and conscientiousness are probably foremost. In the USA or Japan this list would be augmented by a high degree of loyalty to the business; in some companies (or jobs) inventiveness, resourcefulness, dedication, and a critical approach are desired. In places where employees handle money and valuables, honesty is valued highly, although the increasing demand for monitoring apparatus such as CCTV would suggest that it is in short supply. As almost every employment is a collective activity, and its success is largely dependent on good human relationships, employers also value pleasant personal

---

500 One such exception was probably the Prussian bureaucracy, based on military culture. The ideal type of compliant superior was referred to as a 'cyclist' under the communist regime: bent over on top, pedalling away down below.

501 Excepting special emergencies when there is no time for discussion. A soldier or a fire fighter cannot participate in a discussion while in action, the same goes for an airplane crew or a member of a surgical team.

502 A strong contrast is seen especially in the practice of American and Japanese firms. As convivial fun among sales personnel does not make a good impression on customers, some companies regulate that a sales person should for, say, ten seconds look a customer in the eye.

characteristics, such as directness or kindness. Although the salary is a substantial motivator for every employee, we should not overlook others, which, in some areas, might even outweigh it: a scientist's or a design engineer's fascination for their field, the personal interest of a teacher or a musician, or the human concern of a doctor.

The activity of an organisation as a whole also takes place in a sort of 'outer field' of evaluation and value, which happens at several levels. In the case of commercial and manufacturing companies, there is naturally competitiveness and corresponding advertisement campaigns, which strive to build the good name of a brand; the astronomical sums of money commanded by big brands suggest just what a crucial element of a successful strategy that is. Aside from that, many companies deliberately foster a sort of non-commercial image – for example by supporting charitable, cultural, or sporting events.[503] With educational, scientific and cultural organisations, reputation plays a key part; it is painstakingly built up on their expert competence, significant results and public successes – and it can be easily lost on the back of public scandal, plagiarism and the suchlike. The rather individual character of scientific work notwithstanding, it is quite obvious that the success of individual scientists is determined by the reputation of the organisation they work for; and its success is in turn determined by the decency of the actions of each and every one of them. As they are with increasing frequency mechanically evaluated on their 'outcomes', the quality of which cannot easily be judged, the temptation to cheat must be strong. Apart from the fear of being – in all unlikelihood – exposed as a fraud, it is countered only by the 'ethos' of scientific truthfulness.

All these various relationships place the acting person into a conflict of solidarities and loyalties, especially in higher posts, where a multitude of relationships are part of the role. As liberal societies try to curb authoritative decision-making and rely on free competition between partial interests, it also becomes increasingly difficult to find 'independent experts' who are able to carry out factual assessments of what is in the public interest.[504] But where to find independent experts in a society of dependents, and how to hold them under scrutiny, since they do not bear any responsibility? No decision-making can be made without experts and specialists, but if they are to offer advice on matters of public

---

503 Referred to as 'goodwill' in the English-speaking world.

504 Traditional societies relied on the 'elders' (Greek *presbyteros*, Latin *senior*), who are not as much caught up in their own affairs any more. In modern societies though, the elderly often do not understand the problems of the times.

interest, they are placed in a situation of conflict, and they should be well aware of it.

A banker or a businessperson acting as an advisor to state bodies, an expert on a tender committee, or a scientist passing judgment on the work of his or her colleagues are on the one hand beholden to those who entrusted them with the task to maintain their civic and professional integrity; but there are also strong personal interests, the interests of the organisation they work for, and possibly also pressure of professional solidarity, and other factors. Add to this the dilemma of a short- or long-term profit, both personal and to the organisation, the particular field, and society as a whole. For example, from a short-term point of view, it might be advantageous not to own up to a mistake, but by doing so, we run a long-term risk of the loss of credibility should our mistake be uncovered later, to say nothing of our having been caught lying and withholding information.[505] When major decisions are being made, we simply have to reckon with direct and indirect pressure from various pressure groups, lobbies, and so on. Those who have personally experienced this will be likely to be more reserved in uttering moral condemnation of politicians and high-level managers in general.

A person in a role is clearly not entirely autonomous, but functions as a component of complicated social machines – so complex that nobody understands all their details – without which we would most likely not be able to survive.[506] We may tell ourselves that they are human creations after all, and that we therefore hold the reins firmly in our hands; but if we had to answer the question of who really runs the state, we would soon realise that the answer is far from straightforward. Every schoolchild knows that, *de jure*, it is the government, a fairly clearly defined set of certain people. But is that really so? Even top politicians are people, just like us. They have their limitations, their interests and concerns, and they encounter various pressures – the higher their position, the greater these pressures are. Besides, each minister is at the helm of a vast and complex apparatus, which he must rely on, because it consists of people who – unlike the minister himself – have a deep, expert understanding

---

505 All major political scandals – from the Dreyfus affair right through to Watergate and into the present day – tend to quickly snowball out of control: the first mistake or deceit is covered up with more and more of the same, which eventually create a far worse effect that the original would have done on its own.

506 Herein may lie the root of the whole 'feeling of absurdity' and the bulk of the 20th century literature which grew from it. Its success proves that the feeling was real but the surge died down in the meantime – perhaps because we are beginning to better understand the complex relationships or because we have grown accustomed to their opacity.

of their particular sphere, as well as years of experience and contacts. Should an experienced ministerial official wish to push through a matter of personal interest, it would probably not be difficult to 'guide' the minister in that direction.[507] Who, then, runs the state?

Hence the demands on a person in a 'role', especially if they are not directly interacting with clients or parties, are different from those among equals in the private sphere. This is most obviously the case with officials, and those entrusted with power. G. K. Chesterton once wrote that if a drunk sticks his tongue out at a judge, the one thing the judge must not do is stick his tongue back out at him. The judge's authority is directly dependent on not descending to the same level as the accused, and maintaining the distance of his role. Nor can a policeman act according to the categorical imperative: he must act according to orders and rules, and if the subject uses violence, he must not 'reciprocate' with the same measure. For example, when taking measures against demonstrators, a police officer is required to suppress natural affections – getting hit by a stone should not stir up his natural anger, but rather he should maintain unshakable correctness and distance.

We have seen how highly real friendship is valued in private life, but if you are, for example, a member of a jury or a tender committee, any friendship displays are explicitly and strictly forbidden. It is no wonder, then, that in situations where private and institutional morality come into direct opposition people so easily and gladly forget about their roles and start acting as they were not inhabiting a role at the moment.[508] But, as the police informant Brettschneider in Jaroslav Hašek's novel *The Good Soldier Švejk* illustrates, the opposite can happen, too: some people can never step out of their role, it somehow sticks to them even in their private life. But perhaps this is a psychiatric issue rather than an ethical one, as these people lack the 'natural world' setting, where it would be possible to have a normal conversation with them.[509]

507 The British TV series *Yes, Minister* illustrates the risks of well-established bureaucracy – while in the Czech context, a new minister will first of all bring in new senior civil servants, which launches the civil service into rudderless chaos.

508 The importance of private interests of employees and people in public roles is the subject of study of the public choice theory. Chief contributors to the field are among others D. Black, G. Tullock, J. M. Buchanan and K. Arrow. The principal-agent problem theory on the other hand examines these relationships through a focus on information asymmetry.

509 The character of Bretschneider is clearly a caricature, but similar traits can – to a lesser degree – be observed in extremely ambitious people who are also permanently 'in a role' and follow a certain objective even in random personal encounters.

***

This brief overview of the situation of a person in different roles demonstrates that the problem of morality and ethics of acting in a role is anything but simple, particularly because it cannot be reduced to bilateral and symmetrical relationships between two parties. Nor do the golden rule or the categorical imperative apply here. Is it possible to find any basic and general rules for moral (if not necessarily good) action?

The first and simplest rule of institutional morality requires that a person can manage to strictly separate their own interest from their role. However, that is easier said than done, as there are two sides to everything and opportunity makes a thief. There is a temptation for stock keepers, sales assistants, or cleaners, but also for a traffic warden, with whom a guilty driver might want to make a deal – advantageous to both parties – just as they would in a market place. The requirement of separation does not only apply to obviously thievish or dishonest actions. If the mayor of a town receives a visit from a distraught woman with a crying child in her arms, he should certainly offer help – but not out of the municipal coffers. Whatever human emergency the matter might be, it is not a matter of public interest. The mayor would have to have the financial help approved by the councillors, who are not so completely autonomous and who might worry about their electorate objecting to such largesse: why help this woman in particular, and not someone else?[510]

The iron rule of separating what is our own from what has been entrusted to us, and the private person from the role within an organisation, is on the one hand a necessary condition for the smooth running of the organisation. But on the other hand, it excludes certain important human aspects from the behaviour of an organisation. Although a private business owner may wish to make a display of generosity, none of the employees of that business are entitled to act in such a way, not even the top managers. In state and public organisations, only sovereign citizens and 'tax payers' would have this autonomy, but it is impossible to ask them.

Even more serious is the flip-side of this separation, namely the demand of loyalty towards the organisation: an employee must reliably carry out orders given by his or her superiors. This too is a necessary

---

[510] Such objections vanish at times of great natural disasters when people suddenly become reminded of their togetherness.

condition for an organisation to function; it is, however, one with potentially horrifying consequences. The bigger the power and authority these people have been entrusted with, and the mightier the organisation they work for, the more horrifying these consequences can be. An extreme example of such strict separation is the figure of Adolf Eichmann, an unexceptional and inconspicuous person, and dutiful family man, who in his strictly separated role, became a symbol of the systematic genocide of European Jewry. He was captured by Israeli agents in Argentina in 1960 and taken to Jerusalem to stand trial for his part in the Holocaust. Eichmann himself was not an anti-Semite, and in his defence speeches, he repeatedly referred to Immanuel Kant. He appeared to sincerely believe that as a loyal (albeit high-ranking) official he was merely carrying out orders issued by his superiors, ensuring they were properly implemented. He was so convinced of this that he even told a journalist that he had failed in his duty when he helped three Jewish people to avoid the transports.

Hannah Arendt, who followed Eichmann's trial closely and wrote an exceptional book about it, came to this sobering conclusion: while one of the most heinous crimes in human history was carried out against a backdrop of widespread anti-Semitism, it was actually made possible by the terrifying discipline of hundreds of diligent officials.[511] A criminal state is not propped up by common criminals, nor by fanaticised masses, but by the servile functioning of quite ordinary people carrying out their inhuman roles.

This is an extremely valuable lesson, and one which does not only apply to Hitler's regime in Germany. Similar – although less tragic – situations occur in everyday life. The ever-increasing real power of organisations in modern mass societies is constantly in danger of being abused, and the effects can be devastating. As Niklas Luhman describes it, organisations create their own 'functional enclosure', so an ordinary citizen looking from the outside cannot see what is actually happening within. We have already mentioned that even dependent people within an organisation are often in the dark as to what ends are served by the tasks they carry out; they may well consider it to be someone else's problem. Moreover, they are bound by loyalty to the employer's rules, and perhaps also by a degree of solidarity with their fellow workers.

That can only apply up to a certain point though, beyond which people should understand that they are not living tools in the hands of their

---

511 Arendt, *Eichmann in Jerusalem*.

employer, and that even in their role, they remain free, and therefore responsible, human beings. If in this role, they detect serious wrongdoing which nobody else has noticed, they cannot keep that knowledge to themselves. Even keeping quiet about it ranks them among those committing the misdeed. This is a tall order, one requiring a large dose of courage, if not heroism. And the surrounding society must support them and protect them if need be. An employee of a chemical plant who 'blows the whistle' on incorrect or unethical activities must expect some retaliation from his or her superiors, and possibly from colleagues, too, whose life he or she has complicated. Whistleblowers must expect to be called names like 'grass' and 'snitch'. And yet this person is often the only one who can save the whole society from serious damage.[512]

The 'disjunction' of action and responsibility is one of the typical features of modern societies. We may all live as free citizens, but there are an increasing number of things which we cannot understand. We engage in the things which we do understand in our employment, but there, our options for action are limited. A person who buys a complicated industrial product cannot possibly have an idea of all its working parts, and whether any of it might be harmful or toxic. The worker who makes them has no real idea what he or she is making, and the design engineers who thinks them up are under strong pressure to keep that knowledge to themselves. Neither one nor the other, as an expert, is responsible for what he or she does, while private citizens will not even come close to such responsibility. Only insiders and experts who are willing to divulge such secrets to the media and the public – clearly crossing all institutional lines – can hope to remedy this situation.[513]

This, I believe, successfully rebuts the notion that personal morality and ethics can be replaced by rules and law in modern society. As I have tried to illustrate, the circumstances and relationships in these societies are so intricate and opaque, so frequently problematic, that requirements of good actions cannot be formulated as generally valid and enforceable rules. We can certainly not do without those, but they are not enough by

---

512 On the other hand, a false accusation of corruption is an easy and effective way of eliminating competition. The threat increases correspondingly to the importance of the post, thus contributing to many decent people's reluctance to take up such positions. Some then wonder how it is that most people holding high posts are overambitious and uncommonly thick-skinned individuals.

513 The fair-trade movement can serve as a recent example: the person buying coffee beans has no idea what was the coffee's 'journey' to the shop – and he or she may not care very much either. Only an insider will be aware of what a tiny percentage of the purchase price will be paid out to the growers – and therefore be in a position to try and reorganise the trade system.

themselves. They must first be applied, and therefore interpreted, both in the context of the whole legal system and in terms of 'good manners', on which there must be a certain degree of social consensus.

Corruption

With the increase of indirect, mediated relationships and of delegated authority and entrusted assets, the possibility of their misuse – what we normally call 'corruption' – also grows.[514] The term is almost exclusively used for the misuse of entrusted assets and powers to gain unlawful privileges. Some definitions narrow it down to such misuse solely in state and public office, which however does not cover the significant corruption in sport, or cheating and bribery in the business environment.[515] Other definitions emphasise misuse for personal or private gain, but that would exclude the particularly significant corruption within political parties, whose exponents do not acquire 'dirty money' for their own private use but for the party's.[516] As all these occurrences share common features, we will adhere to the wider definition, adding just one other obvious feature: corrupt actions must always be conducted covertly. Just as 'dirty money' is usually characterised by nobody wanting to own up to it, so that they do not have to explain where it came from, a telling symptom of corruption is its 'photodysphoria'.[517] The best remedy to counter corruption is therefore transparency, and perhaps even the need to make relevant information available to the public.

514 Corruption derives from the Latin *corruptio*, the verb *co-rumpere*, 'to destroy', 'spoil', 'distort'. This highly-charged word was already employed as a technical term for bribery in Antiquity, which seems to support the conjecture that it was a serious issue even then. Cicero drily notes that 'people admire especially the man who is indifferent to money' (*De officiis*, 2.38).

515 For example Frič & Kabele, in P. Frič (ed.), *Korupce na český způsob* (*Corruption – the Czech way*), p. 13. The proposal of the UN Convention defines it more broadly as on the one hand 'the promise, offering or giving of an undue advantage to the official himself or herself or another person or entity, in order that the official act or refrain from acting in the exercise of his or her official duties', and on the other 'solicitation or acceptance of an undue advantage, for the official himself or herself or another person or entity in order that the official act or refrain from acting in the exercise of his or her official duties' (Ibid. P. 18). The definition looks too long-winded but due to the incorporation of 'intention', it can distinguish a corrupting gift or promise – given in advance – from a gift given as an expression of gratitude.

516 For example 'Transparency International' defines corruption as 'abuse of entrusted power for private gain' (quoted Ibid. p. 19).

517 'Corruption does not like to be seen' (M. Burian in P. Frič et al., *Korupce na český způsob*, p. 293).

The issue of corruption plagues modern societies the world over, wealthy and poor alike. A certain correlation between poverty and the degree of corruption, and how it is viewed by the members of that particular society, can be interpreted in various ways.[518] On the one hand, there is the conviction of the whole moral tradition from Plato to Friedrich von Hayek, as summed up by Socrates: 'I tell you that virtue does not come from money but from virtue comes money and all other good things to man, both to the individual and to the state.'[519] On the other hand, there is the theory of 'primary accumulation', which maintains that, through accumulation of capital, an improvement of morals will eventually be achieved. In post-communist countries, this theory was often mentioned in the context of privatisation. We also have a socio-psychological theory at our disposal: the Corruption Perceptions Index (CPI), which does not measure actual levels of corruption, but rather how corruption is perceived within the society. Thus, it tends to indicate the level of mutual distrust, in poorly organised societies of course high.[520]

Before we look in detail at the various forms of corruption, we ought to note the obvious fact that corruption (unlike theft or embezzlement) always involves at least two parties: the 'corrupter' and the 'corruptee', if you will. Instances of corruption may take the form of various offers, persuasion, and temptation, or a straightforward exchange of the *quid pro quo* variety, or even the sinister methods of blackmail and threats. The external, forensic perspective of the police or the courts must however be limited to provable facts or events, which severely restrict its differentiation ability. The inventiveness of corruption seems almost limitless, but it should be noted that not every gift or 'handout' is a sign of corruption. A distinction should always be made between a suspicious gift presented beforehand, just 'to be noticed', and a gift given perhaps as an expression of gratitude after a successful surgery, although that too could be construed as keeping one's side of a prearranged, and therefore corrupt arrangement.

Corruption is typically instigated by someone who needs something and often cannot achieve it by regular or opens means. Petty corruption is, therefore, rife wherever there is a shortage of some kind, whether it is goods, an administrative act, a university degree, or a job promotion. Such shortages may actually be 'cultivated' by officials, especially if the

518 Cf. the graph in the quoted book by P. Frič et al., p. 281, source not given.
519 Plato, *Apology*, 30d.
520 On criticism of CPI (Corruption Perception Index) see *A User's Guide to Measuring Corruption*, UNDP 2008.

supplicants have no other recourse. There are also examples in the literature of officials themselves offering such services, with these 'offers' seamlessly changing into blackmail and threats.[521] It is more common however that the instigator must, not without risk, seek out a suitable partner. Much then depends not only on the legislation and the functionality of the justice system in the given society, but also on how the society, including the perpetrator's closest environment, looks upon such behaviour. It clearly matters whether you have to keep such actions secret even from your closest friends and family, or whether you can openly boast about them in the pub.

Petty everyday corruption can easily come from familial and friendly relationships. In traditional societies – as we have seen – kinship solidarity was one of the most basic human obligations, and if such societies rapidly adopt bureaucratic forms of government, this solidarity will smoothly metamorphose into corruption.[522] After all, no society has as yet managed to completely eradicate mild forms of favouritism, and it is likely that no society ever will. In typically modern situations, on the other hand, such as 'publishing shortages', or the awarding of research grants, there arise completely fresh forms of corruption, such as promoting one's students or friends, or a particular scientific school of thought. Unlike shortage situations, where customers bribed the shop assistants, nowadays there are various common ways of bribing the customer, especially distributors in foreign markets. Indeed, in some countries, firms are allowed to write this 'expense' off from their taxes.[523]

We have already established that initiating a corrupt relationship carries a certain risk. If petty corruption is widespread within a society, chains of connections and 'reliable partners' begin to form in order to reduce such risk. Sociologists speak of a 'stage of spontaneously regulated corruption', which can evolve into a stage of organised corruption when these chains actively seek out 'clients'.[524] This dangerous process, which gives rise to a general climate of corruption, is, according to Weinberg and Rubington, based on three main factors: a collision of several social cultures (such as kinship and bureaucracy), the failure of the legitimate channels, and an absence of regulatory control. From our own recent

---

521 Bodrock, 'Die Erpressung', in *Harvard Business Manager. Ethik*, Hamburg 2009.

522 See a very enlightened expose of the Chinese situation in Yan, *The Flow of Gifts*.

523 Cf. M. Burian, 'Korupce ve světě (Corruption in the world), in P. Frič et al., *Korupce na český způsob*, pp. 255–293.

524 Frič a Kabele, 'Korupce jako sociální fenomén (Corruption as a social phenomenon)', in: P. Frič et al., *Korupce na český způsob*.

experience in the post-communist world, we could add exceptionally rapid changes of ownership, such as took place during privatisation: the urgent need to change the ownership structure of the whole economy presented an unparalleled impulse to create widespread corruption networks, no matter how politicians vowed to fight it.

At the other end of the spectrum, there is 'big' corruption, such as when political parties obtain funds for their increasingly expensive election campaigns by courting 'willing' big business – whether by tailor-made legislation or granting public tenders and so on. Professional mediators come into play here, and where the stakes are high enough, the underworld and the mafia will often act as the executive power. This 'big' corruption, often sprouting from the fertile ground prepared by petty corruption, may so transform the situation in society that it infiltrates even those state organisations which are supposed to fight against it. But for all that, the apocalyptic images of the state completely usurped by mafia are not entirely convincing. The mafia is such a parasitic structure that it needs a more or less functioning state for its activities – for example, in order to allow its members to enjoy their profits in peace and security. So even in a worst-case scenario, they will behave rather like the sabre wasp larva which feeds of a caterpillar in such a way that no vital centres are damaged.

Yet another form of corruption is misuse of state structures by top politicians. On the Czech political scene, we have seen large contracts being tendered out in unclear circumstances, as well as undue influence exerted on the prosecutor's offices or the police. R. Brooke mentions an interesting case from London: in 1978 and in 1990, two Tory-led local councils decided to privatise tens of thousands of council flats to attract wealthier people into these boroughs and thus avoid losing the impending election. This did indeed lead to electoral victory in both cases; it also led to criminal investigations and convictions. In other countries, constituency boundaries have been redrawn for the same purpose, a move which would be hard to prosecute.

Although individual forms of corruption are extremely varied, corruption can only occur in situations when people are handling money, authority or other resources that have been entrusted to them. While this is usually regulated by a set of rules, there must be some scope for the individual employee or official to exercise certain discretion. One of the ways to counter corruption would then be to further specify the rules and regulations; this would however make the running of an organisation more difficult and might in the end have the opposite effect:

what cannot be achieved legally, needs must be delivered through corruption.[525] It is also true that excessively detailed rules make people 'unlearn' responsibility, so they may in fact undermine moral constraints which people would otherwise feel. As Kant says: 'People like to stick to the rules so that it would appear that they have a character... because they do not trust their own judgment that they would be able to make decisions without them.' [526]

The opposite strategy is to strengthen independent assiduity and responsibility – by providing further qualifications, good salaries, a guarantee of steady employment and so on. An ideal balance between the two strategies will be different in a small business where everybody knows each other and there is no one who would write the rules, in a large bank with many employees and branches, and finally in the vast organisation of government administration, where good organisational rules are a must. "Young' organisations which must rely fairly heavily on improvisation can live off their 'founders' élan' of shared worries and first successes. Sooner or later though, they will reach the stage of consolidation, which inevitably requires the introduction of rules and monitoring procedures. As well as preventative control devices such as group decision-making, approving larger projects in stages, and a requirement of detailed documentation, subsequent checks are usually also introduced, and eventually sanctions.

A certain degree of regular subsequent checks is necessary in any organisation, although its effectiveness is diminished by its regular pattern. On the other hand, random and unexpected checks can evoke an atmosphere of 'policing' and in the long run undermine the employees' loyalty. If the management and employees engage in a game of 'cops and robbers', it will antagonise both groups towards each other, which can bring nothing positive to the organisation. Although it might at a casual glance seem that the sanctions should be as tough as possible, the general experience concurs with the opinion offered by penology, that exceedingly harsh sanctions make the job of uncovering corruption much more difficult, as the perpetrators will take greater pains to avoid being found out.[527] Natural human solidarity among employees – highly developed in our part of the world, as we have already mentioned – also presents an obstacle

---

525 Hasty and rash 'anti-corruption' rules can actually in the end lead to dutiful officials breaking these in the interest of the matter at hand, even if that means risking prosecution and punishment. Only a very conscientious judge can distinguish such cases.

526 Kant, *Lose Blätter*, Nr. 1159, AA XIV, p. 513.

527 Cf. expert discussions on the subject of capital punishment.

and makes bosses to stick up for the culprits and defend them against 'attacks from the outside'. After all, they have their own reasons for it: they depended a good deal – as we have seen – on their subordinates and to replace an experienced team manager or official is no easy task.

Researchers who study corruption cite a superficially surprising experience, and that is that even public officials frequently are not at all aware of their corrupt actions.[528] But we should bear in mind that humans naturally live '*teleologically*' – they follow specific objectives. In private life we act based on our own decisions and the traditional morality which we are guided by, does not take into account regulations and handling entrusted assets. As we have established, opportunities for corruption are manifold and we can often find ourselves in situations which we are not prepared for. In any case, nearly all experts agree that the first step to curbing corruption is through a sort of edification – clarifying and explaining when corruption occurs and why.

Some organisations, such as banks, are entirely dependent on the trust of their clients. They therefore try to influence the behaviour of their employees directly through various ethical codices, which are nowadays also becoming increasingly important in medicine, biology and law. Such actions are not dissimilar to the purpose of this book – and similarly, they can be regarded with scepticism. If anybody expected that the employees who have undergone such training would never cheat again, might have a surprise coming, the critics will argue. But their objective can also be more modest and realistic, simply to remind where and how (im)morality manifests itself in their everyday activities and that while morality or ethics cannot be weighed or measured, nevertheless, it wields a strong influence over us and sometimes actually impacts on measurable factors, too.[529]

Institutions as Inheritance

Public institutions do not enjoy very much popularity in our modern times, particularly among young people. Perhaps therein lies the enduring charm of westerns and gangster movies – they are set in an 'organisa-

---

528 'Many MPs have no idea that they are acting in a way which could be construed as corruption,' says M. Hunt of the British House of Commons, in Chapman (ed.), *Ethics in Public Service*, p. 53.

529 This is well illustrated by the detailed manuals issued e.g. to pilots or nurses. Simple reiteration of seemingly obvious tasks which 'everybody knows' may appear like a formality but it has been proven to actually reduce the number of air accidents and unsuccessful operations alike.

tion-free' situation, where people act for themselves and based on their own decisions, and there is a clear-cut distinction between heroes and villains. That is something which is lacking in modern reality – partly because it has become so densely intertwined with impersonal organisations.[530] They are omnipresent and matter-of-course, at best grey and uninteresting, often dull, cold, even pointless. In a famous quote, Nietzsche likened the state to 'the coldest of all cold monsters'.[531] If you add to that the countless occasions of misuse (for the majority of seriously large-scale villainy has been committed and is still committed through organisations) it is no wonder that the general public do not have a high opinion of such institutions.

Contrast that with this surprisingly unambiguous statement by Heraclitus: "The people must fight for the law as for the city wall.'[532] This, I think, expresses the perception of a person who could still imagine a city 'without law'– he may have even personally experienced it. Modern societies may no longer rely on the city walls but anybody who has experienced, if only temporarily, a 'lawless' society – during the war, after a natural disaster, or a revolution – will clearly understand his warning. Emile Durkheim called this state *anomy* and he devoted his writing to discover how to prevent it.

Our generations in this part of the world have been largely spared the experience of a war defeat or a radical revolution manifested in a total collapse of social institutions. The war happened a long time ago now, and it did not affect the Czech lands nearly as much as it did most of Europe. We are fortunate not to live in an earthquake zone and have so far not been a target of a terrorist attack. But it only takes a fairly local and temporary occurrence, such as a gale-force wind or a flood, for us all to suddenly realise all the things that we take for granted in our everyday life – and we quite spontaneously turn to the public institutions to fix it: how come the electricity is off, why is there no running water and why have the trains been cancelled? In France, where large-scale strikes are part of life, the railways and municipal transport systems sometimes appear to have been afflicted by just such a catastrophe, and the public

---

530 Hegel actually believed that 'Once the state has been founded, there can no longer be any heroes. They come on the scene only in uncivilised conditions' (*Philosophy of Right,* § 93, addition). As any large-scale disaster shows, this is not true, but it does very precisely capture the direction of 'institutional' thinking: it is the task of organisations to make sure that there is no need for heroes. Cf. a surprisingly 'bourgeois' utterance from the German dramatist Bertold Brecht: 'Pity the country that needs heroes.'

531 *Thus Spoke Zarathustra*, I.11.

532 Heraclitus, Fragment DK 22 B 44.

view them in that light. In countries where the state has recently collapsed, it is fairly certain that at least the current generation will not forget about it quickly; and the authoritarian tendencies in countries such as Russia make great play of these experiences.

Public organisations are very powerful and, under normal circumstances, the incessant complaints from the general public or the revelation of various scandals are not enough to put them in serious danger. The real danger lies elsewhere, namely in the sweeping disdainful indifference, which is precisely what makes it possible for them not to function properly. If everything is corrupt and rotten to the core, how can you be surprised? That is why it is well worth reviewing the function of institutions from another angle. Organisations – both public and private – are, on a higher, more general level, a part of the division of activities. Private, for-profit organisations try to capture and organise our needs ('demand') and their success depends on how well they manage to do that. The current distribution of workforce suggests how this 'demand' has changed: about 3 % of the Czech workforce presently work in agriculture and mining, about 33 % work in manufacturing. All the rest work in the 'service' sector, which includes services provided by the state. Each of these fairly broad sectors is subdivided into hundreds and thousands of individual businesses and organisations, who contribute to them with an ever more sophisticated division of tasks.

A testimony to the efficacy of this arrangement is the vast difference between societies where the majority of people subsist, i.e. make their living individually and independently of others, as traditional farmers, and societies with a highly advanced division of labour. The former are referred to euphemistically as 'developing' countries, possibly because they are, with all their might, trying to get out of this state of things and to 'develop', above all, the division of labour. The first step, as we have seen, was the early Neolithic specialisation of crafts, followed by the division of individual operations in factories, and also the division of activities between businesses and organisations. In the for-profit sphere, where modern societies rely on the influence of the free market, this system is uncompromisingly enforced by the principles of modern economics. Whatever we may think of them, we would have to concede that owing to advanced specialisation and institutionalisation, a considerable part of the world's population has experienced an unprecedented rise in living standards.

But for the economy to function, public institutions must provide a framework of certain basic conditions: peace, security of the individual and property, effective law enforcement, a stable currency and many other conditions, which must, in principle, be kept separate from the profit motive. The task of the police force, law courts, or the army is most certainly not to make a profit, but rather to provide such conditions as would allow others to focus on making a profit. Adam Smith was already aware that this includes a broad infrastructure and certain public assets which are 'indivisible' (in the modern sense), and which we would want everyone to have access to, including the less successful: healthcare and education, a certain level of social care, and care for the environment.

So here, too, an advanced institutional specialisation is required, but we must search for ways to improve its functionality without the automatic pressure of economic competition.[533] No matter that organisations tend to be conservative, they are after all cultural products, too, and therefore should be passed on, developed, criticized, and transformed to suit the changing times. There is no doubt that we need public institutions on a daily basis in order for them to professionally maintain the running of society.

In our context of practical philosophy, we should however not overlook another aspect of their activity, and that is a certain division of responsibilities. Just as the increasingly more complex coordination of all aspects of human societies requires to be provided by specialised organisations, the increasing volume of cumulative cultural 'inheritance' is out of the reach of individual or voluntary groups. It is easy to trace the historical origins of this situation: up until the end of the 18th century, exceptional polymaths, versatile 'Renaissance men', such as Aristotle, Leonardo da Vinci, Leibniz, Goethe, or Kant, could still attempt to encompass the whole of culture. Since the early 19th century though, such attempts have been regarded as a sign of naive dilettantism.[534] Diligent care for the maintenance, critical refinement, and transmission of culture in the broadest sense is no longer possible without appropriate division of responsibilities. It was perhaps Kant who first realised this when, in

---

533 Much has been written on the topic of how market economy needs an 'extra-market' social and legal framework and possibly correction. See Sokol, *Moc, peníze, právo* (*Power, money and law*), esp. chap. 12.

534 It is also beyond any doubt that this situation poses a serious problem for cultural transmission, and it very likely requires new, better-informed versions of 'dilettantism' or 'popularisation' – some philosophers and philosophically-minded scientists provide a good example. In this sense, we should perhaps also amend Husserl's attempt to reform sciences, as proposed in *The Crisis of the European Sciences*: a shared common ground of understanding is not so much needed by sciences for their own inner goings-on, it is however badly needed in order to pass on knowledge and learning, not just in scientific areas but in public institutions as such.

the introduction of a polemical treatise on a dispute between faculties, he praised the university for attempting to divide academic work 'almost as in a factory' into individual fields. The professors of each discipline are something like a public 'depository' and, as a whole, they represent the 'sum of learning' thus entrusted to the university.[535] People who work in the individual fields, making their livelihood in that way, at the same time take on a particular responsibility for 'their' discipline.[536] Without such practical division, any general declarations of cultural responsibility and learning as a whole are rather unrealistic, certainly ineffective, and therefore in a sense irresponsible.

* * *

As we have seen, public institutions are endowed with considerable amount of power and assets, which inevitably attracts droves of predators, too, intent on plundering rather that maintaining them. The low level of interest among the general population in institutions as such only makes it easier for them. There is one other reason why institutions are more vulnerable than other parts of the human inheritance. Young children are able to attract attention to their needs, and love of children – our own but to a certain extent of other people's too – is part of our basic natural equipment. Various areas of economy, science, and culture are also attractive enough to draw in 'fresh blood'. But who will take care of the grey, mundane public institutions, so that they do not fall prey to voracious predators?

The English doctor and agnostic T. H. Huxley reminded his readers that 'virtue and goodness' strictly demanded 'that each man who enters into the enjoyment of the advantages of a polity shall be mindful of his debt to those who have laboriously constructed it; and shall take heed that no act of his weakens the fabric in which he has been permitted to live.'[537] Nobody questions the need to criticise public institutions: they

535 '... den ganzen Inbegriff der Gelehrsamkeit gleichsam fabrikenmässig, durch Verteilung der Arbeiten zu behandeln' (Kant, 'Der Streit der Fakultäten', in *Werkausgabe* XI, p. 279). Kant also mentions that beside those organised in a 'guild', there are freelance ('*zunftfreie*') learned people who either come together under the umbrella of various academies or societies, or they ply and further their field of science individually, as amateurs (*Liebhaber*).

536 This is still – albeit in a general manner – incorporated in the graduation pledge at Charles University. Sadly, it is read out in Latin, and therefore most of the participants are unaware that by joining the 'guild' of the learned, they each accept responsibility for how they manage the very specific cultural assets entrusted to them.

537 Huxley, *Evolution and Ethics*.

often deserve criticism. Nevertheless, we should expect more of educated people – after all, it is they who are most dependent on the quality of such institutions. In every society, there are plenty of people who might quite happily do without public freedoms, and who will get what they need no matter what the regime. But for intellectuals, scientists and artists, freedom is of the utmost importance, and if they do not want to spend their lives barred from what they do and reduced to cleaning windows or stoking boilers, they should pay closer attention to public institutions – offering criticism rather than just generalised moaning and grumbling. After all, as Cicero quite bluntly reminds us philosophers, for the matters of public interest, it is not enough to 'dispute in our dens' but our ideas should be realised in the running of the *polis*.[538]

4.5 Summary

The increasingly complicated organisation of the modern world forces us to live in a dual mode. On the one hand, our ancestors won for us our privileges of individual freedom (available, ideally, to all); but on the other hand, the indispensible division of labour compels us to combine our individual freedoms in large-scale, fixed organisations. Most of us also have to learn to act in this dual mode of the private heir and the contractually entrusted steward. In one mode, we live our own personal life, we act for ourselves, handle our own possessions, and bear an undivided responsibility for both. In the other, we accept an authorised role, we carry out allotted work according to someone else's will, we handle entrusted assets and exercise entrusted powers, for which we bear responsibility defined by the scope of our limited freedom of decision-making. The ability to distinguish between the two is a natural presupposition for the successful running of the modern society. Organisations cannot tolerate their employees handling that which has been entrusted to them as if it were their own.

Acting in organisations is guided by established customs and rules; the aim of these customs and rules is to support their activities and the achievement of stipulated goals: productivity, diligence, and reliability (in public organisations also impartiality and transparency). From a purely sociological point of view – such as Luhmann's theory of systems for example, which methodically excludes the acting people as in-

---

538 Cicero, *De re publica* I.2.

dividuals – it might seem as though these rules could completely replace morality and ethics. Practical philosophy should certainly not accept this viewpoint – just as an acting person should not. In recent times we have experienced some egregious examples of the complete 'functional enclosure' of institutions and organisations, and a totalitarian regime or a concentration camp cannot be made legitimate because of how perfectly they function, i.e. achieve their goals. Organisations need permanent control and criticism – including criticism of their goals. That cannot be achieved through any number of rules, but through the vigilance of people who are well-informed about their running. So not even when acting in a role can we be absolved of our unconditional human responsibility for what we participate in through our actions. And it makes no difference that applying this responsibility in mass, organisation-based societies is much more difficult, and that it itself requires a certain cooperation and a level of organisation.

Neither can the concept of inheritance and the responsibility for inherited assets substitute ordinary, indivisible human morality, as it has been developed and nurtured by religious movements and philosophical schools for millennia. It would be self-defeating to emphasise the importance of inheritance, while ignoring that which inheritance itself stems from. We have observed how various starting points and approaches to practical philosophy complement each other: Kant's starting point of rationality and equality, and the notion of moral sense amending and complementing each other. The criterion of utility necessarily needs the counterbalance of conscience and honour, so that it does not turn into the concept of 'the end justifying the means.' The Stoic morality of virtue must be complemented by the eudaimonic notion of happiness, and *vice versa*, otherwise it would become a sort of violation of life, as Nietzsche very aptly noted. This counterbalance is equally necessary for all kinds of hedonism, which are based on a false conception of humanity and promises something which it cannot deliver. 'It is not better for men to get all they wish to get', as Heraclitus already knew, and if the end purpose should be to just take pain and suffering away, we would have to concede, in the end, that the best solution to life is (painless) death.[539]

The complementary, indeed partial nature of moral theories also explains why diligent practical philosophy is unable to answer concrete questions with concrete answers. On the contrary, its task is to remind us that even seemingly unambiguous situations can be regarded from vari-

---

539 Fragment DK 22 B 110.

ous angles and that 'good' decision-making is almost always problematic; if we achieve something, we must often reconcile ourselves to losing something else. The understandable desire to simplify decision-making – especially by converting it to a single parameter, for example of money and price – is in fact a distortion of the true situation. An acting person will never be able to completely avoid this, but should however be aware of it. This is, after all, why political decisions are decided by vote, or why court rulings are made by a judge, a live person able to consider all the incommensurable pros and cons, and not a computer.

The ancient concept of 'inheritance' as the responsible handling of one's life and the world can be found in virtually all human cultures. Much as it has been misused in various ways over the course of history, and as much it has been programmatically suppressed in modern times, it can complement this polyphony with elements which are nowadays markedly absent from it. In an unexpectedly expanded form, augmented by the scientific study of living organisms, it above all disabuses practical philosophy of modern-age anthropocentrism, renewing the notion of our belonging to, and solidarity with, the world. If there is any 'positive knowledge' which practical philosophy can lean on, is it this. As it is grounded so deeply in pre-human reality, it is not weighed down by any cultural exclusivity. However, the concept of inheritance stresses the irreplaceable role of man and human culture in contrast to biological reductionism, and to the non-human nature and the world. Unlike the one-sided focus on morality and law, which regards morality merely as a restriction, it offers to each human life a sense of orientation and purpose. In contrast to the myopic concentration on various problems and pseudo-problems of the day, it bears in mind the view to the future, which is beyond our individual lives, without suffering from the shortcomings of naïve fetishes of 'progress'.[540]

---

540 That this, too, should be incorporated in the study of practical philosophy is expressed by Kant in his third question: 'What may I hope?' (*Critique of Pure Reason*, A 805, AA III).

5. Conclusion

Unlike individual sciences, which strive to amass factual knowledge, and in so doing to expand human possibilities, practical philosophy poses the question of how to utilise these possibilities. To quote Socrates, it asks 'how we should live'. As human possibilities have changed dramatically throughout history, practical philosophy cannot be expected to provide a definitive solution to this basic quandary of human life. On the contrary, it must confine itself to searching for and offering rules and points of view which we can apply in our evaluations and decision-making. There is no pressing need for philosophical ethics in times of stability, when everyone knows what they should and should not do, but it is needed in times of change when there is a lack of respected authority and role models, and when opinions differ. It is precisely because human judgment and action is always set within a society, and yet in unstable times there is an absence of commonly recognised authority and models, that we need philosophy: that is to say, we need clarifying terms and the search for universally plausible reasons and arguments.

Over the past two and a half thousand years, practical philosophy has amassed an array of views, many of which are still relevant, but which we must nonetheless critically appraise, organise, complement and expand to fit the new situation. Our rapidly-changing world brings with it several challenges: apart from a weakening of traditional authorities, also a categorical requirement of universality, and as well as new demands, there are new scientific discoveries which it is necessary to take into account. All this strengthens the importance of practical philosophy, despite its notorious weakness and limited effectiveness in comparison with traditional – especially religious – morality.

A necessary prerequisite of philosophical thinking is the clarification and distinction of basic terms, in our case terms such as freedom, morals, morality, and ethics, and especially life, a term which plays an important part in this work. The world which, when viewed from close up, seems merely to change, in the eyes of modern science also evolves – that is, forms a vast, yet closely-knit whole, an irreversible event. Practical philosophy can then no longer regard man as a being strictly separated from the whole of life as such but rather as a part of it – albeit a very specific part. Even a cursory glance at the phenomenon of life has revealed to us the aspects of finiteness, dependency, self-regulation, reproduction, and evolution, which can play an important part in philosophical argumentation.

On the other hand, practical philosophy must stand up to all attempts to reduce man to a 'mere animal'. It cannot overlook the obvious fact that man is a social creature in a much stronger sense than the ant, the bee, or the wolf. The cultural development of man and mankind certainly follows from his biological evolution; it is however not only guided by the given conditions but also by more or less conscious goals, often actively going against the perceived 'nature' of the reductionists. It has, over the course of human history, been taking over the initiative and it clearly has the upper hand in the sphere of social evolution.

While modern-age man has achieved some remarkable successes and has created a flattering notion of an absolutely independent, self-sufficient and autonomous individual, this ideal has become increasingly divorced from reality. In spite of the unparalleled emphasis on freedom, autonomy and individuality which characterises our times, we live in ever more complex dependencies on thousands of other, mostly anonymous people, without whom we would not be able to manage. Nor can practical philosophy nowadays be content with the model of the individual as an absolute starting point, one making decisions and acting purely of his own accord and for himself; none of us can live in that way. More and more, we live off things and impulses created for us by others, and we spend a considerable part of our lives in the service of organisations, where we are not our own masters – nevertheless we would like to remain free within them too.

Apart from this excursion into the sphere of institutions and organisations, I have tried to enrich the repertoire of practical philosophy by including the topic of inheritance. This is a principle which is closely related to the area of life, to genetic 'heredity', though it is significantly altered by the fact that man is aware of this inheritance and has reflected upon it ever since ancient times. The modern age has however also seen the factual content of this 'heritage' dramatically broadened: it can no longer mean passing down a portion of land and customs within one family, but it should encompass all that constitutes our daily lives and all that has been handed down to us through generations – primarily the language, culture, law, science, institutions and organisations without which the relatively safe and comfortable life of the wealthy part of the modern world would be unthinkable.

We may have taken over this immeasurable wealth, continuously enriched by new artistic, scientific, and technical output, for free but certainly not only for our own use and consumption. By taking it on, we have also accepted the responsibility to develop it, critically refine it and to pass it on to those who will come after us. This truly unlimited responsibility is not merely a burden, a limitation of our possibilities; it could actually provide a shared sense of purpose to our lives, something which is very often missing from modern life. I consider the fact that at least some our contemporaries have begun to realise that the cornerstone of this 'heritage' is life itself, the Earth and nature which carries and sustains us, to be the most significant moral progress of modern humanity.

* * *

The author first embarked on this adventure many years ago with 'awe and trepidation' and he kept putting off the task of writing this book, as he was hoping to prepare the ground for it with his previous books on the human person, on time, on religion, and on the social power and law. This is by way of an explanation and an apology for referring to them so frequently. Finally, I would like to:

- apologise to those who have been disappointed by the book's generalist approach;
- thank those who inspired me to write this book, and who have also helped me, especially by providing invaluable criticism; and
- apologise to all those whose books I should have read and yet have not.

My final wish for this book is that it may find readers who will take something from it.

Prague, August 2010

The first edition of this book sold out gratifyingly quickly. For the second edition, I have made certain additions and I have completely reworked the fourth part. I wish to thank all those who have helped me with their comments and criticisms, and I hope to have improved the readability of the book and made its arguments more convincing.

Prague, July 2014

For the English edition, I would like to express my gratitude to the translators and to the publisher for their efforts and patience. I have reduced the number of citations of untranslated Czech works, as these would prove unhelpful to an English-language reader with no command of Czech. We have attempted to find suitable English translations of all works originally cited in other languages. Where we were unable to consult printed copies of these, I have replaced page numbers with less specific markers (chapter headings, etc.) wherever this was possible. I offer my apologies for any inconvenience this may cause the reader.

Prague, July 2015

Bibliography

Aglietta, M. – Orléan, A., *La monnaie souveraine*. Paris: Odile Jacob 1998.

Alain, (Émile-Auguste Chartier), *Propos sur le bonheur*. Paris: Gallimard 1993.

Arendt, H., *Eichmann in Jerusalem*. New York: Penguin 2006.

Aristoteles, *Nicomachean ethics*. Trans. H. Rackham. Cambridge (Ma.): HUP 1990.

— *The Nicomachean Ethics*. Trans. D. Ross. Oxford: Oxford UP 2009.

— *Nikomachische Ethik*. Trans. O. Gigon. Munich: DTV 1991.

— *The Politics*. Oxford: Oxford UP 2009.

Aronson, E., *The Social Animal*. New York: Freeman 1984.

Avesta. *Vendidad. http://www.avesta.org/vendidad/vd_tc.htm.*

Barša, P., *Imanence a sociální pouto* [Immanence and the social bond]. Brno: CDK 2001.

Bateson, G., *Steps to an Ecology of Mind*. Northvale: Aronson 1987.

Bayertz, K. (ed.), *Evolution und Ethik*. Stuttgart: Reclam 1993.

Beck, U., *The Reinvention of Politics: Rethinking Modernity*. Oxford: Polity Press 1997.

Benedict, R., *Patterns of Culture*. Boston: Houghton Mifflin 2005.

Bergson, H., *The Two Sources of Morality and Religion*. Notre Dame (In.): UNDP 1977.

— *Creative Evolution*. New York: Palgrave Macmillan 2007.

Berlin, I., *Four Essays on Liberty*. Oxford: Oxford UP 1984.

Bible. The New English Version. Oxford: Oxford UP 1970.

Biocca, C., *Yanoáma : The story of Helena Valero, a Girl Kidnapped by Amazonian Indians*. New York: Kodansha 1996.

Bleicken, J., *Die athenische Demokratie*. Paderborn: Schöningh 1994.

Blondel, E., *La morale*. Paris: Flammarion 1999.

Bodrock, P., 'Die Erpressung', in *Harvard Business Manager. Ethik*. Hamburg: MMV 2009, 7–15.

Bolzano, B., *Von dem besten Staate*, Prague: Královská česká společnost nauk 1932, (B. Bolzano's Schriften, iii.).

Bourdieu, P., *Practical Reason: On the Theory of Action*. Cambridge: Polity 1998.

Brague, R., *On the God of the Christians*. South Bend: St. Augustine's Press 2013.

— *Les ancres dans le ciel*. Paris: Seuil 2011.

Brentano, F., *The Origin of our Knowledge of Right and Wrong*. New York: Humanities 1969.

Buber, M., *I and Thou*. New York: Scribner 2000.

Buchanan, J. M., *The Limits of Liberty: Between Anarchy and Leviathan*. Indianapolis: Liberty Funds 2000.

Burkert, W., *Creation of the Sacred*. Cambridge (Ma.): HUP 1996.

Caillois, R., *Man, Play, and Games*. New York: Glencoe 1969.

Carrithers, M. (ed.), *The Category of the Person*. Cambridge: Cambridge UP 1986.

— *Why Humans Have Cultures*. Oxford: Oxford UP 1992.

Cennini, C., *Il libro dell'arte: a new English translation*. London: Archetype 2015.

Chapman, R. A. (ed.), *Ethics in the British Civil Service*. London: Routledge 1988.

Childe, G. V., *What Happened in History*. Harmondsworth: Penguin 1954.

Cicero, *De officiis*. Stuttgart: Reclam 2003.

— *De legibus*. The Latin Library. http://www.thelatinlibrary.com/cic.html.

— *De re publica*. The Latin Library. http://www.thelatinlibrary.com/cic.html.

— *De domo sua*. The Latin Library. http://www.thelatinlibrary.com/cic.html.

Clastres, P., *Chronicle of the Guayaki Indians*. New York: Zone 1998.

Coderc, H., 'Fighting with Property'. *Monthly of the AmEthnSociety*, 8 (1950), 68.

Comenius, J. A., 'Mundus moralis', in *De emendatione rerum humanarum*. ii., Prague: Academia 1992.

— *Panorthosia or Universal Reform*. Sheffield: Sheffield AP 1995.

Comte, A., *Cours de philosophie positive*. Paris: Schleicher 1908.

— *Auguste Comte and Positivism : The Essential Writings*. New Brunswick: Transaction Publishers 1998.

Comte-Sponville, A., *A Small Treatise on the Great Virtues*. New York: Metropolitan 2001.

Coreth, E., *Was ist der Mensch? Grundzüge philosophischer Anthropologie*. Innsbruck: Tyrolia 1986.

Count, E. W., 'The Biological Basis of Human Sociality', in A. M. F. Montagu, *Culture*, London: Oxford UP 1968, 114–158.

Cornu, M., *La confiance dans tous ses états*, Geneve 1997.

Creveld, M. van, *The Transformation of War*. New York: Free Press 1991.

Dante Alighieri, *La divina comedia*. www.gutenberg.org<http://www.gutenberg.org/>.

— *The Divine Comedy*. Trans. C. H. Sisson. Oxford: Oxford UP 1980.

Darwin, Ch., *On the Origin of Species.* www.gutenberg.org<http://www.gutenberg.org/>.

Davy, G., *La foi jurée.* Paris: Alcan 1922.

Derrida, J., 'Hospitality, Justice and Responsibility', in R. Kearney – M. Dooley (eds.), *Questioning Ethics.* London, Routledge 1999, 65–83.

.— *Donner le temps.* Paris: Galilée 2011.

Descartes, R., 'Principia philosophiae', in Descartes, *Oeuvres.* Paris: Pléiade Gallimard 1953.

— 'Lettres', in Descartes, *Oeuvres.* Paris: Pléiade Gallimard 1953.

— *Discours sur la méthode,* www.gutenberg.org<http://www.gutenberg.org/>.

— *Les passions de l'âme.* Art. II, p. 146. www.gutenberg.org<http://www.gutenberg.org/>.

Diels, H. – Kranz, W. (ed.), *Die Fragmente der Vorsokratiker.* Hamburg: Rowohlt 1957.

Diogenés Laertios, *Lives of Eminent Philosophers. X. Epikuros.* http://www.epicurus.info/etexts/Lives.html.

Durkheim, E., *The Elementary Forms of Religious Life.* Oxford: Oxford UP 2001.

— *Physik der Sitten und des Rechts.* Frankfurt on the Main: Suhrkamp 1991.

— *Sociology and Philosophy.* New York: Free Press 1974.

Eastman, L. E., *Family, Field and Ancestors.* New York: Oxford UP 1988.

Eibl-Eibesfeld, I., *Die Biologie des meschlichen Verhaltens.* Munich: Piper 1984.

— *Der Mensch – das riskierte Wesen.* Munich: Piper 1991.

— *Liebe und Hass.* Munich: Piper 1998.

— *Wider die Misstrauensgesellschaft.* Munich: Piper 1994.

Eliade, M. *The Sacred and the Profane.* New York: Harper and Row 1961.

— *The Myth of the Eternal Return.* Princeton: PUP 2005.

— *A History of religious ideas.* Chicago: CUP 1978.

Engels, E.-M., 'Spencers Moralwissenschaft – Ethik oder Sozialtechnologie?', in *Evolution und Ethik.* Edited by K. Bayertz, Stuttgart 1993, 243–287.

Fink, E., *Spiel als Weltsymbol.* Freiburg: Alber 2010.

Floss, P., 'Ztracené paradigma?' [A lost paradigm?], *Proglas,* 2 (1995), 11–71. https://phil.muni.cz/fil/etika/texty/studie/floss1.html.

Fraňková, S. – Klein, Z., Úvod do etologie člověka [Introduction to human ethology]. Prague: HZ 1997.

Frič, P. et al., *Korupce na český způsob* [Corruption – the Czech way]. Prague: G plus G 1999.

Friesen, S. J., (ed.), *Ancestors in Post-Contact Religion.* Cambridge (Ma.): HUP 2001.

Fukuyama, F., *Trust: The Social Virtues and the Creation of Prosperity.* New York 1996.

Fung Yu-Lan, *Selected Philosophical Writings.* Beijing: Foreign Languages Press 1998.

Furger, F., *Etika seberealizace, osobních vztahů a politiky* [Ethics of self-realisation, of human relations and politics]. Prague: Academia 2003.

Fustel de Coulanges, *The Ancient City*. Baltimore: John Hopkins UP 1980.

Gadamer, H.-G., *Le probleme de la conscience historique*. Louvain: University of Louvain 1963.

— Mensch und Sprache, in *Wahrheit und Methode*. Tübingen: Mohr Siebeck 1986, ii., 146–154.

Gauchet, M., *La condition politique*. Paris: Gallimard 2007.

Gehlen, A., *Man, His nature and Place in the World*. New York: Columbia UP 1988.

Gellner, E., *Plough, Sword, and Book: The Structure of Human History*. London: Paladin Grafton 1991.

— *Nations and Nationalism*. Ithaca: Cornell UP 2008.

Gernet, L., *The Anthropology of Ancient Greece*. Baltimore: John Hopkins UP 1981.

Gide, A. *Journal I. (1889–1939)*. Paris: Pléiade 1951.

Goffman, E., *Stigma: Notes on the Management of Spoiled Identity*. New York: Simon & Schuster 1986.

— *The Presentation of Self in Everyday Life*. Harmonsworth: Penguin 1990.

Greisch, J., 'Ethics and Lifeworlds', in R. Kearney – M. Dooley (eds.), *Questioning Ethics*, Lonon and New York: Routledge 1999, 44–60.

Habermas, J.: *Moral Consciousness and Communicative Action*. Cambridge (Ma.): MIT Press 1990.

Haffner, S., *Germany: Jekyll and Hyde*. London: Libris 2005.

Hegel, G. W. F., *Outlines of the Philosophy of Right*. Oxford: Oxford UP 2008.

Heidegger, M., *Poetry, Language, Thought*. New York: Perennial 1975.

— *Being and Time*. Albany: SUNY Press 2010.

— *The Fundamental Concepts of Metaphysics*. Bloomington: Indiana UP 2005.

— *The Essence of Truth*. New York: Continuum 2002.

Hobbes, T., *Leviathan*. www.gutenberg.org<http://www.gutenberg.org/>.

Hocart, A. M., 'The purpose of Ritual', in *The Life-Giving Myth*. London: Methuen 1970.

Höffe, O., *Lesebuch zur Ethik*. Munich: C. H. Beck 2002.

— *Lexikon der Ethik*. Munich: C. H. Beck 1992.

— *Gerechtigkeit als Tausch?* Baden-Baden: Nomos 1991.

Honneth, A., *The I in We: Studies in the Theory of Recognition*. Cambridge: Polity 2012.

— *Pathologien des Sozialen: die Aufgaben der Sozialphilosophie*. Frankfurt on the Main: Fischer 1994.

Hoquet, T., *La vie*. Paris: Flammarion 1999.

Hume, D., *A Treatise on Human Nature*. 3.1.1. www.gutenberg.org<http://www.gutenberg.org/>.

Husserl, E., *The Crisis of European sciences and Transcendental Phenomenology*. Evanston: Northwestern UP 1970.

— 'Vorlesungen über Ethik und Wertlehre 1908–14'. *Husserliana* xxviii. Dordrecht: Kluwer 1988.

Hutcheson, F. *Inquiry Concerning Moral Good and Evil*. OLL. http://oll.libertyfund.org/index.php.

— *Essay on the Nature and Conduct of the Passions*. OLL. http://oll.libertyfund.org/index.php.

Huxley, T. H., *Evolution & Ethics*. Princeton: PUP 2009.

Jablonka, E., – Lamb, M. J., *Evolution in Four Dimensions*. Cambridge (Ma.): MIT Press 2005.

Janďourek, J., *Sociologický slovník* [Dictionary of sociology]. Prague: Portál 2001.

Jankélévitch, V., *Le paradoxe de la morale*. Paris: Seuil 1981.

— *Le pur et l'impur*. Paris: Flammarion 1960.

— *Forgiveness*. Chicago: Chicago UP 2005.

Jaspers, K., *The Origin and Goal of History*. New Haven: Yale UP 1953.

— *The Question of German Guilt*. New York: Fordham University Press 2000.

Jonas, H., *Philosophical Essays: From Ancient Creed to Technological Man*. Englewood Cliffs: Prentice-Hall 1974.

— 'Evolution and Freedom: On the continuity among life-forms', in *Mortality and Morality: A Search for the Good after Auschwitz*. Evanston: Northwestern University Press, 1996, 59–74.

— *The Imperative of Responsibility*. Chicago: Chicago UP 1984.

Kant, I., *Akademie-Ausgabe der Gesammelten Schriften*. (AA). http://virt052.zim.uni-duisburg-essen.de/Kant/verzeichnisse-gesamt.html.

— *Anthropology, History, and Education*. Cambridge: CUP 2009.

— *Practical Philosophy*. Cambridge: CUP 1996.

— *Anthropologie in pragmatischer Hinsicht*. Frankfurt on the Main: Suhrkamp 1983.

— 'Die Metaphysik der Sitten', in *Werke*, v., Cologne: Könneman 1995.

— 'Werkausgabe', xi., in *Schriften zur Anthropologie, Geschichtsphilosophie, Politik und Pädagogik 1.*, edited by Wilhelm Weischedel. Frankfurt on the Main: Suhrkamp 1977.

Kearney, R. – Dooley, M. (eds.), *Questioning Ethics: Contemporary Debates in Philosophy*. London: Routledge 1999.

Kekes, J., *Moral Wisdom and Good Lives*. Ithaca: Cornell University Press, 1995.

Keller, J., *Úvod do sociologie* [Introduction to sociology]. Prague: SLON 1995.

— *Sociologie organizace a byrokracie* [Sociology of organizations and bureaucracy]. Prague: SLON 2007.

Kenny, A., *The Anatomy of the Soul*. Oxford: Blackwell 1973.

Kirschner, M. W. – Gerhart, J. C., *The Plausibility of Life*. New Haven: Yale UP 2005.

Knapp, V., *Teorie práva* [Theory of law]. Prague: C. H. Beck 1995.

Kohák, E., *Člověk, dobro a zlo* [Man, the good and the evil]. Prague: Ježek 1993.

Kohen, A., *In Defense of Human Rights: a Non-Religious Grounding in a Pluralistic World*. New York: Routledge 2007.

Kolář, P. – Svoboda, V., *Logika a etika: úvod do metaetiky* [Logic and ethics – introduction to metaethics]. Prague: Filosofia 1997.

Küng, H., *A Global Ethic and Global Responsibilities*. London: ECM 1998.

Laozi, *The Tao Teh King*. www.gutenberg.org<http://www.gutenberg.org/>.

Levin, R. W. – Reynolds, F. E. (eds.), *Cosmogony and the Ethical Order*. Chicago: UCP 1985.

Lévinas, E., *Otherwise than Being*. Pittsburgh: Duquesne UP 1998.

— *Ethics and Infinity*. Pittsburgh: Duquesne UP 1998.

— *Quelques réflexions sur la philosophie de l'hitlérisme*. Paris: Payot et Rivages 1997.

— *Totality and Infinity*. Pittsburgh: Duquesne UP 1998.

Lipovetsky, G., *Le crépuscule du devoir*. Paris: Galimard 1992.

Livius, T., *The History of Rome*. www.gutenberg.org<http://www.gutenberg.org/>.

Locke, J., *An Essay on Human Understanding*. www.gutenberg.org<http://www.gutenberg.org/>.

— *The Treatises on Governement*. Cambridge: Cambridge UP 1988.

Lorenz, K., *Das sogenannte Böse*. Wien: Borotha 1964.

Luhmann, N., *Law as a Social System*. Frankfurt on the Main: Suhrkamp 1997.

— *Die Wirtschaft der Gesellschaft*. Frankfurt on the Main: Suhrkamp 1996.

— *Social Systems*. Stanford: Stanford UP 1995.

— 'Paradigm Lost.' *Thesis Eleven*. 29 (1991), 82–94.

Machek, V., *Etymologický slovník jazyka českého* [Etymological dictionary of Czech]. Prague: Academia 1970.

MacIntyre, A., *After Virtue*. Notre Dame (In.): UNDP 2007.

Maine, H. S., *Lectures on the Early History of Institutions* (1875). http://webu2.upmf-grenoble.fr/DroitRomain/.

Malinowski, B., *Argonauts of the Western Pacific*. London: Routledge 1922.

Mansfeld, J. (ed.), *Die Vorsokratiker. Griechisch /Deutsch*. 2 vols., Stuttgart: Reclam 1990.

Manu, *The Laws of Manu*. Trans. by W. Doniger and B. Smith, London – New York: Penguin Group 1991.

Marcel, G., *Being and Having*. Boston: Beacon 1951.

Maturana, H., *Autopoiesis, structural coupling and cognition*. http://www.isss.org /maturana.htm.

Mauss, M., *The Gift*. London: Routledge 2002.

Mill, J. S., *Utilitarianism*. London 1962.

Mitchell, S., *Gilgamesh: A New English Version*. New York: Free Press 2006.

Mitscherlich, A., *Auf dem Weg zur vaterlosen Gesellschaft*. Munich: Piper 1965.

Montagu, A. (ed.), *Culture: Man's Adaptive Dimension*. London: Oxford UP 1968.

Moore, G. E., 'Principia ethica'. In *Fair use repository*. http://fair-use.org/g-e-moore /principia-ethica.

Moural, J., 'Život, svět, hodnoty a dějiny' [Life, world, values and history.], in B. Velický et al., *Spor o přirozený svět* [Dispute over inherent world], Prague: Filosofia 2010, 113–126.

Možný, Ivo, *Rodina a společnost* [Family and society]. Prague: SLON 2008.

— *Rodina vysokoškolsky vzdělaných manželů* [Family of academics]. Brno: UJEP 1983.

Murphy, M., 'The Natural Law Tradition in Ethics', in *Stanford encyclopedia of philosophy*. Edited by E. N. Zalpa. Stanford: Stanford University 1997.

Němec, J. (ed.), *Bolest a naděje. Deset esejů o osobním zrání* [Pain and hope. 10 essays on personal maturity]. Prague: Vyšehrad 1992.

Nietzsche, F., *Thus Spoke Zarathustra*. Trans. R. J. Hollingdale. Harmondsworth: Penguin 1969.

— *Friedrich Nietzsche, Werke*. Edited by K. Schlechta. Berlin: Directmedia 2002 (CD-ROM).

—*Götzen-Dämmerung*, Leipzig: Kröner 1921, (Nietzsches Werke. x.).

Nilsson, M. P., *Greek Folk Religion*. New York: Harper 1961.

Nussbaum, M. C., *The Fragility of Goodness : Luck and Ethics in Greek Tragedy and Philosophy*. Cambridge UP 2001.

Ogien, R., *L' éthique aujourd'hui. Maximalistes et minimalistes*. Paris: Gallimard 2007.

Ost, F., *La nature hors la loi*. Paris: Découverte 2000.

Palouš, R., *Paradoxy výchovy* [Paradoxes of education]. Prague: Karolinum 2009.

Parry, J., 'The Gift, the Indian Gift and the "Indian Gift"'. *Man*. (n. s.) 21 (3), 1996, 453–473.

Pascal, B. Pensées. OLL. https://archive.org/details/pensesedde167000pasc.

Patočka, J., *Sebrané spisy* [Collected works]. Prague: Oikúmené.

— *Plato and Europe*. Stanford: Stanford UP 2002.

— 'Ještě jedna Antigona a Antigoné ještě jednou' [Antigone once more], in J. Patočka, *Umění a čas I. Sebrané spisy 4*. Prague: Oikúmené 2004.

— *Přirozený svět jako filosofický problém* [The natural world as a philosophical problem]. Prague 1936, 1970 ff.

Petrusek, M. (ed.), *Velký sociologický slovník* [Encyclopaedia of sociology]. 2 vols. Prague: Karolinum 1996.

Piaget, J., *The Insights and Illusions of Philosophy*. New York: World Publishing 1971.

Pichot, A., *Histoire de la notion de vie*. Paris: Gallimard 1993.

Pico della Mirandola, *Oration on the Dignity of Man*. New York: CUP 2012.

Pinker, S. *The Better Angels of our Nature: Why Violence Has Declined*. New York: Penguin 2011.

Plato, *Complete Works*. Indianapolis: Hackett 1997.

Popper, K., *The Open Society and its Enemies I/II*. London: Routledge 2002.

Pospíšil, L., *The Ethnology of Law*. Menlo Park 1978.

Postman, N., *Amusing Ourselves to Death*. New York: Viking 1985.

Prudký, L., *Kudy ke dnu* [The way to bottom]. Prague: Socioklub 2010.

Radbruch, G., *Rechtsphilosophie*. Heidelberg: Müller 1993.

Rádl, E., Útěcha z filosofie [Consolation from philosophy]. Prague: Svoboda 1994.

Rappaport, R. A., *Pigs for the Ancestors*. New Haven: Yale UP 1984.

— *Ritual and Religion in the Making of Humanity*. Cambridge UP 1999.

Rawls, J., *A Theory of Justice*. Cambridge: Belknap HUP 1999.

— *Political Liberalism*. New York: Columbia UP 1996.

Reale, G., *Toward a New Interpretation of Plato*. Washington: Catholic University 1997.

Rich, A., *Business and Economic Ethics*. Leuven: Peeters 2006.

Ricken, F., *Allgemeine Ethik*. Stuttgart: Kohlhammer 1998.

Richerson, J. P. – Boyd, R., *Not by Genes Alone*. Chicago 2005.

Ricoeur, P., *Oneself as Another*. Chicago: UCP 1992.

Ridley, M., *The Origins of Virtue*. London: Viking 1996.

Rist, J. M., *Stoic Philosophy*. Cambridge: CUP 1977.

Ritter, J – Gründer, K., *Historisches Wörterbuch der Philosophie*. 12 vols. Basel: Schwabe 1981.

Rosenzweig, F., *The New Thinking*. Syracuse, SUP 1999.

Ross, E. A., *Sin and Society*. New York 1973.

Rotter, H., *Person und Ethik*. Innsbruck: Tyrolia 1973.

Ruse, M., *Taking Darwin Seriously: A Naturalistic Approach to Philosophy*. Oxford: Blackwell 1986.

Ruyer, R., *Paradoxes de la conscience*. Paris: Albin Michel 1966.

Scheler, M., *Formalism in Ethics and Non-Formal Ethics of Values*. Evanston: Northwestern UP 1973.

— 'Ordo amoris', in *Selected Philosophical Essays*. Evanston: Northwestern UP 1973.

— *O studu* [On shame]. Prague: Mladá fronta 1993.

Schiffauer, W., *Die Bauern von Subay*. Stuttgart: Klett-Cotta 1987.

Scholtz, G., *Ethik und Hermeneutik*. Frankfurt on the Main: Suhrkamp 1995.

Seneca, *Ad Novatium de ira*. The Latin Library. http://www.thelatinlibrary.com/sen/sen.ira1.shtml.

Shaftesbury, A. A., *Characteristicks of Men, Manners, Opinions, Times.* Oxford 1999.

Simmel, G., *Kant.* Stuttgart 1997.

Smith, A., *Theory of Moral Sentiments.* Edited by Sálvio M. Soares. MetaLibri 2005, v1.0p.

Snell, B., *The Discovery of the Mind: The Greek Origins of European Thought.* New York: Dover 1982.

Sokol, J., *Thinking about Ordinary Things.* Prague: Karolinum 2013.

— *Mensch und Religion.* Freiburg: Alber 2007.

— *Filosofická antropologie* [Philosophic anthropology]. Prague: Portál 2003.

— *Moc, peníze a právo* [Power, money and law]. Plzeň: A. Čeněk 2007.

Spaemann, R., *Happiness and Benevolence.* Notre Dame (In.): NDUP 2000.

— *Basic Moral Concepts.* London: Routledge 1989.

Spinoza, B., *Die Ethik. Lateinisch/Deutsch.* Stuttgart: Philip Reclam Jun. 1977.

St Augustine, *The City of God.* Trans. Marcus Dods, Peabody: Hendrickson 2009.

St Thomas Aquinas, *Summa theologica I–V.* Roma 1925.

Stanford Encyclopedia of Philosophy. Edited by E. N. Zalpa. Stanford: Stanford University 1997.

Stewart, F. H., *Honor.* Chicago 1994.

Sutor, B., *Politische Ethik.* Paderborn: Schöningh 1991.

Sweet, W., 'The Bases of Ethics', in *Questia*, Milwaukee: MUP 2001

Teilhard de Chardin, P., *The Appearance of Man.* New York: Harper and Row 1975.

— *The Phenomenon of Man.* New York: Harper and Row 1975.

Tomkins, F., *The commentaries of Gaius on the Roman law.* Holmes Beach: Gaunt 2002.

UNDP: *A Users' Guide to Measuring Corruption.* UNDP 2008.

Velický, B. (ed.), *Spor o přirozený svět* [The cause of the natural world]. Prague: Filosofia 2010.

Vico, G., *New Science: Principles of the New Science Concerning the Common Nature of Nations.* London: Penguin 2001.

Waal, F. de, *Good Natured. The Origins of Right and Wrong in Humans and Other Animals.* Cambridge: Harvard UP 1998.

Watzlawick, P. – Bavelas, J. B. – Jackson, D. D., *Pragmatics of Human Communication.* New York: Norton 1967.

Weber, B., 'Life', in *Stanford Encyclopedia of Philosophy.* http://plato.stanford.edu /entries/life/, substantive revision Mon Nov 7, 2011.

Weber, M., *Economy and Society: An Outline of Interpretive Sociology.* Berkeley: UCP 2013.

— 'Politics as a vocation', in *The vocation Lectures.* Indianapolis: Hackett 2004.

Wesel, U., *Frühformen des Rechts in vorstaatlichen Gesellschaften.* Frankfurt on the Main: Suhrkamp 1985.

Wesson, R. G., *Beyond Natural Selection*. Cambridge (Ma.): MIT Press 1991.

Williams, B., *Ethics and the Limits of Philosophy*. London: Fontana 1987.

Wilson, D. S. – Wilson E. O., 'Rethinking the Theoretical Foundation of Sociobiology'. *The Quarterly Review of Biology*, 82 (4), December 2007, 327–348.

Wilson, E. O., *Naturalist*. Washington: Island Press 2006.

— *On Human Nature*. Cambridge (Ma.): HUP 2004.

— *Nature Revealed: Selected Writings*. Baltimore: John Hopkins UP 2006.

Wittgenstein, L., *Blue Book*. http://www.geocities.jp/mickindex/wittgenstein/witt_blue_en.html.

— *Philosophical Investigations*. Oxford: Blackwell 1997.

— *Personal Recollections*. Ed. by R. Rhees. Totowa: Rowman 1981.

— *Tractatus logico-philosophicus*. London: Routledge 2014.

Worms, F., *La vie qui unit et qui sépare*. Paris: Payot 2013.

— *Bergson ou les deux sens de la vie*. Paris: PUF 2004.

Wright, R., *The Moral Animal*. New York: Vintage 1995.

Yan, Yung-xiang, *The Flow of Gifts. Reciprocity and Social Networks in a Chinese Village*. Stanford: Stanford UP 1996.

Zrzavý, J., *Proč se lidé zabíjejí. Homicida a genocida* [Why people kill each other]. Prague: Triton 2004.

Internet resources

Encyclopedia Britannica 1911: http://1911encyclopedia.org/.

Ethik-Werkstatt: http://www.ethik-werkstatt.de.

Fair use repository: http://fair-use.org.

Kant-Archiv: http://virt052.zim.uni-duisburg-essen.de/Kant/verzeichnisse-gesamt.html.

MetaLibri: http://www.ibiblio.org/ml/libri/.

OLL: http://oll.libertyfund.org/index.php.

Project Gutenberg: http://www.gutenberg.org/.

Stanford encyclopedia of philosophy: http://plato.stanford.edu/.

The Latin Library: http://www.thelatinlibrary.com.

UNDP: http://www.lulu.com/product/paperback/a-users-guide-to-measuring-corruption/3473656.

Wikipedia: http://en.wikipedia.org.

Wikisource: http://en.wikisource.org/wiki/Main_Page.

Index